Ancient Greece

—AN ILLUSTRATED HISTORY—

Marshall Cavendish
Reference
New York

Marshall Cavendish

Copyright © 2011 Marshall Cavendish Corporation

Published by Marshall Cavendish Reference
An imprint of Marshall Cavendish Corporation

Website: www.marshallcavendish.us

Library of Congress Cataloging-in-Publication Data
Ancient Greece : an illustrated history.
    p. cm.
  Includes index.
  ISBN 978-0-7614-7932-1 (alk. paper)
  1. Greece--History--To 146 B.C. 2. Greece--Civilization--To 146 B.C.
  DF215.A55 2010
  938--dc22
                                        2010002924

Printed in Malaysia

14 13 12 11 10   1 2 3 4 5

MARSHALL CAVENDISH
Publisher: Paul Bernabeo
Project Editor: Brian Kinsey
Production Manager: Mike Esposito

THE BROWN REFERENCE GROUP PLC
Managing Editor: Tim Harris
Designer: Lynne Lennon
Picture Researcher: Laila Torsun
Indexer: Ann Barrett
Design Manager: David Poole
Editorial Director: Lindsey Lowe

Other Marshall Cavendish Offices:

Marshall Cavendish International (Asia) Private Limited, 1 New Industrial Road, Singapore 536196 • Marshall Cavendish International (Thailand) Co Ltd. 253 Asoke, 12th Flr, Sukhumvit 21 Road, Klongtoey Nua, Wattana, Bangkok 10110, Thailand • Marshall Cavendish (Malaysia) Sdn Bhd, Times Subang, Lot 46, Subang Hi-Tech Industrial Park, Batu Tiga, 40000 Shah Alam, Selangor Darul Ehsan, Malaysia

Marshall Cavendish is a trademark of Times Publishing Limited

All websites were available and accurate when this book was sent to press.

PHOTOGRAPHIC CREDITS
Front Cover: Shutterstock: Raimond Siebesma (main), David H Seymour (background).
Back Cover: Shutterstock: Raimond Siebesma (main), David H Seymour (background).
Inside: AKG: 21, 75, 92, 103, 135, 136, 148, 149, 156, 179, Andrea Baguzzi 87, 171, Pietro Baguzzi 153, Orsi Battaglini 178, Herve Champollion 145, 170, Peter Connolly 19, 60, 73, 157, Gerard Degeorge 102, Electa 61, Rainer Hachenberg 48, John Hios 10b, 56, 77, 97, 113, 116, Andrea Jemolo 47, Tristan Lafrancis 49, 58, 167, Erich Lessing 7, 8, 10t, 15, 16, 20, 22, 24, 25, 33, 39, 62, 67, 68, 72, 76, 78, 83, 84, 86, 89, 98, 106, 114, 117, 118, 120, 123, 127, 139, 141, 159, 165, 168, 175, 176, Nimatallah 44, 45b, 53, 59, 105, 112, 155, 173, Jean-Louis Nou 38, Ullstein Bild-Agelou 142; **Ancient Art and Architecture Collection:** B. Wilson 82; **Art Archive:** Archaelogical Museum Eretria/Gianni Dagli Orti 42, 45t; **Corbis:** Barney Burstein 146, Gianni Dagli Orti 46, Hulton-Deutsch Collection 151; **Lebrecht:** 37, H. J. Shunk/Interfoto 163; **Mary Evans Picture Library:** 57, 124, 150; **Science Photo Library:** 131; **Shutterstock:** 70, Cornelie LEU 1, Elpis Ioaninidis 63, Nikita Rogul 79, Scion 3, Valery Shanon 5, Olga Shelego 140, Nikolas Strigins 12; **Still Pictures:** 126; **Superstock:** Yiorgos Depollas 54; **Topham:** 11, 23, 27, 51, 91, 101, 104, 137, 147, 162, 172, Alinari 32, 65, 69, 81, 95, 143, 152, 177, 183, Mike Andrews 35, Ann Ronan Picture Library/HIP 125, 128, 130, 132, Arena PAL 93, Art Media/HIP 133, 160, British Library/HIP 34, 36, 74, 94, 100, 111, 119, 161, Fortean 129, HIP 41, 85, 90, 134, 164, Image Works 18, 107, 144, Prisma-Vew 121, Roger-Viollet 13, 180, 181, Charles Wallker 115; **Werner Forman:** 71, 108, British Museum, London 109.

CONTENTS

Foreword   4

Bronze Age Greece   6

The Minoans   14

Mycenae and Troy   26

The Dark Age and
Greek Expansion   40

Sparta and Athens   52

From Tyranny to
Democracy   64

Greek Religion   80

The Birth of Drama   88

The Persian Wars   96

The Age of Pericles   110

The Great
Philosophers   122

The Peloponnesian
War   138

Macedon and Alexander
the Great   154

After Alexander   166

The Greek Legacy   174

Glossary   184

Major Historical Figures   187

Index   188

FOREWORD

In the preface to his lyric drama "Hellas" (1821), written the year before he died, the poet Percy Bysshe Shelley declared to readers throughout the English-speaking world that: "We are all Greeks. Our laws, our literature, our religion, our arts, have their root in Greece." For citizens of the West, Shelley's statement is as true now as it was then. Take, for example, the evidence from our everyday language. Nouns in common usage such as "democracy," "tragedy," "odyssey," "tyrant," "theater," and "poet," as well as the adjectives "spartan," "stoic," "comic," "olympic," "epic," and "platonic," testify to the enduring influence of the Hellenic past.

At no time in recent history have the peoples of Europe and of Western civilization in general been as engaged as they are today in areas of the globe that were involved for centuries in repeated conflicts and continuous cultural exchange with the Greeks. Scarcely a day passes in which an event in the Near East, western Asia, or South Asia does not make up some aspect of the daily news cycle. Looking back to the last century, the British invasion of Iraq during the Anglo-Iraqi War in May 1941 marked the first time since Alexander the Great's siege of the island city Tyre in 333 BCE that armed forces of any nation had marched east from the eastern shores of the Mediterranean Sea to the Mesopotamian city of Babylon. That invasion occurred roughly 70 years ago. How little the world changes!

Covering the major periods of Greek history, *Ancient Greece: An Illustrated History* brings the past alive to a new generation of students and gives them the background needed to interpret current circumstances. Such background is sorely needed, for the past has always served as the prologue to the future. Beginning with a survey of Stone Age culture from the Paleolithic era and a study of the life of the island peoples inhabiting Crete and the Cyclades, this book then introduces its readers to the Bronze Age warrior culture populated by the men and women who were made immortal by the poet Homer in the *Iliad*: Agamemnon, Helen, Hector, and Achilles, among others. When the Mycenaean hegemony fell apart, there followed a prolonged period of decline, from whose ruins rose a system of city-states such as those of Sparta, Corinth, Thebes, and Athens. These cities in turn created economic engines, forms of art and architecture, structures of government, techniques of diplomacy, methods of warfare, and systems of philosophy, religion, and law that are now applied worldwide. The successes, failures, biases, and shortcomings of these systems remain of great consequence to us. The warning made by the Greek historian Herodotus to his audience in the fifth century BCE still pertains: the divinities who sanction prosperity will just as frequently destroy it.

Over time, this pan-Hellenic network of Greek-speaking city-states absorbed and was itself absorbed by neighboring cultures. The network became truly multicultural as it spread westward throughout the Mediterranean region into Sicily, portions of Italy, southern France, and the Iberian Peninsula, southward into Africa, and eastward as far as the Hindu Kush and northern India—where Alexander the Great made the final thrusts of his military campaign. Alexander's death in Babylon in 323 BCE marked the beginning of the Hellenistic Age. It may indeed be no exaggeration to say that we are still living in the Hellenistic Age, because the Greek cultural diffusion, quickened by Alexander's wide reach and later extended by the Romans and the Byzantines, has not yet ended.

Ancient Greece: An Illustrated History has many merits and is a commendable asset to the 21st-century classroom. Its prose is clear and well-paced, and its pagination and format are visually attractive. In addition to the neat summations of information arranged in time lines and the valuable details of geography conveyed by the volume's many maps, a positive boon is the book's illustrations.

The images are large, mostly in color, and their varied arrangement—depicting actual artifacts as well as presenting modern views of ancient sites—sustains the reader's interest. Instructors will enjoy teaching from this book and students who learn from it will come away with a strong sense that "the glory that was Greece," vis-à-vis Edgar Allan Poe's poem "To Helen" (1845), is no frothy sentiment of poetic hyperbole, but in fact an assertion well worth the scrutiny and analysis of every generation.

Michele Ronnick

Michele Ronnick is president of the Classical Association of the Middle West and South and a professor in the Department of Classical and Modern Languages, Literatures, and Cultures at Wayne State University, Detroit, MI.

Additional related information is available in the 11-volume *History of the Ancient and Medieval World*, second edition, and the corresponding online *Ancient and Medieval World* database at www.marshallcavendishdigital.com.

BRONZE AGE GREECE

TIME LINE

c. 6500 BCE

Farming communities established on Greek mainland.

c. 3000 BCE

Distinctive culture emerges on Cycladic islands in Aegean Sea.

c. 2800 BCE

Invaders with knowledge of metalwork arrive on Greek mainland; beginning of Early Helladic I period.

c. 2600 BCE

Beginning of Early Helladic II period. Sophisticated stone settlements built.

c. 2100 BCE

Migrants from central Asia arrive on Greek mainland to establish Minyan culture.

c. 1500 BCE

Traditional date given for eruption of volcano on Greek island of Thera.

In the third millennium BCE, a relatively sophisticated culture grew up on both the Greek mainland and the surrounding islands. In particular, the inhabitants of the Cyclades began to produce beautiful works of sculpture.

Greece consists of mainland Greece on the Balkan Peninsula and a mass of islands, large and small, scattered over the Aegean Sea and extending as far south as Crete in the Mediterranean. The climate is volatile, with extreme fluctuations in temperature, strong winds, and sudden downpours of torrential rain. The main agricultural products are olives, grapes, and figs. In ancient times, both cattle and horses were grazed in the eastern central regions of mainland Greece.

Greece in the Stone Age

There is evidence of Stone Age hunters living in mainland Greece in the Paleolithic Age, and by the seventh millennium BCE it seems that farming communities were established. These early farmers lived in villages of circular mud huts, grew grains, peas, and lentils, and kept animals, such as pigs, cattle, goats, and sheep, for meat and milk. The farmers supplemented their diet by hunting and fishing and made stone tools such as axes and chisels. By the end of the Neolithic Age, people were living in walled towns, in which some large houses had a central hall—indicating that some individuals had now become wealthier than others, or had even become chieftains.

On the mainland, metalworking invaders arrived in the first part of the third millennium BCE. In addition to a knowledge of bronze, the invaders introduced the swing-plow, which greatly improved farming methods. The period between around 2800 and 2600 BCE (called Early Helladic I) was a time of great change. Walled hilltop villages appeared, with a chief who ruled over the surrounding farmland. Trading with other communities, some of them overseas, led to the emergence of a wealthy class, who built their houses of stone rather than mud bricks. Along with the rise of this merchant class came the craftsman class and the use of symbols to mark goods and seal containers.

During the period called Early Helladic II (c. 2600–2100 BCE), this civilization peaked, building settlements surrounded by towering stone walls and containing houses with several rooms. Excavations at Lerna have uncovered what was probably an important civic building, the massive House of Tiles, which was built two stories high with a balcony on the upper story. The house takes its modern name from a number of small, flat tiles of baked clay that were found in its ruins. The tiles may have covered a sloping roof and are thought to be the earliest roof tiles ever discovered.

From 2100 BCE onward, successive waves of hostile migrants from central Asia swept through the Balkan Peninsula

and destroyed most of the fortified towns. In their place, the invaders built dwellings of more primitive, one-storied, houses. The invaders brought with them a new kind of pottery, which was made on a wheel and whose angular shapes seemed to imitate metal pots. This pottery was first discovered by the German archaeologist Heinrich Schliemann, who uncovered it in the late 19th century CE when he was excavating at Orchomenus, a city in Boeotia that rose to prominence in the Mycenaean era. Schliemann named both the pots and the people who had produced them Minyan. These Minyans spoke an Indo-European language and have since come to be considered the first Greeks.

This marble sculpture, made on the island of Keros around 2000 BCE, depicts a musician playing the harp.

This gold goblet dates to around 2100 BCE, an era known to archaeologists as the Early Helladic II period.

The invaders eventually integrated with the indigenous inhabitants and learned from them seafaring skills that had been notably lacking. The general level of culture remained low, however, for the Minyans. They lived in simple "long houses" arranged in villages, and some of the villages were enclosed within walls.

Island cultures

Prior to the Early Helladic I period on the Greek mainland, another culture had started to develop on the Cycladic islands. Located in the southwestern Aegean Sea, the Cyclades are a group of more than 30 major islands formed from the peaks of mountain ranges submerged long ago. The islands are rocky and volcanic and are rich in minerals such as gold, silver, obsidian, and marble, as well as the ores of lead, iron, and copper.

The Cyclades get their name from the Greek word *kyklos*, meaning "circle," because they are arranged roughly in a circle around the island of Delos, which was considered sacred to the god Apollo (see box, page 11). The islands have been inhabited since very early times. There is evidence of settlements on the larger islands, such as Kythnos, Mykonos, Naxos, and Milos, dating from the sixth millennium BCE.

These early Neolithic settlers probably came from southwestern Anatolia (present-day Turkey), and as they were seafaring people, they settled near the coasts on the chosen islands. The settlers grew barley and wheat, raised pigs, sheep,

GREECE IN THE BRONZE AGE

and goats, and caught fish, particularly tuna, in the Aegean. There is evidence from some excavated sites that these people were familiar with copperworking from around 4000 BCE.

Cycladic art

From around 3000 BCE, the Cycladic islanders began to develop a distinct culture of their own. They became expert at carving small, elegant figurines in the pure white marble that they found on the islands of Paros and Naxos. Archaeologists have discovered these statuettes in burial chambers. To achieve a smooth surface, the figures were rubbed with emery stones, a dark, very

hard rock that the sculptors obtained from Naxos. Details were then often picked out in red and blue paint.

The figurines are extremely distinctive in their style. To begin with, they almost always portray women rather than men. The elongated figures stand upright with the head tilted back, while the arms are usually folded across the chest, with the left arm above the right. The legs and feet touch one another. The statues vary in size enormously; the smallest are only 2 inches (5 cm) tall, while the largest are almost life-size.

Archaeologists are unsure about the purpose of these statuettes. Because many of these figurines were found in

The early inhabitants of Greece were skilled at metalworking. This gold headband from around 2100 BCE depicts a group of warriors.

This ancient Greek sculpture depicts a man carrying a calf. Much of Bronze Age Greek life revolved around farming.

tombs, and because the form was usually female, it is thought they may represent goddesses who would protect the dead. They could also have been votive figures (objects of prayer).

The first modern discoveries of Cycladic figurines were made in the 1880s CE. In the early 20th century CE, the statuettes became fashionable with art collectors who admired them for their purity and simplicity of form.

Cultural developments

This Early Cycladic era is divided into two separate periods: Early Cycladic I (c. 3200–2700 BCE) and Early Cycladic II (c. 2700–2400 BCE), based on significant burial-site finds at Grotta-Pelos and Keros-Syros, respectively. Besides the female figurines, other artifacts found in tombs of this Early Cycladic period include a seated male marble figure, depicted playing a musical instrument, plus items such as bowls, bottles, and vases. Because the quality and quantity of goods vary from grave to grave, archaeologists believe that different levels of society were beginning to be seen on the Cyclades at this time.

As well as the beautiful white marble of the Cyclades, another substance of benefit to the whole region was obsidian. This black, glassy volcanic rock was found on Milos and was prized for making knives or scraping tools. The islanders were able to profit by trading in obsidian.

Moving inland

A significant shift in the population of the Cyclades took place around 2500 BCE. The communities that had been living in simple villages close to the coasts to facilitate their fishing activities started to move into the central parts of the islands and to build citadels, making the people less vulnerable to attack. One particular citadel, found at Kastri on Syros, was encircled by a wall with six towers.

From around 2000 BCE, the grave goods become more sophisticated, and it is thought that the Cycladic islanders may have had contact with, and been influenced by, the Minoan civilization that was developing on the nearby island of Crete. In more than 500 tombs excavated near Kastri, terra-cotta, marble, and gold vessels have been found, along with pins made of bronze and silver that were probably used to fasten garments. The fact that these pins are engraved with designs also found in Egypt and mainland Greece suggests that the Cycladic islanders were regularly trading with those countries.

Volcanic eruption

Some time around 1500 BCE (or possibly earlier; see box, page 12), a volcano on the southerly island of Thera (present-day Santorini) erupted with cataclysmic

DELOS

The island of Delos figures in many Greek legends. The very creation of the island was the subject of a myth. Poseidon, the god of the sea, together with Zeus, king of the gods, was supposed to have used columns made of diamonds to secure an enormous rock to the sea bed; this rock became Delos. Delos was destined to be the birthplace of the moon goddess Artemis and her twin brother, the sun god Apollo, who was also the god of poetry and music and is often depicted holding a lyre (a form of small harp).

When the Ionians occupied the Cyclades, they designated the island of Delos as their religious capital, because they believed themselves to be descended from Apollo. By the eighth century BCE, a large religious festival dedicated to Apollo was being held annually on Delos.

results. Ash and volcanic debris rained down on Thera and the surrounding islands. The explosion was so violent that it actually split Thera into several pieces, resulting in one large island and several smaller ones; much of the original island disappeared into the sea. Volcanic debris was lifted high into the atmosphere and deposited thousand of miles away.

One town that was devastated by the eruption was Akrotiri. As the vol-

Cycladic art is highly distinctive. This statuette from around 2600 BCE depicts a woman standing with her arms folded.

THE EXPLOSION AT THERA

The volcanic eruption on the island of Thera was one of the major events to occur in the Mediterranean region in the second millennium BCE. Ash from the explosion was thrown so far into the sky that some of it has been found in Greenland and North America. The eruption would have caused huge tidal waves to crash into other Aegean islands, including Crete, which is why the aftereffects of the explosion have sometimes been blamed for the downfall of the Minoan civilization.

Traditionally, the date of the Thera eruption has been placed at around 1500 BCE. That date was originally put forward in 1939 because pottery found buried by the eruption on Thera closely resembled Egyptian pottery from 1500 BCE. For several decades, this theory was acknowledged to be true. However, from the 1970s onward, archaeologists increasingly began to dispute the date, as radiocarbon evidence began to suggest that the disaster may have occurred much earlier, around 1625 BCE.

In 2006, a new theory was proposed in an article published in the magazine *Science*. Research by Danish geologist Walter Friedrich suggested that the eruption occurred between 1627 and 1600 BCE. Friedrich's conclusion was based on radiocarbon dating of an olive branch that was buried in the lava. Friedrich's theory did not settle the argument, however. While many geologists and archaeologists have supported his claims, others have questioned his findings.

The island of Santorini, called Thera in ancient times, is now a popular tourist destination.

cano exploded, enormous boulders came crashing down on the town and the sky darkened with ash. Next, tons of molten lava engulfed the hapless town, which was buried under 16 feet (5 m) of debris and so preserved almost intact, rather like the later Roman town of Pompeii.

Cycladic life

When the town of Akrotiri, on Thera, was eventually excavated, it gave a very clear picture of what life was like in the Cyclades before around 1500 BCE. The people lived in houses consisting of several rooms, arranged on either two or three stories. The narrow streets of the town were equipped with a simple drainage system for removing sewage. The houses contained wooden furniture and pottery and, on the ground floor, large earthenware jars for storing foodstuffs such as grain, vegetables, dried fish, wine, and oil.

One room in each house was arranged as a shrine and decorated with wall paintings (frescoes) showing landscapes with animals, birds, and flowers such as lilies and crocuses. In other houses excavated at Phylakope on Milos, frescoes have been found depicting battles, festivals, and, in one famous painting, a school of flying fish.

Because no human remains have been found at Thera, it is thought that the inhabitants may have had time to escape, but where they went is a mystery. Another mystery linked to Thera is that of the lost world of Atlantis, which was the subject of later Greek legends. It has been thought that these legends may refer to Thera.

End of Cycladic culture

From around 1500 BCE, the Cyclades came increasingly under the influence of the Mycenaeans on mainland Greece, and Cycladic culture was gradually absorbed into that of the Mycenaeans. The Cyclades were also in contact with the Phoenicians, who visited the islands to trade for precious metals. By around 1000 BCE, the Cycladic culture had completely disappeared. Most of the islands had been settled by Ionians from Anatolia, while Dorians from northwestern Greece had occupied Milos and Thera.

See also:
The Minoans (page 14) • Mycenae and Troy (page 26)

Two young boys box in this fresco found in the town of Akrotiri.

THE MINOANS

The Minoan culture, which flourished on Crete between around 2500 and 1450 BCE, was one of the first major cultures to emerge in Europe. Much of what is known about the Minoans has been gained through excavations at Knossos.

TIME LINE

c. 3000 BCE

People living in Aegean begin to make bronze by mixing copper and tin; dawn of Minoan culture on Crete.

c. 2000 BCE

First large palace complexes built at Knossos and Phaistos.

c. 1700 BCE

Early palaces destroyed, either by invaders or by an earthquake; later rebuilt.

c. 1525 BCE

Kings based at Knossos reach height of power.

c. 1500 BCE

Volcanic eruption on nearby island of Thera results in vast quantities of ash showered over Crete.

c. 1450 BCE

Minoan civilization comes to end. Palaces burned down, possibly by Mycenaean invaders.

In the spring of 1900 CE, there was great excitement on the island of Crete in the Mediterranean Sea. British archaeologist Arthur Evans and his team had just unearthed the first signs of a sophisticated Bronze Age civilization on the island. The excavations were centered on a large mound, called Kephala (or Knossos), in the north of the island. Local legend had it that this was the site of a great palace belonging to the mythical King Minos. According to the legend, Minos's palace was home to a monster known as the Minotaur, which lived in a labyrinth and devoured young men and women as sacrificial victims (see box, page 20).

The first finds were fragments of pottery decorated with images of sea creatures such as starfish, dolphins, sea urchins, and octopuses. The subject matter of the designs suggested that the pottery was produced by a seagoing people. Even more exciting were the fragments of a wall painting that showed a man in a loincloth carrying a vase. Similarly clothed figures had been painted on the walls of ancient Egyptian tombs, where they were identified as the Keftiu (island people) paying tribute to the pharaoh. It seemed that the Cretans and the Keftiu could have been one and the same.

Very soon, evidence of walls, floors, and columns came to light, indicating the presence of an enormous palace extending over 6 acres (2.4 ha). Evans named it the Palace of Minos (see box, page 18). The 1,400 rooms, which included ceremonial chambers, were connected by corridors and staircases, and many of the walls were decorated with elaborate paintings showing young men and women and more sea creatures. There were also paintings of bulls, suggesting that the palace was indeed the source of the Minotaur legend.

The site that Evans had discovered was the center of a Bronze Age culture that flourished on Crete from around 2500 to 1450 BCE. It was the first sophisticated civilization to develop in Europe; it was a civilization centered on trade and an efficient bureaucracy, and unlike most other early civilizations, it seemed entirely unwarlike. Prior to the Minoans (as Evans called these people), life on Crete had been primitive.

The Neolithic period

Before around 6000 BCE, Crete may have been uninhabited, but in the sixth millennium BCE, groups of people from Anatolia settled in mainland Greece and on Crete, bringing with them a knowledge of farming. These early

This mosaic depicts the Greek hero Theseus killing the Minotaur. According to legend, the Minotaur lived in a maze on Crete.

Cretan settlers found a large island (the fifth largest in the Mediterranean) with mountains covered in trees and a large fertile plain in the center. The warm climate made it a favorable area for growing crops. The farmers grew barley, oats, and wheat, as well as pulses and peas. They kept goats, sheep, cattle, and pigs and supplemented their diet by hunting and fishing. They fashioned pots out of clay by hand and made axes and chisels from stones that they ground to a sharp edge.

The Bronze Age

Around 3000 BCE, people living in the region of the Aegean discovered how to make bronze by mixing copper with tin, so beginning the period known as the Bronze Age. The people living on Crete in the early Bronze Age built houses of mud bricks. The houses had separate living rooms, kitchens, and workrooms. The Cretans became skilled metalworkers, producing beautiful jewelry in gold and silver.

At the same time that the Minoan civilization was developing on Crete, other cultures were developing in different parts of the Mediterranean region. One culture arose on a group of islands in the Aegean called the Cyclades. The early inhabitants of the Cyclades are most famous for the finely wrought figurines that they carved out of stone. The Greek mainland saw the rise of another culture, the Helladic, which in its later stages was known as the Mycenaean civilization.

When Arthur Evans was excavating the palace at Knossos, he divided Minoan history up into three main periods:

This ivory figurine was found in the palace at Knossos. It dates to around the 17th century BCE.

Early Minoan (3000–2000) BCE), Middle Minoan (2000–1600 BCE), and Late Minoan (1600–1050 BCE). However, other historians have chosen to divide Minoan history into three alternate periods spanning a shorter time: First Palace (1900–1700 BCE), Second Palace (1650–1540 BCE), and Third Palace (1450–1200 BCE).

During the Early Minoan period, the Minoans started to use bronze to make metal tools such as daggers, adzes, and double-headed axes. They grew olives and grape vines and traded the resulting olive oil and wine with neighboring peoples in the Aegean, taking to the sea in ships propelled by a combination of oars and square sails attached to masts. The Minoans used seals to stamp impressions on wet clay, possibly to seal storage jars to guard against theft. They also began building extensive settlements, although few traces of them now remain.

The age of the palaces

It was in the Middle Minoan period that the Minoans started to build great palaces at sites such as Knossos, Phaistos, Mallia, and Zakro. These palaces consisted of a complex of buildings surrounding a large open court and the main royal residence. The buildings, which served as the island's administrative center, included workshops for craftsmen and artisans, plus special storage rooms for oil, wine, grain, and other farming produce.

The first palaces have disappeared almost completely, but there have been numerous smaller finds from this period.

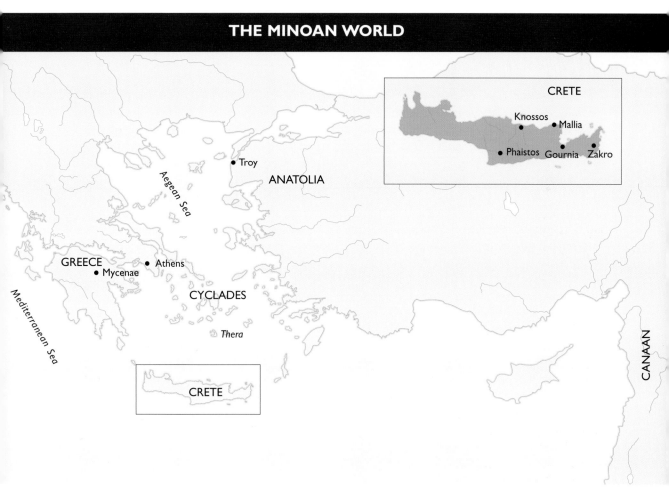

THE MINOAN WORLD

One of the most striking of these finds is a type of thin-walled pottery called Kamares ware, which was produced on a potter's wheel and decorated with spirals and plant motifs in red, orange, yellow, and white on a blue-black background. This refined pottery was crafted by specialized potters both for the domestic market and for export.

A collection of small plaques found in the palace at Knossos gives a good idea of the architecture of this period. The plaques are made of faience (a fine grade of pottery covered with a glaze) and depict city houses built of stone, bound together with large wooden beams. All the houses have a least two floors and a flat roof, and many appear to have a small central court that possibly served as an air and light shaft. Some of the houses are shown with window openings painted bright red, which might indicate that the early inhabitants of Crete used oiled parchment as an early type of windowpane.

The palace at Knossos

Around 1700 BCE, all the Minoan palaces were destroyed, either by earthquakes or invaders. They were all soon rebuilt, however. The new palace at Knossos became even more elaborate than its predecessor, with at least three stories and many rooms, including a magnificent throne room. The kings of Knossos reached the peak of their power

THE PALACE OF MINOS

The Palace of Minos excavated by Arthur Evans at Knossos is one of the most fascinating archaeological sites of the ancient world. The site covers a vast area around 3 miles (5 km) from the north coast of Crete, and it is thought that as many as 30,000 people lived and worked there in its heyday.

Digging down, Evans discovered a palace five stories high in places, with the floors connected by a grand staircase. The whole palace was skillfully designed to let light in and allow air to circulate—and to protect the occupants from the fierce summer heat. In winter, the doors would be closed so that fireplaces could provide warmth.

One very grand room was the throne room, which opened off the central courtyard. Inside was a stately throne carved out of gypsum and backed by a colorful mural depicting griffins (a kind of mythical animal). Evans thought that this room might have been used by the king to receive visitors, although others have suggested it might have been used for religious ceremonies.

The eastern side of the palace contained the royal apartments. The king's room was a large double room with a light well at one end and a veranda facing east. Motifs of double axes were carved on stone blocks found in the room, and for this reason it was named the Hall of the Double Axes. The queen's hall was decorated with paintings of dolphins and a dancing girl. It contained a bathroom in one corner, with an earthenware bathtub that was probably filled by servants. A hole in the floor leading to the drains made emptying it simple. In an adjoining room, there was a toilet. This was simply a hole in a stone slab with a drain beneath that carried the waste away to a stream.

As well as these grand rooms, there was a multitude of smaller rooms, all connected by corridors and staircases, together with vast numbers of underground storage rooms for the goods brought in from the surrounding countryside. The palace was a hive of activity. In addition to the king, queen, and nobles, there were priests, storekeepers, accountants and scribes, plus many servants and slaves. In the workshops around the palace, there were craftspeople such as jewelers, painters, potters, and carpenters busily plying their trade to produce the wonderful artifacts of the Minoan culture.

A pithos, or storage jar, stands amid the excavated ruins of the palace at Knossos. The palace complex at Knossos contained many storage rooms that would have contained pithoi such as this. Pithoi were usually used as containers for wine and olive oil.

between around 1550 and 1500 BCE, dominating the Aegean region and trading extensively with the Greek mainland, the Aegean islands, Anatolia (present-day Turkey), Egypt, and the Canaanite Syrian coast.

The basic plan at Knossos—which was echoed in the other palaces—was that of a large central courtyard surrounded by reception halls, living quarters, workshops, and storerooms. The palace was not protected by fortifications, and its western side looked out over wide agoras (public courtyards used for ceremonies and gatherings). The whole palace was supplied with water through an elaborate system of pipes, while drains and conduits removed waste water and sewage from the site. The storerooms at Knossos are particularly striking. They were long, narrow basement rooms containing rows of enormous storage jars called *pithoi* in which grain, oil, and wine were kept.

Social structure

Minoan society was divided into several regions and groups. Presiding over the country as a whole was the king. Below the king were the nobles, who were provincial rulers living in country mansions. A group of officials controlled the operations of the merchants, who contributed to the region's wealth through trade. In particular, merchants supplied imported materials such as ivory to the craftsmen who lived and worked in the palace. Below these classes came the farmers, who produced the agricultural goods that were so important for the

This artist's illustration depicts how the palace at Knossos may have looked. The palace was spread over a large area and contained several floors.

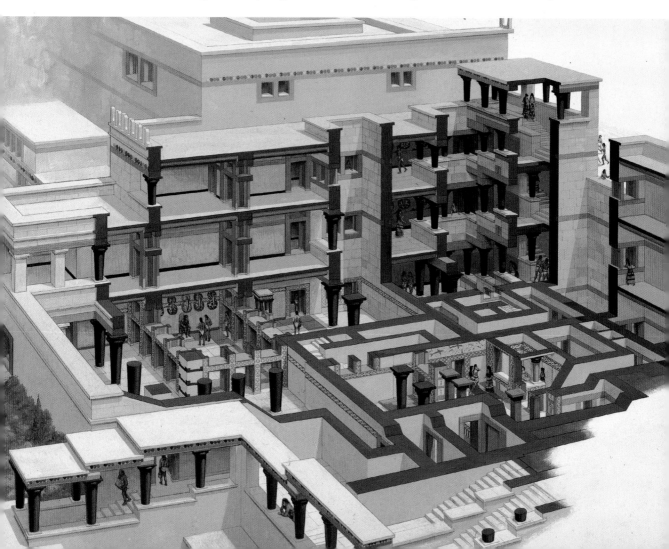

THE LEGEND OF THE MINOTAUR

According to Greek mythology, the god Poseidon sent a snow-white bull to King Minos of Crete, intending that the king should sacrifice the bull to Poseidon. When Minos refused to do this, Poseidon, in revenge, made Pasiphaë, the wife of Minos and queen of Crete, fall in love with the bull. As a result of this affair, she bore a child—a monster with a human body and a bull's head—that was called the Minotaur.

To keep the Minotaur safe, Minos commissioned the architect Daedalus to build a labyrinth so complex that nobody could find the way through it. When the maze was completed, the Minotaur was locked inside.

When the son of Minos was murdered by the king of Athens, Minos demanded that every nine years Athens should send seven young men and seven young women to Minos in compensation. These young people were fed to the Minotaur. Finally, the Athenian hero Theseus decided to put an end to this practice. He offered himself as one of the victims and sailed with the others to Crete. Ariadne, the daughter of Minos, fell in love with Theseus and offered to help him escape his fate. She gave him a ball of thread, which he tied to the entrance to the maze and unwound as he went. At the center of the maze, he found the Minotaur asleep and killed him. Then, with the help of the thread, Theseus made his escape, together with the intended victims he had rescued.

This drinking vessel made in the shape of a bull's head was found at Knossos. It was made between around 1900 and 1400 BCE.

Minoans' wealth. There was also a class of scribes, who were kept busy recording stocks of produce on clay tablets.

The Minoans had a highly developed religious life, and many priests and priestesses lived in the palaces. Rather than building temples to their gods, the Minoans held religious ceremonies in their houses, at hilltop shrines, or in special rooms in the palaces. Many gods and goddesses were worshipped, but it seems that one goddess, the mother (or earth) goddess, was supreme. She watched over animals and plants and symbolized fertility. Every year, she married a young god who died when winter came around but who came back to life in the spring. Another important goddess was the snake goddess. Usually portrayed holding a snake in each hand, she was seen as the guardian of the house.

Many replicas of bull's horns carved in stone have been found in Crete, suggesting that the bull played an important part in some religious cult. There are also several wall paintings that show young men and women somersaulting over a charging bull. This sport possibly took place in the palace courtyard and may have been part of a religious ritual.

Minoan towns and villas

Minoan palaces were encircled by large cities, which were connected to each other and to other Cretan towns by paved roads. One famous Minoan town is Gournia, which stands on a ridge overlooking the sea around 38 miles (60 km) east of Knossos. This town, excavated at around the same time as Knossos, consisted of a maze of winding streets connecting small square houses and courtyards. The houses were up to three stories and had flat roofs. The first floor usually contained workshops or storerooms, while the living quarters were on the second floor, which was reached by an outside staircase. From the tools found in the workshops, it is clear that the town's inhabitants included potters, weavers, metalsmiths, and carpenters, as well as fishermen and farmers.

A number of villas have also been excavated on Crete, and they were all built to the same plan as the palaces,

Athletes are shown vaulting over a charging bull in this fresco from the east wing of the palace at Knossos. Experts are divided over whether bull leaping was a religious ritual or just a dangerous sport.

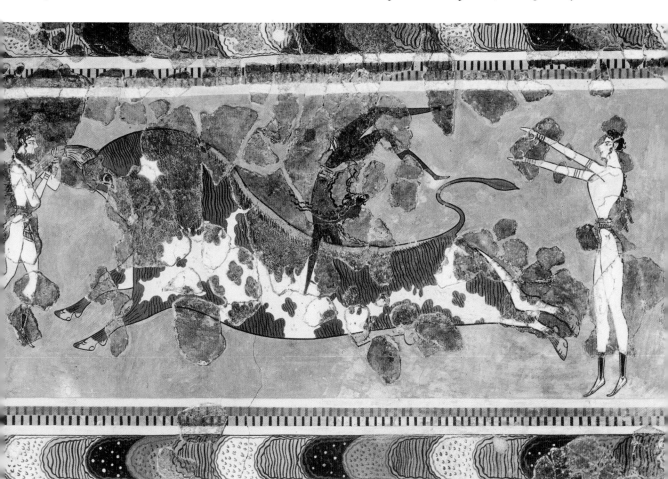

The remains of the Minoan town of Gournia are extremely well preserved. Like a number of other Minoan towns, Gournia was the site of a large palace.

THE PALACES AT PHAISTOS

Knossos was just one of the many locations where Minoan palaces were built. Another location was Phaistos, in the south of the island. The site was occupied by around 4000 BCE, but the first palace at Phaistos was not built until around 2000 BCE, roughly the same time as the palace at Knossos. What is now known as the "old palace" at Phaistos was destroyed by fire around 1700 BCE. Another palace was built in its place.

Like the palace at Knossos, the "new palace" at Phaistos was built around a magnificent central courtyard, lined with pillars. The royal quarters stood to the north. Workshops were found to the east, while storerooms were located to the west. The west wing also contained rooms that were used for religious purposes; religious figurines were found there and pictures of double axheads (a religious motif) were carved into the walls. Like the other great palaces, the palace at Phaistos was destroyed around 1450 BCE when the Minoan civilization came to an end.

albeit on a smaller scale. Some historians believe that these villas, which are all located within 7 to 10 miles (11 to 16 km) of each other, were the regional offices of a central power.

Minoan art

The interiors of the palaces were decorated with colorful murals, some made up of abstract patterns, others depicting plants, animals, and people. These paintings are often called frescoes, but true frescoes are painted on wet plaster, whereas the Minoan murals were painted on dry plaster walls. The so-called House of the Frescoes at Knossos is famous for its murals showing a park where various flowering plants are complemented by high-spouting fountains and a blue bird. Murals showing dolphins and flying fish have been found in several other places.

The paintings of men and women provide a clear idea of how the Minoans looked and dressed. When taking part in rituals, men often covered their bodies with a type of red powder for ceremonial purposes, so the men are often shown painted red. Men usually wore their hair long, but were clean shaven. In some paintings, men are shown wearing just a leather belt and a loincloth, while in others they wear a kilt. Women wore dresses with a long flounced skirt and an open bodice that left their breasts and arms bare, their jewelry consisted of rings, bracelets, necklaces, and earrings, and they had elaborate hairstyles with strings of beads braided into their long hair.

Women often occupy a prominent position in these paintings. They are shown dominating ceremonies from a place of honor and performing dances in beautiful costumes. In the famous bull-leaping fresco at Knossos, two young women are shown taking equal part with a young man in the ceremony.

This fresco probably shows a Minoan priestess. The woman depicted is sometimes known as La Parisienne because she resembles the subjects of paintings by French artist Henri Toulouse-Lautrec.

MINOAN WRITING

The Minoans were one of the earliest peoples to develop writing. From around 2000 BCE onward, they began using a system of hieroglyphic or pictographic writing, with signs in the shape of animals or objects. This form of picture writing may have originated through contact with the Egyptians, who were also writing in hieroglyphics at this time. Nevertheless, very few of the Minoan signs resemble those of the Egyptians.

Around 300 years later, the Minoans started writing in a simplified linear script, which used signs to represent the different syllables in a word. This script was usually scratched on clay tablets, although there is evidence that some kind of paper (perhaps similar to the papyrus of the Egyptians) was also used, together with a form of ink. Tablets in this script found at Knossos bear stockkeeping records of textiles, grain, animals, oils, and spices. Arthur Evans named this script Linear A.

No large statues from the Minoan civilization have survived, but the pedestals of what were presumably wooden statues have been preserved. A number of small statues have been found. These are made of ivory (sometimes inlaid with gold), bronze, or faience, and they depict goddesses or priestesses, praying figures, acrobats, animals, and a few tableaus, such as a stable with cattle or a group of dancers. Occasionally, children are portrayed.

This ivory figurine depicts a Minoan acrobat taking part in a bull-leaping ritual. The figurine was found in the palace at Knossos and was made around 1550 BCE.

HUMAN SACRIFICE

It seems clear that some religious rituals practiced by the Minoans involved the slaughter of animals as a sacrifice to the gods. However, there may have been an even more dramatic and sinister practice. In 1979, a major sanctuary was excavated in the mountains around 4.5 miles (7.2 km) south of Knossos. Among the items found were a cult statue and a number of votive offerings. What caused the greatest excitement was evidence that when the sanctuary was destroyed by an earthquake, a human sacrifice had been in progress. The body of a young man found tied to a low altar had died as a result of having his throat cut. Other finds in Knossos have included children's bones that show knife marks, suggesting that child sacrifice took place—or even cannibalism. There have been further archaeological indications to support the idea that these were not isolated instances.

The pots and ceramic ware from this period show that there was a great technical and artistic tradition. Motifs from the plant kingdom, inherited from the earlier Kamares ware, were mingled with images of marine creatures. These decorations were painted in dark colors on a light background.

It is obvious from a number of other found items that sections of Minoan society were very affluent. Beautiful jewelry was wrought in gold, while elegant stone vases were made of rock crystal, obsidian (a kind of volcanic glass), alabaster, or marble. Gold signet rings engraved with scenes of rituals have also been found.

Other important sources of information on Minoan life are the numerous seals that have been found. They were engraved with many designs, including geometric patterns and representations of human beings and animals. After 2000 BCE, the seals bear a type of writing that Arthur Evans termed hieroglyphic. Three

centuries later, this writing was replaced by a simplified script called Linear A (see box, page 23). Seals were used for placing a personal or official stamp on objects as a signature. They were also used as ornaments and charms.

The Third Palace period

Around the 15th century BCE, the Minoan people suffered a series of disasters. At the beginning of the century, the volcano on the island of Thera in the Cyclades erupted violently, causing catastrophic destruction over a wide area. Around 50 years later, many Minoan centers were destroyed by fire, and the palaces and other settlements may have been ransacked before being put to the torch. Whatever the reason, the existing social order was overthrown.

Invaders, probably Greek-speaking Mycenaeans from the mainland, came to dominate Crete. They made Knossos, which had suffered relatively little damage, their administrative center, but by 1300 BCE, the town appears to have been destroyed by unknown attackers. Occupied by the Mycenaeans, Crete became a Greek city-state, and the Minoan civilization that had flourished for more than 1,000 years was at an end.

See also:

Bronze Age Greece (page 6) • Mycenae and Troy (page 26)

This fresco depicts a Minoan ship entering a port. The Minoans were highly successful traders.

MYCENAE AND TROY

TIME LINE

c. 3000 BCE

First settlement appears at Troy.

c. 1600 BCE

Mycenae becomes major power on Greek mainland.

c. 1450 BCE

Mycenaeans invade Crete, making Knossos administrative center; fortress at Tiryns built around this time.

c. 1275 BCE

Tomb known as Treasury of Atreus built at Mycenae.

c. 1250 BCE

Mycenaean era comes to end, possibly as result of invasion from the north. Troy VIIa, the Troy of Homer, destroyed.

c. 1050 BCE

Troy VIIb destroyed; city abandoned for several centuries.

The Mycenaean civilization was the first major culture to develop on the Greek mainland. It flourished from around 1600 BCE until around 1250 BCE. According to legend, a major rival of the Mycenaean kingdoms was the Anatolian city of Troy.

Around the same time that the Minoan civilization was flourishing on Crete, another culture was developing on the Greek mainland. This new culture was the Mycenaean culture, which was named after the ancient city of Mycenae, one of the culture's centers. The Mycenaean civilization was not a single kingdom; it consisted of a group of city-states united by a common language and way of life. Other great centers of Mycenaean society were the cities of Athens, Thebes, Pylos, Tiryns, and Gla.

Unlike the Minoans, the Mycenaeans were a warlike people. However, they were also successful traders and skillful craftsmen. Their origins are still a mystery. Some historians believe they were a Greek-speaking people from the northeast who migrated to mainland Greece around 2000 BCE. Other experts, while accepting that such people did arrive in Greece, remain unconvinced that they were the Mycenaeans. Wherever they came from, the Mycenaeans had become a major power in the Aegean region by 1600 BCE. They were to dominate the region for the next 400 years. Around 1450 BCE, they invaded Crete, where they made the city of Knossos their administrative center. They also occupied many other Aegean islands and their commercial empire extended throughout the Mediterranean region.

Most of the knowledge about the Mycenaeans is of fairly recent origin. The obsession of a German archaeologist, Heinrich Schliemann (1822–1890), with the story of Troy led to the city of Mycenae being discovered in the 19th century CE. That Mycenaeans spoke Greek was only established in 1952, when a cryptographer succeeded in deciphering the script on clay tablets that had been found at Pylos and Mycenae (see box, page 30).

Schliemann and Homer

The epic poems the *Iliad* and the *Odyssey*, attributed to the Greek poet Homer, describe a Greek world in which Agamemnon ruled Mycenae, the paramount Greek city, while his brother Menelaus was king of Sparta and Pylos and Ithaca were ruled by Nestor and Odysseus respectively. Both of these epics were once regarded as complete fiction, but historians now accept that they give some very valuable glimpses into the Mycenaean civilization of the 12th century BCE.

In the late 19th century CE, nothing was known about Greek history prior to 800 BCE, but Heinrich Schliemann became convinced that the world described by Homer was based on fact and that Troy and Mycenae had really existed. In 1876, Schliemann set out to

prove that Mycenae was the city of Agamemnon. While excavating a burial ground close to the ruins of Mycenae, Schliemann came across a tomb containing many exquisite gold objects, including a gold death mask—a replica of a dead person's facial features. Schliemann was convinced he had found the tomb of the Mycenaean king. "I have looked upon the face of Agamemnon," he declared triumphantly in a telegram written to the king of Greece. Schliemann was mistaken, however. It

Dating from the 16th century BCE, this gold death mask was discovered in a shaft burial at Mycenae. At the time, it was mistakenly believed to have belonged to the legendary king Agamemnon.

has since been established that the mask dates from the 1550s BCE, around 300 years before the time of the Trojan War.

The city of Mycenae

Like many other cities in the ancient world, Mycenae had been built on a hill to make it easy to defend if attacked. At the top of the hill was the upper city, or citadel, which contained the royal palace. During the Late Mycenaean period (c. 1550–1100 BCE), the citadel was surrounded by a defensive wall almost half a mile (805 m) long, 30 feet (9.1 m) high, and at least 20 feet (6.1 m) thick. The wall was constructed of massive limestone blocks so heavy that later generations believed the wall must have been built by the Cyclopes, a mythical race of one-eyed giants. As a consequence, this type of masonry is called Cyclopean.

On the west side of the fortress, the Lion Gate, the main gateway into the city, was an impressive structure, crowned by two stone lions standing on their hind legs on either side of a column. The lions are thought to have been a symbol of kingship. The gate was closed by a set of double doors, and the spindle holes for these doors can still be seen in the threshold and the massive lintel. The doors were hung on the spindle ends that protruded from the holes. A feature of the gate that seems to bring the ancient city to life is the fact that the threshold still shows traces of wear from the constant passage of chariots and carts.

HEINRICH SCHLIEMANN

Heinrich Schliemann, born in January 1822, in Germany, was the son of an impoverished pastor. Schliemann left school at 14 and, after a succession of odd jobs, sailed for California, where he made a fortune during the Gold Rush. Schliemann next established himself in Russia, where he became a successful businessman and eventually grew rich enough to retire in his late thirties, devoting himself to archaeology.

Schliemann had been obsessed with the stories of the Trojan War since childhood, and he used the fortune that he had amassed to pursue his dream. He not only excavated the cities of Troy and Mycenae, but also the city of Tiryns. Schliemann publicized his discoveries through books and letters to British newspapers.

Schliemann died in Naples on December 26, 1890, as the result of an ear infection.

At the center of the citadel lies the palace, which covers an area of 200 by 180 feet (61 by 55 m). Built on uneven terrain, the palace probably gave the impression of being a stepped or terraced structure. The entrance to the palace was approached by a grand staircase, some of which still survives.

A royal residence

The palace was an enormously important building. Besides housing the royal family, it acted as a regional center and a military headquarters. In addition to a throne room, the palace contained halls, storerooms, and workshops. The core room was the megaron—a large rectangular room where the king presided over state business. This audience chamber had a large central hearth where a fire was kept burning, and the walls were painted with colorful scenes of daily life.

The citadel, which contained several houses as well as the palace, had many underground vaults and a system of underground drains. A reliable water supply was crucial to the city, particularly in time of siege, and Mycenae had a secret underground reservoir outside the wall of the citadel. Historians believe that the water was brought into the citadel by an underground channel.

In addition to the king and his relatives, the citadel housed a number of other noble families, probably in separate houses. Most of the houses were spacious and had two stories. In the late 1960s, a sanctuary containing the remains of terra-cotta figures 2 feet (0.6 m) high was found within the walls. These figures were possibly cult statues.

From the remains of a number of dwellings found on the hillside outside the citadel, it has been assumed that a substantial town extended from the foot of the city walls. In times of war, the population of the town would have taken refuge within the citadel.

THE MYCENAEAN CIVILIZATION

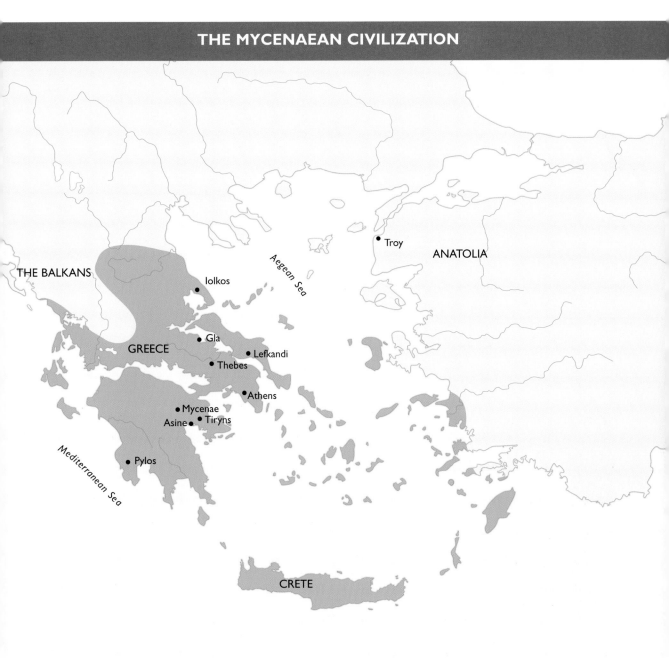

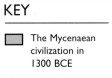

KEY

The Mycenaean civilization in 1300 BCE

Tombs

Two styles of Mycenaean tombs have been discovered. When Schliemann was excavating Mycenae, he found an extensive burial site in the northwest corner of the citadel. Archaeologists call this location Grave Circle A. The site contains a number of royal tombs dating from around 1600 BCE. These tombs were composed of simple shafts, which were dug deep into the ground. Each tomb contained the bodies of several generations of royalty, together with their possessions. When a tomb was full, it would be covered with stones and the shaft filled with earth. Later, a second circle of shaft tombs, called Grave Circle B, was discovered outside the citadel walls.

The treasures that were buried with the deceased in these shaft tombs are a testimony to the power and wealth of Mycenae in those days. As well as gold death masks, the graves yielded many richly decorated weapons, including a number of daggers inlaid with gold or silver. Some of the daggers featured entire scenes, including hunts and battles, depicted in inlay work. The hilts of the daggers were often made of wood or bone to which reliefs of hammered gold were applied.

The deceased were not only provided with weapons, however. A number of other splendid objects have also been found in the burial shafts. These objects include vases, dishes, golden *rhytons* (an ornate type of drinking vessel), beautifully crafted diadems, earrings, hairpins, necklaces, and bracelets, as well as hundreds of tiny gold disks, which were probably used to decorate clothes. Archaeologists have also found a number of cylinder seals and signet rings.

Another type of Mycenaean tomb was the *tholos* tomb, which was used from around 1500 BCE. These more elaborate tombs were built by master craftsmen. Schliemann excavated many of these tombs, which appear to have been reserved for the elite. The *tholos* tomb had a dome-shaped roof, and because of the domed appearance, the tombs are also known as beehive tombs.

In a *tholos* tomb, the burial space consisted of a round hole in the ground covered by a dome of stone blocks. The blocks were laid in such a way that each layer protruded inward over the layer below, leaving only a small opening at the top. The opening was then closed with an apex stone. The stone blocks were covered with soil and pebbles, and the mound thus created was given an identifying mark or gravestone. Inside the tomb, the protruding portions of the stone blocks were removed, and the surface was smoothed, creating a conical dome.

A *tholos* tomb was often built into the side of a hill and was approached by a

MYCENAEAN WRITING

When archaeologist Arthur Evans was excavating the Minoan city of Knossos in the early 20th century, he unearthed a number of clay tablets inscribed with three distinct types of script. Evans called these scripts hieroglyphic (the earliest form), Linear A, and Linear B. Evans never succeeded in deciphering any of these scripts.

In 1939, excavations at the Mycenaean palace at Pylos turned up many more Linear B tablets, and thousands more were subsequently found at Mycenae, Tiryns, and Thebes. Using the tablets from Pylos and Knossos, a cryptographer, Michael Ventris, set about deciphering Linear B in the 1950s. Most people believed that the script represented an unknown language of the Minoans, because the signs of Linear B were clearly based on those of Linear A.

Ventris tried to establish a phonetic value for the syllable signs, based on assumptions about the place names on the tablets. Starting from such names as Konoso and Aminiso (Knossos and Amnissos), Ventris was able to uncover an archaic form of Greek. In 1953, together with John Chadwick, a specialist in Greek historical linguistics, Ventris published his findings. The initial article was controversial, but the decipherment is now generally accepted—the language of the Mycenaeans was Greek.

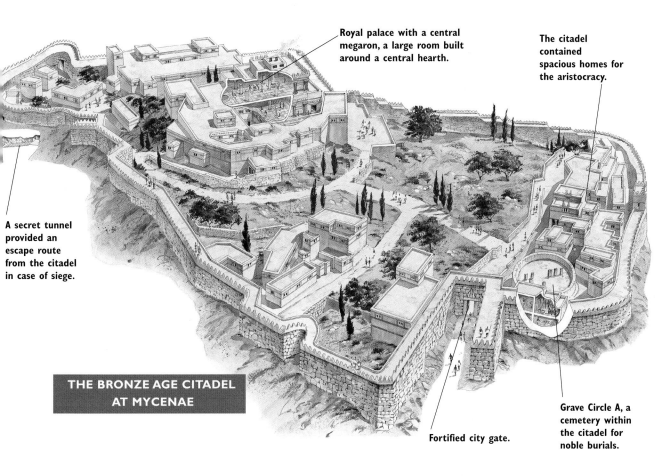

Royal palace with a central megaron, a large room built around a central hearth.

The citadel contained spacious homes for the aristocracy.

A secret tunnel provided an escape route from the citadel in case of siege.

THE BRONZE AGE CITADEL AT MYCENAE

Grave Circle A, a cemetery within the citadel for noble burials.

Fortified city gate.

long open corridor called a *dromos*. One particularly splendid *tholos* tomb discovered in the citadel of Mycenae was named the Treasury of Atreus (see box, page 32).

Other Mycenaean centers

Although Mycenae was the mightiest center of the Mycenaean world, other royal fortresses and palaces of similar or even greater size were built at Tiryns, Asine, Pylos, Athens, Thebes, and Iolkos.

At Tiryns, a fortress was built in three stages some time after 1450 BCE. This fortress has mighty walls that surpass those of Mycenae both in height and in the size of their stone blocks. Several palace buildings, including a megaron,

have been found in Tiryns. Probably the most striking features of these buildings are the covered corridors and casements enclosing impressive galleries.

The floorplan of one building, Nestor's Palace at Pylos, has been particularly well preserved. Named after one of the city's semimythical kings, Nestor's Palace comprised several buildings, which were not protected by massive surrounding walls but were probably guarded by fortresses along the coast. At the gateway to the citadel, there was a guardroom, as well as another room where records were kept of the daily business of the palace, produce received in taxes, and work to be carried out by officials. At the center of the citadel was

This artist's illustration depicts how the citadel of Mycenae may have appeared.

THE TREASURY OF ATREUS

The so-called Treasury of Atreus was a huge, handsome domed grave at Mycenae that dates from the early 13th century BCE. Atreus was a mythical king of Mycenae who was involved in a bitter and tragic battle with his brother Thyestes for the city's throne. The identity of the real-life king who was buried in the tomb remains a mystery, however.

One of the most spectacular features of the dome is its impressive *dromos* (entrance passage), which measures 120 feet (36.6 m) long and 20 feet (6.1 m) wide. This *dromos* leads up to a majestic doorway that is 30 feet (9.1 m) tall and would have been elaborately decorated. A gigantic stone block weighing 120 tons (108,862 kg) closes off the top of the entrance. Inside the tomb, the vast dome has a diameter and height of approximately 45 feet (13.7 m) each and consists of 33 layers of stone blocks fitted snugly together. Remnants of bronze nails suggest that the inside of the dome may well have been decorated with bronze rosettes and friezes.

Using evidence from this and other tombs, archaeologists have tried to imagine what a royal funeral would have been like. It probably started with the funeral procession—consisting of the body of the king drawn on a chariot, followed by priests and mourners—moving slowly along the *dromos* toward the entrance to the tomb, where great doors of bronze would open to admit the procession. Inside the tomb, the king would be laid to rest on a golden carpet. He would be dressed in his robes of state, and around him would be laid his provisions for after death— food and wine, together with his weapons. Animals would be sacrificed, roasted on fires lit within the tomb, and eaten by the mourners. Everyone would then have withdrawn, the doors would have been closed, and the entrance would have been filled up.

The dromos (entrance passage) of the Treasury of Atreus. The Treasury of Atreus is one of the most splendid examples of a tholos tomb.

the palace itself, with an open courtyard, anteroom, and state room (megaron), all surrounded by pantries and storerooms, together with the queen's apartments, which consisted of a smaller megaron, a boudoir, and a large bathroom with a terra-cotta bath.

Many clay tablets have been recovered from the palace at Pylos. When the palace was destroyed by fire around 1200 BCE, the fire may have actually preserved the tablets by baking them. The tablets generally record administrative matters, listing goods, palace personnel, and other details of housekeeping. By doing so, the tablets provide a snapshot of the palace administration just before the destruction. In addition, the tablets reveal much information about Mycenaean social life.

Mycenaean society

Despite its loose political organization, the Mycenaean world was surprisingly united in its social, religious, and linguistic aspects. Each region had its own king (*wanax*), who acted as its head. Under him was the *lawagetas* (people's leader), who was possibly an army commander. Then there were the *telestai*, who are thought to have been wealthy landowners. Freemen were referred to as *damos*. Each class had its own kind of landownership or tenancy.

Everything was controlled by the palace—the ownership and use of land, the labor employed, and the products of craftsmen. The tablets that have been recovered make it clear that most Mycenaeans were poor farmers who worked on land that was owned by the king. They grew crops such as barley and wheat and kept groves of olive trees to produce olive oil. They raised animals such as goats and sheep, which provided both meat and wool, and grew flax to make linen. Most of this produce had to be taken to the palace. It was then sold to

Tiryns, the ruins of which are seen here, was one of the most important Mycenaean cities.

help support the royal family, priests, bureaucrats, and the army.

Another section of Mycenaean society included the skilled craftsmen. The most important of these were the bronzesmiths, who made the weapons for the army. There were also jewellers, potters, carpenters, and cabinetmakers, who carried out intricate inlay work. Large-scale textile manufacturing was carried out by spinners and weavers, most of whom were women. Many slaves were employed in Mycenaean society; most of them had been bought in slave markets in Anatolia.

The Mycenaeans were aggressive and warlike, and each king kept his own standing army, which he had to feed, clothe, and arm. The commanders of the

MYCENAEAN RELIGION

There appear to have been many similarities between the Mycenaean and Minoan religions, but the two were not identical. Still, it seems that both civilizations did worship a mother goddess, whose divine son died at the death of the old year and was born again in the spring. Many Bronze Age paintings show people making offerings to this goddess.

Mycenaean tablets also mention the names of many gods, including Zeus, Athena, Artemis, Poseidon, and Dionysus, who were worshipped by later Greeks. At Pylos, Poseidon, the sea god who was the brother of Zeus, was an important deity who was depicted in the form of a horse. The name of Dionysus, the god of wine, is also found on Mycenaean tablets, which suggests that he too may have been worshipped at this time.

The Mycenaeans tended not to build temples to their gods. Instead, the people worshipped the gods at small shrines, some of which may have been located outdoors but most of which were found inside houses. Small terra-cotta idols in the shape of female figures have been recovered from Mycenae and other places, suggesting that the cult of the goddess was widespread. However, larger idols of both female and male figures have also been found, and it is possible that these idols represent the Greek gods.

These Mycenaean terra-cotta figures date to between 1400 and 1200 BCE. Archaeologists believe that the figures' flattened headdresses indicate that they depict goddesses.

Priests were an important part of Mycenaean society, and they would have carried out the religious rituals, which included sacrificing animals to the gods. The priests would also have conducted burials, and it is evident from the grave goods found in royal tombs from the period that the Mycenaeans believed that their kings would have a life after death.

army wore heavy armor made of bronze and leather helmets made fearsome with the addition of boar's tusks. The infantry wore tunics of leather and carried shields, swords, and daggers. Chariots, which usually carried two men and were drawn by two horses, played an important role in the army. Chariots were used both to lead charges in battle and to carry information back to headquarters.

The Mycenaeans came to dominate most of the Aegean area, subjugating Knossos on Crete and occupying other parts of the island. The influence of the Mycenaeans reached to all corners of their world—Asia Minor, Syria, Egypt, southern Italy, and the Mediterranean islands of Sicily, Cyprus, and Sardinia.

From the 1600s BCE onward, the Mycenaeans dominated sea trade in the Mediterranean. Trading posts were set up in southern Italy and Anatolia, and Mycenaean merchants traded goods such as cloth, pottery, grain, and oil with countries as far away as North Africa, Scandinavia, and the Middle East.

Decline and fall

Over the course of the 13th century BCE, the Mycenaeans carried out a significant amount of construction in their territory. Many new buildings were erected, and the fortresses of Tiryns, Mycenae, and Athens were expanded and reinforced. Even in Pylos, where there were no surrounding walls, the palace was modified to make it less open. Storerooms were enlarged and measures were taken to secure supplies of drinking water.

At the same time, in central Greece, a gigantic fortress was being erected near Gla, which is locat-

This Mycenaean jar is decorated with a picture of an octopus.

ed on the edge of Lake Kopaïs in Boeotia. This fortress had walls 2 miles (3.2 km) long and covered a total area of 50 acres (202,343 m^2). In comparison, Mycenae had walls slightly over 0.5 miles (0.8 km) long encircling an area of 7.5 acres (30,351 m^2). The fortress at Gla was probably intended to be a central refuge for the entire surrounding area, at a time when Mycenaeans all over Greece were apparently feeling a threat of invasion.

This theory is borne out by clay tablets found at Pylos, which mention sending sentinels to the coast, drafting soldiers, and hiring rowers. One of the tablets refers to an unprecedented sacrifice of 13 golden vases and 10 people, obviously an attempt to secure the favor of the gods at a time of great emergency.

That the threat was not imaginary was proved by the widespread destruction that took place after 1250 BCE. This destruction has frequently been explained as the result of an invasion by the Dorians, a tribe from the Balkans and northern Greece. The Dorians are said to have annihilated the Mycenaean civilization, but this idea is flawed. There is no gap in the archaeological record that would correspond to the arrival of a huge group of newcomers. On the contrary, the overall impression is one of continuity after the destruction. Many of the former settlements were rebuilt, and the existing Mycenaean culture simply continued. However, the size of the population dropped dramatically, and society as a whole descended to a lower cultural plane.

So what caused the decline if it was not the Dorians? The whole eastern Mediterranean area was in ferment

This cup, which was found in a Mycenaean tomb on the island of Rhodes, was made between 1350 and 1300 BCE.

at this time. The Hittites disappeared from Asia Minor while the Egyptians were battling with the Sea Peoples. It may be that these enemies of Egypt swept through the Mycenaean palaces, or there may have been civil war between the Mycenaean kingdoms. There may have been natural disasters, such as earthquakes, or the administrative and political systems may simply have collapsed as a result of famine or the cutting off of trade routes. Whatever the reason, the Mycenaean civilization disintegrated, and the so-called Dark Age dawned in Greece.

Troy

While the Mycenaean culture was dominant on the mainland of Greece, a city was flourishing in northwestern Anatolia. This city was Troy, the legendary adversary of Greece. As with Mycenae, much of what is known about Troy is the result of work carried out by the archaeologist Heinrich Schliemann.

The legendary city of Troy had fascinated Schliemann since boyhood, when his father had told him the stories of the *Iliad* and the *Odyssey* (see box, page 38) and Schliemann had come across an illustration of how the ancient city might

have looked. The city was supposed to have been encircled by a massive wall, punctuated by towers, and to have been the site of the Trojan War, the subject of the *Iliad*.

Troy did in fact exist more than 5,000 years ago. Bronze Age Troy was situated at the entrance to the Dardanelles, the route for ships passing between the Aegean Sea and the Black Sea. The city also occupied a crucial position on the land route between Europe and Asia. For these reasons, Troy became a prosperous mercantile city and a center of culture. In the third and second millennia BCE, it was the leading city of the region, with a royal house ruling over the surrounding farming villages. Troy continued to prosper until the middle of the 11th century BCE.

Schliemann's excavation

The true history of Troy was unknown in the mid-19th century CE, but several archaeologists, including Frank Calvert (1828–1908), were interested in discovering the site of ancient Troy (if it in fact existed). Calvert was an English amateur archaeologist working as a consular official in the Dardanelles area. He had read a book by Charles Maclaren (published in 1822) that suggested that a hill called Hissarlik on the Aegean coast of western Turkey might be the site of the city. Calvert's brother Frederick, who was also based in the area, bought a farm in 1847 that extended over 2,000 acres (8 km²) and took in part of Mount Hissarlik. Over the next few years, Frank made some exploratory excavations on his brother's land.

Since his retirement from the world of business around 1860, Heinrich Schliemann had been busy. He had studied archaeology, written a book on Troy, and traveled widely to visit sites of archaeological interest. In 1868, he met Frank Calvert in Turkey and learned of the preliminary excavations at Hissarlik. However, a full-scale excavation of the site would require considerable financing, which Calvert could not provide. Schliemann could, and he persuaded Calvert to let him take over the excavations on the Calvert half of the Hissarlik. Schliemann also obtained permission from the Turkish government to dig on the other half of the mound, as long as any discovered treasure was shared with the government.

Schliemann hired 70 local workmen and started digging in 1871. Very soon, he uncovered an ancient wall, built of immense boulders, just 15 feet (4.5 m) below the surface. Encouraged by this discovery, he then sank shafts and dug trenches into the hillside. To his amazement, he discovered the remains of not just one city, but nine cities, each built on the ruins of the last.

The treasure of Priam

Schliemann had certainly discovered an important archaeological site, but was it Troy? Although he called himself an archaeologist, Schliemann was primarily a treasure hunter. Later, at Mycenae, he would hope to unearth treasure belonging to Agamemnon. At the supposed site of Troy, he longed to find what he called "the treasure of Priam." Convinced that the Trojan War was grounded in historical fact, Schliemann felt sure that King Priam had hidden his treasures to save them from the Greeks.

Around noon on a day in June 1873, Schliemann spotted the gleam of gold at the base of a wall in the excavations. Schliemann and his wife, Sophia,

Neoptolemus is given the armor of his father Achilles by the Greek hero Odysseus. This vase illustration dates to around the eighth century BCE.

unearthed a cache of golden objects, including bracelets, earrings, diadems, and many gold rings. The Schliemanns hid the treasure and smuggled it off the site and, eventually, out of Turkey. When news of the find leaked out, the Turkish authorities were outraged at the deception. Schliemann had to pay a very heavy fine before he was allowed to continue excavating. Although Schliemann remained convinced he had discovered the treasure of King Priam, later research established that the golden horde dated from more than a thousand years before the time of the Trojan War.

Believing that the Troy of Homer would probably lie at almost the lowest level, Schliemann hired more men to dig down to that level. Unfortunately, since Schliemann understood nothing of the scientific method of archaeology, much valuable evidence was destroyed during the dig. Later archaeologists established that Homer's Troy lay at a much higher level.

The nine cities

The nine levels of Troy start with the first Troy, which was a small fortified citadel dating from around 3000 BCE. This citadel would have provided a safe shelter for the surrounding villagers when danger threatened. The second level was Troy II, dating from around 2600 BCE. The town was much larger and became wealthy by trading with the Mycenaeans of mainland Greece. The evidence points to Troy II being destroyed by fire, which was why Schliemann believed it was the Troy of

THE *ILIAD* AND THE *ODYSSEY*

The background to the story of the *Iliad* is the siege of Troy by a coalition of Greeks, called Achaeans in the poem. The reason for the war is that Helen, the beautiful wife of Menelaus, king of Sparta, has been abducted by Paris, a Trojan prince. When Menelaus discovers that his wife is gone, he and his brother Agamemnon, king of Mycenae, call upon the princes of Achaea to assist in punishing Troy and bringing Helen home. A fleet is prepared, and the warriors sail for Troy, where a drawn-out siege follows.

In the Greek camp outside Troy, a dispute arises between the Greek prince Achilles and the supreme commander, Agamemnon, who has abused his authority by taking a beautiful slave away from Achilles. Achilles, deeply insulted, refuses to continue fighting. Without Achilles, the Greeks prove to be weaker than the Trojans, and disaster threatens. Achilles finally agrees to allow his friend, Patroclus, to take part in the conflict, and Hector, the Trojan commander, kills Patroclus. The grieving Achilles feels compelled to avenge the death of his friend and in turn kills Hector, which heralds the beginning of the end for the Trojans.

The *Iliad* ends with the burial of Patroclus and the return of Hector's body to his father, King Priam.

The *Odyssey*, a sequel to the *Iliad*, deals with the difficult voyage home of one of the Greek princes, Odysseus of Ithaca. The tale opens with the stress that his prolonged absence has caused his household. Since no word has been heard from him for 10 years, Odysseus is assumed to be dead. Greedy suitors are ruining his property as they court his wife, Penelope.

Odysseus himself then relates his adventures to the king and queen of Scheria. Among other escapades, Odysseus tells them of his encounter with the man-eating giant Polyphemus and the temptations of the goddess Calypso, who offered Odysseus immortality.

The *Odyssey* ends with the return of Odysseus to the island of Ithaca, where the hero discovers what has been going on in his absence. He kills the suitors who have been besieging his supposed widow and is reunited with his wife, son, and aged father.

This Roman mosaic depicts Odysseus being tempted by the sirens.

The walls of the ancient city of Troy stand in northwestern Anatolia.

Homer. The three succeeding Troys were each larger than the one before.

Troy VI was heavily influenced by the Mycenaeans and attracted many new settlers. It was destroyed around 1300 BCE, to be succeeded by what is called Troy VIIa. Most archaeologists now believe that this is the Homeric Troy. Fragments of pottery found at this level indicate that the city dates from the mid-13th century BCE. Some human remains, one of which is a human skeleton showing injuries to the head and a broken jawbone, have been found in the streets, which suggests the city was destroyed by war. There is also evidence that Troy VIIa was put to the torch. The next city, Troy VIIb, also seems to have been destroyed by fire. Historians believe this destruction happened around 1050 BCE.

The fall of Troy

After the destruction of Troy VIIb, the city seems to have been abandoned for several centuries, but at the start of the seventh century BCE, the site was reoccupied by Greeks and became known as Ilium. Around 85 BCE, this city was attacked and taken by the Romans, who then built Troy IX, which became an important trading city until it was eclipsed by Constantinople in the fourth century CE. Around 400 CE, the site was finally abandoned and gradually disappeared under the mound of Hissarlik, until the cities were finally rediscovered by Schliemann.

Schliemann died in 1890, and the work at Hissarlik was carried on by his assistant, Wilhelm Dorpfeld, who made further excavations in 1893 and 1894. After that point, nothing more was done until the 1930s, when the American archaeologist Carl Blegen (1887–1971) carried out careful excavations over a seven-year period, from 1932 to 1938. He took many photographs and was instrumental in establishing much of the chronology of the city. In particular, it was Blegen who established that the Troy of Homeric legend was almost certainly Troy VIIa.

See also:

Bronze Age Greece (page 6) • The Minoans (page 14)

THE DARK AGE AND GREEK EXPANSION

After the fall of the Mycenaean civilization, Greece entered a period that is now known as the Dark Age. Gradually, however, Greece emerged from this era, and exiles from the country founded colonies all around the Mediterranean region.

TIME LINE

c. 1250 BCE

Influx of Dorian invaders from north heralds beginning of end of Mycenaean culture.

c. 1100 BCE

Greece enters Dark Age, period marked by poverty and depopulation.

c. 850 BCE

Greeks begin migrations to Cyprus, Crete, Aegean islands, and Anatolia.

c. 750 BCE

Beginning of Archaic period; developments include reintroduction of writing, increased trade, and emergence of poleis.

c. 700 BCE

New style of poetry emerges in works of Hesiod and Archilochus; poems contrast with epics of Homer.

By the mid-13th century BCE, the cities and palaces of mainland Greece were feeling under threat. New construction surrounded many of the cities with strong fortified walls, and measures were taken to protect underground water supplies, suggesting that imminent invasion was feared. This fear seems not to have been misplaced. By the end of the century, all the palaces had been burned, and the once great Mycenaean civilization was in terminal decline.

The cause of this collapse was a vast influx of Dorian peoples from central Asia. These aggressive tribesmen swept down mainland Greece from the north, traveling in ox-drawn covered wagons and inspiring terror with their horned helmets. By 1100 BCE, all the main Mycenaean centers had fallen to these invaders, and for the next few centuries, Greece entered what is called the Dark Age, about which very little is known.

An age of poverty

Archaeological excavations suggest that Greece became impoverished and partially depopulated in the turbulent period following the collapse of the Mycenaean culture. The arrival of the Dorians resulted in a change in the spoken dialect and in iron being used in preference to bronze, but the number and size of both settlements and burial grounds declined sharply, while the primitive style of buildings and earthenware show that the people lived in great poverty. The complete disappearance of the complex society once centered on the palaces meant that writing skills were also lost. The social organization seems to have broken down into small communities, each led by a *basileus*. In the palace hierarchy, this title had been used for a subordinate figure, but in the Dark Age, the title referred to a powerful chieftain who held independent authority.

It seems that the population increased again in the ninth century BCE, possibly due to a reduction in mortality or an increase in migration. What is certain is that the Greeks began to migrate from the mainland around this time, some to Cyprus, Crete, and the Aegean islands, others to Anatolia. Over the course of the ninth century, representatives of three main dialect groups (see box, page 44) settled in much of the coastal region of Anatolia and on the islands off this coast. Those speaking the Aeolic dialect settled on the island of Lesbos and in the region from north of the Dardanelles on the northwest coast of Anatolia down to

The Temple of Hera on the island of Samos in the Aegean Sea. Samos was settled by Ionians during the Dark Age and later became an important trading center.

This terra-cotta figurine, known as the Lefkandi Centaur, was found on the island of Euboea. The figurine dates to the 10th century BCE and is a rare relic from the Dark Age.

Smyrna. Ionians settled on the central part of the coast from Smyrna to Miletus and on the islands of Chios and Samos. Dorians settled in the southern part from Halicarnassus down to the southernmost coast and on the islands of Rhodes and Cos. Some of the many settlements created on these islands and in the coastal regions developed into important cities—in particular, the 12 Ionian settlements called the *dodeca poleis* (the 12 cities).

The migration to the various islands and to Anatolia stimulated further exploration, and the former trading routes with the east were soon restored. Linking large parts of the Mediterranean world with the Greek world, these routes had declined during the Dark Age but had never been completely severed. Toward the end of the ninth century BCE, Greek seafarers could once again be found in the harbors of northern Syria and Phoenicia.

The Archaic period

The restoration of trade with the east had momentous results for the Greeks. The Greek world emerged from its temporary isolation and began to experience such great changes that a new era is defined as beginning around 750 BCE. The new world that was developing bore little resemblance to the old Bronze Age civilization. Historians call this new era the Archaic period.

During the Archaic period, increased contact with the east brought the Greeks new ideas regarding pottery, sculpture, architecture, mythology, religion, and the use of iron and bronze. Most important of all was the reintroduction of writing, this time using an alphabet derived from Phoenician examples (see box, page 46). It is not clear exactly when the Greeks started to adapt the Semitic alphabet to their own needs, but the oldest inscriptions using the new alphabet date from the second half of the eighth century BCE. After that, the use of the alphabet spread rapidly, making it possible to record the *Iliad* and the *Odyssey*; these

THE GREEK WORLD IN THE DARK AGE

two epics were almost certainly first composed in the oral tradition.

The beginning of the Archaic period also saw the emergence of the polis (plural: poleis), which was an autonomous political unit covering a small territory, usually averaging between 50 and 100 square miles (260 km²), with a population of between 2,500 and 4,500. Some poleis were larger than this, particularly those of Sparta, Argos, Corinth, Athens, and Thebes. There were also some very small units covering a territory of no more than 15 square miles (39 km²) and having a population of only around 250. However large or small, each polis had at least one settlement that was called a city (also, confusingly, called a polis), no matter how small or unlike a city it actually was.

Each polis was completely independent. In theory, all the freemen who were its citizens organized the political affairs of the polis (from which the term *politics* is derived) in community assemblies, but in fact, much of the real power rested with the aristocracy. The basileus, who in the Dark Age had ruled as a king, was replaced in most cases by magistrates who were elected annually from the ranks of the nobles. These aristocrats owed their dominant position to a combination of

THE GREEK DIALECT GROUPS

Dialect was a significant factor in the Greek migrations of the ninth century BCE because people tended to settle into linguistic groups. Doric was the dialect of northwest Greece. It was also spoken along the west of Greece and on the islands of Crete, Cos, and Rhodes as a result of Dorian conquests between 1200 and 1000 BCE. Doric spread to Anatolia as Dorian speakers settled there in the ninth century BCE.

The non-Doric dialects were Ionic, Aeolic, and Arcado-Cyprian. Ionic was the language of Attica and the island of Evvoia, while Aeolic was spoken in the northeast and center of mainland Greece. Arcado-Cyprian, the dialect spoken in Arcadia on the Peloponnese and on Cyprus, is closely related to Mycenaean Greek, in which the Linear B inscriptions were written. This affinity to Linear B may be due to the fact that there was little migrant influence in the wild and rugged Arcadian region and that Cyprus had served as a haven for refugees from the mainland during the time of the invasions.

The greatest differences were those between the Dorians and the Ionians, two groups who spoke different tongues, had different customs and religious practices, and who each built up a position of power. These differences led to the Peloponnesian War (431–404 BCE).

This portrait from a Roman mosaic is believed to depict the poetess Sappho, who wrote in the Aeolic dialect.

These gold earrings were found at Lefkandi on Euboea and date to the mid-ninth century BCE.

power and wealth, which, in the early Archaic period, was often expressed in the number of horses one owned. After 700 BCE, the possession of bronze armor was another indicator of status.

Colonization

The emergence of the poleis took place during a time of rapid population growth. This rise in population led to the conquest of sparsely populated regions and to armed conflicts between neighboring poleis in attempts to expand their territories. The rise also encouraged further emigration of Greeks from the mainland. In the eighth century BCE, Sparta subjected the region of Laconia and began the conquest of neighboring Messenia. Argos extended its power over the Argolis region, while Athens united the peninsula of Attica into one polis. The emigration of many Greeks to settlements on the Mediterranean and Black Sea coasts led to what is called the Archaic colonization.

Developments such as colonization and the subsequent flourishing of trade, the growing contact between the various poleis, and the use of writing to record the laws and decrees of a polis community all had an influence on the relations between the many small states of the Greek world. Within the poleis, social relations were changing as some citizens became a great deal richer than others. An elite of aristocrats and wealthy citizens emerged as a result of trading with the east. In several poleis, these small groups of aristocrats managed to seize control and end the community assemblies, thereby undermining the fundamental principle of the poleis. As the majority of the citizens still had to work to survive, they were often forced into a

This sixth-century-BCE Greek vase painting shows Ajax carrying the body of Achilles. The tales of Homer were not written down until the Archaic period.

THE GREEK ALPHABETS

The word *alphabet* comes from the first two letters of the Greek alphabet—alpha and beta—and denotes a writing system in which a single character (grapheme) represents a single sound (phoneme). Non-alphabetic systems of writing use signs that represent whole words or syllables. The Mesopotamian cuneiform system used a combination of word and syllable signs, while Egyptian hieroglyphs used signs that represented words together with signs that represented a group of consonants or a single consonant. Around 1500 BCE, elements of the Egyptian hieroglyphic script were adapted to create a script in which each individual sound of a language (apart from vowel sounds) was represented by a single symbol—that is, an alphabet. This adaptation took place somewhere in the Syro-Palestinian region, and the inventors of the new script spoke a Semitic language.

The new alphabetic script soon took on different forms as its use spread among different peoples over the course of the following centuries. One script developed in the 14th and 13th centuries BCE in the city of Ugarit on the coast of Syria

consisted of a cuneiform (wedge-shaped) alphabet of 30 characters. One of the principal variants was the Northwest Semitic alphabet, from which nearly all alphabetic scripts in use today are ultimately descended. A short version, using 22 letters, was being used to write the Phoenician language from the 11th century BCE, and from Phoenicia it spread to neighboring regions in the Middle East.

The Greeks adopted this short Phoenician alphabet in the eighth century BCE and modified it by adding two or more consonant symbols. They also began to use some of the symbols to represent vowel sounds. For a time, they experimented with writing from left to right and from right to left, but by around 500 BCE, they settled on left to right. As the Greek alphabet spread, it was adopted and modified by various Mediterranean peoples, including the Etruscans, the Umbrians, the Oscans, and the Romans. The last were to be the most influential, since the Roman alphabet, used to write Latin, was subsequently to be used by all the languages of western Europe.

This tablet found on the island of Pylos is inscribed with Linear B script. The Greeks later adopted the Phoenician alphabet.

The Temple of Ceres at Paestum. Paestum, a Greek colony in southern Italy, was founded around the beginning of the seventh century BCE.

dependent relationship with rich land-holders. Many of the poorer citizens were exploited, and if they got into debt, they could be sold into slavery.

In Sparta, attempts were made to resolve the internal tensions by making all citizens equal, at the expense of an underprivileged group that was excluded from citizenship and left with no rights at all. In Athens and Corinth, rivalry between aristocrats led to internal political conflict. In some cases, an aristocrat would succeed in seizing absolute power and set himself up as an all-powerful sovereign—this was a new kind of monarch that the Greeks called a *tyrannis* (tyrant).

After the horrors of the Dark Age, the Archaic period saw the Greeks emerging into an era of prosperity that in turn led to a flowering of new ideas and artistic achievement. The spread of writing had a profound effect on law and government. Because the results of law suits could now be recorded, leading to the establishment of legal codes, any citizen could appeal against an arbitrary ruling by a corrupt magistrate and cite legal precedent to uphold the appeal. This change led to more rational government and the rule of law.

Greek expansion

The period of Greek overseas settlement that began in the middle of the eighth century BCE lasted for more than 200 years. During that time, Greeks founded dozens of settlements on the fringes of the Aegean, Mediterranean, and Black seas. The impetus behind this colonizing movement may have originally been trade, but the settlements soon became new, independent states. These colonies (not a strictly accurate term for the settlements) inherited various social and political aspects—such as religious cults, political organizations, and spoken dialect—from their metropolis (parent city), but the colonies themselves were completely independent entities.

An overseas polis often started as a trading post (*emporion*), which then developed into a settlement as colonists followed. Trade was certainly the motivating factor in some of the very early Greek colonies, such as Al Mina in Syria and Pithekoussai in Italy. Greek traders were looking to buy iron ore, silver, and slaves, while offering wine and olive oil in return. A trading post that turned into a colony was called an *apoikia*, meaning a "settlement elsewhere." Most *apoikiai* started with no more than one or two hundred people, to be joined by other colonists at a later stage. The new colony would always hold its parent metropolis in esteem and would preserve the religious customs of the parent city despite any political differences. The metropolis and satellite polis would send official envoys to each other's religious festivals, and the special relationship was sometimes demonstrated by the provision of military aid by the parent to the colony. For example, Corinth helped the city of Syracuse to fight the Athenians during the Peloponnesian War, because Syracuse was Corinth's colony.

The spread of settlements

Colonies fanned out in all directions from the Greek mainland. Some of the earliest settlements were on Sicily and in southern Italy, where the colonists were attracted by the good harbors and fertile land to support farming. The Greek presence there became so dominant that the area was called Magna Grecia (Great Greece). In the fifth century BCE, Syracuse on Sicily became the most highly populated of all Greek cities. Other new settlements were situated on the Aegean islands along the northern coast of the Aegean Sea; on the northern coast of Anatolia along the Hellespont and the Bosporus; around the Black Sea; on the north African coast in Cyrenaica (present-day Libya); and on the south coast of France and the northeastern coast of Spain.

The Greek colonists avoided areas where other peoples had a significant presence. These areas included the eastern coast of the Mediterranean, which was already well occupied, and the northeast African coast, which was largely avoided because of the dominance of Egypt in the area. The African coast to

The Sicilian town of Syracuse, the site of this ancient Greek theater, was settled by exiles from Corinth in the eighth century BCE.

Elea, the ruins of which are shown here, was a Greek colony on the mainland of Italy. The colony was founded in the sixth century BCE.

the west of Cyrenaica was entirely in the hands of the Phoenicians, as was the western part of Sicily, the whole of Sardinia, most of the smaller islands in the western Mediterranean, and a large part of the Spanish coast.

Adventurous colonists

Why the Greek colonists wanted to leave the mother country is not completely clear. The theory that they were escaping overpopulation on the mainland has been largely discredited, but they may have been fleeing from an unsatisfactory political situation at home, or seeking land of their own, or simply searching for adventure. When a group of emigrants boarded a ship or—as some sources imply—were taken aboard forcibly, the people were already well prepared for their enterprise. They knew where they

wanted to go and had consulted an oracle before setting out to ensure a favorable outcome to the voyage. At least, that is what they were supposed to do. Colonies that did not possess the text of an oracle, or that could not point out the tomb of an original founder, often produced forgeries in order to ensure their standing.

When the immigrants disembarked at their destination, the first thing they did was to drive away the native population, if there was one. It is not known whether it was common practice to subdue the original inhabitants and bind them in servitude to the Greeks, but this undoubtedly happened from time to time. The second task was to find a site where the new city could be built and divide the surrounding land equally among the colonists. This practice served

49

A POET FARMER

One poet who seems to mark the transition between the heroic epic poetry of Homer and the more practical, personal work of writers such as Archilochus is Hesiod, a farmer who lived in Boeotia around 700 BCE. Whereas the two epic poems of Homer, the *Iliad* and the *Odyssey*, portrayed a legendary time of super-heroes who fought with formidable foes and overcame huge obstacles with the help of the gods, Hesiod's poetry dealt with his own world. Although his poetry retained the traditional epic form, the content of it was novel. Hesiod saw the world as a chaotic place where the individual was on his own in trying to achieve good relations with the gods and his fellow men. Hesiod sometimes featured himself in his poems, and in his "Contest between Homer and Hesiod," he awards the prize to himself, claiming that he stands for peace and plowshares rather than swords and slaughter.

to create an aristocracy of the earliest settlers, who had first choice of land and became premier citizens. Immigrants who arrived later would probably be granted civil rights and a small piece of land, but they would almost certainly be accorded a subordinate position in the new society. This practice explains the existence of the extensive elite groups that occupied the aristocratic councils in many of the colonies. It is not clear whether women accompanied the original colonists. They may have been sent for later, or they may have been sought—or abducted—from neighboring regions.

When a trading post developed into a more permanent community, it usually took the form of an agricultural settlement. No matter how much trading took place, arable land was of prime importance, and most Greek colonies were founded in regions with good agricultural land. Some commentators have deduced from this pattern that Archaic colonization was motivated by a shortage of land in the homeland. While many of the colonists were probably driven to emigrate for economic reasons, this motivation would not have applied to the aristocratic and wealthier colonists who may have left a parent city for political reasons.

Exporting a culture

The natural consequence of Greek colonization was not only a migration of people but a migration of their whole culture, including their technological skills, their customs, their religion, and their concepts and attitudes. The Greeks took with them everything, from specific agricultural methods and crops like the olive and grape to architectural and building skills and an entire hierarchy of gods. This export of culture from the Aegean region to, particularly, the Italian region was to have a profound effect on European history. The colonies of "Great Greece" were to form a bridge between east and west, just as the Mycenaeans and the Phoenicians had done previously.

A good example of this influence can be seen in the colony at Pithekoussai on Ischia, an Italian island in the Bay of Naples. Excavations carried out there since the mid-20th century CE have established that this settlement was founded by colonists from the Aegean island of Evvoia. Certainly not a typical colony, Pithekoussai was a very early settlement of the eighth century BCE and was located right on the northern frontier of what was later to become the Greek world. The colony appears to have started as an *emporion* and subsequently developed into an *apoikia*. Greek settlements functioned as a corridor through which eastern influences reached the Iron Age cultures of Italy and beyond, stimulating major changes. In the seventh and sixth centuries BCE, a Mediterranean urban culture began to take root in the Etruscan region of central Italy.

In addition to generating changes in the occupied regions, the Greek colonies also stimulated developments in the motherland. The existence of strong and independent colonies overseas boosted trade considerably. Grain from Sicily and southern Russia was brought to mainland Greece, while wine, bronze plate, and high-quality pottery were the main commodities sent from the motherland to the colonies. The colonial Greeks then often sold on these products to indigenous rulers in the hinterland.

Finds of pottery and other artifacts in various locations have enabled archaeologists to trace trade movements and map the contacts between Greeks and non-Greeks. It has been discovered, for instance, that Carthaginian and Greek traders supplied bronze products, pottery, wine, and other luxury articles via intermediaries to chieftains who lived in remote inland parts of western and central Europe. These goods were exchanged for silver, tin, or slaves. The Celtic chiefs of Gaul were among those who prospered from trade with the Greeks, as evidenced by the number of luxury Greek items found in their burial chambers. One particular example was a Greek bronze krater (a vessel for mixing wine with water) that was found in the tomb of a ruler in Vix in the Seine valley.

Poetry of the colonies

Besides bringing Greek architecture, sculpture, and art to the new settlements, the colonists also imported Greek poetry. One of these colonial poets was Archilochus, who, in the seventh century BCE, left his birthplace on the island of Paros to go to Thasos (an island off the Thracian coast), where the inhabitants of Paros were founding a colony.

Archilochus was one of the first Greek lyric poets. Unlike the epic poems of Homer, Archilocus's work describes everyday life and the poet's personal feel-

This bust depicts the Greek poet Hesiod, who lived in the eighth century BCE.

ings about the world around him. Often sarcastic in tone, the poems convey strong feelings about his new life abroad.

Joining an early emigrant voyage to Thasos, Archilochus experienced firsthand the rigors of life on the frontier at that time. The settlement was under constant threat from Thracian tribesmen, and the settlers found life hard. Archilochus himself lamented his stay in the "triply dreadful city of Thasos," where, as he put it, "the dregs of the entire Greek nation" came together to fight "the Thracian dogs." Archilochus's view of Thasos gives a fascinating glimpse into the mind of the Greek colonist, with his idealistic view of the paradise over the horizon.

See also:

Mycenae and Troy (page 26)

SPARTA AND ATHENS

TIME LINE

c. 1200 BCE

Twelve cities of Attica united by Theseus according to legend; form city-state of Athens.

c. 950 BCE

Dorian invaders settle on Eurotas Plain; over next two centuries, they form city-state of Sparta.

c. 725 BCE

Spartans conquer neighboring region of Messenia; numerous revolts occur during following century.

c. 650 BCE

Spartan state reorganized; changes credited to lawgiver named Lycurgas.

c. 625 BCE

Social inequality leads to unrest in Athens.

c. 600 BCE

Athenian statesman Solon makes changes to Athenian society, including abolishing debt slavery.

The rivalry of the two city-states Sparta and Athens formed an important part of the history of ancient Greece. Both cities underwent changes in their political structure from the eighth century BCE onward.

The eighth century BCE saw the emergence in Greece of the polis (plural: poleis), the city-state. Two city-states that had very different histories and characteristics were Sparta and Athens.

Sparta

The polis of Sparta had its origins in several small settlements on the Eurotas Plain in Laconia in the southern part of the Peloponnese. In the 10th century BCE, the Eurotas Plain was invaded by warriors who spoke the Doric dialect. Subduing the native population, the invaders moved into several villages grouped near the hills in the center of the plain and formed the settlement that was to become Sparta. Over the next two centuries, the Spartans, as they came to be called, developed a regime that differed considerably from that of other Greek city-states. The highest level of the social hierarchy of this new polis consisted of the conquering warriors—the Spartans—who were led by two kings. The conquered people consisted of helots, or serfs, and *perioikoi*, who were neighboring freemen who recognized the authority of the Spartan kings.

By the eighth century BCE, Sparta had expanded to such an extent that there was not sufficient land in Laconia to provide a reasonable living for all the warriors of the growing population. On the other side of the Taygetus Mountains lay the highly fertile region of Messenia. After a lengthy war, the Spartans succeeded in conquering Messenia toward the end of the eighth century. From that time onward, the original settlement on the Eurotas Plain remained the heart of the state, while Messenia was regarded as occupied territory.

The Messenians found the regime under the Spartans so oppressive that they revolted in the seventh century BCE; the rising was only finally put down after decades of strife. During this period, the Spartan poet Tyrtaeus wrote battle songs, and his verses constitute the oldest written record of Sparta's history. In one song, Tyrtaeus describes the rewards that the conquerors would enjoy when all the Messenians were made into helots: "Like heavily laden donkeys, they will be forced by hard means to hand over to their masters half of what they harvest in their fields." This prophecy was soon to be fulfilled.

The helots

By the mid-seventh century BCE, Sparta had finally subdued the Messenians and was the largest of all the Greek city-states. Sparta had an immense labor force of helots to work its fertile lands, making it also one of the most prosperous city-states. The helots functioned as serfs,

This statue is a copy of the Athena Promachos, a giant statue of the goddess Athena that stood in Athens. The deity was the city's patron, and the original statue was destroyed in the 13th century CE.

carrying out all the agricultural work while their Spartan masters concentrated on military matters. In time of war, helots were used to row the long galleys or as low-ranking soldiers in the field. They had no civil rights, but in contrast to slaves, helots could not be owned by individual Spartans.

Best described as "slaves of the state," the helots belonged to particular plots of land and could not be bought and sold individually. When land was allocated to a Spartan citizen, it came complete with helots, and he was not allowed to sell or release them. The state determined the percentage of the harvest that the helots had to hand over to their masters. The helots were allowed to keep the remainder of the food for themselves.

There were a few legal ways for a helot to secure freedom. A Spartan father could adopt any children he had by a helot mother, making the children Spartan citizens. From the fifth century BCE onward, helots could earn the status of freeman by fighting with the Spartans as full-fledged soldiers in wartime. In neither case did the helot acquire full Spartan civil rights.

Although they were essential for the agricultural economy, helots were by no means always well treated. Spartan citizens were vastly outnumbered by helots and lived in constant fear of an uprising. Consequently, the Spartans attempted to keep the helots firmly under control by systematic humiliation and intimidation. This treatment included the *krypteia*—a kind of secret police in which young Spartans were enrolled to hunt and kill helots in the wilderness. This practice seems to have been a sort of initiation ritual that involved a period of isolation followed by the killing of an "enemy." However, it is probable that only a few helots were murdered in this way; a large-scale culling of the workforce would have had serious negative economic implications.

Perioikoi

The other people who were not entitled to Spartan civil rights were the *perioikoi*—usually translated as neighbors or out-dwellers. These people were

Greek ruins in the Messenia region, which was conquered by Sparta in the eighth century BCE.

SPARTA, ATHENS, AND THEIR RIVALS

freemen descended from the pre-Dorian inhabitants of the region and lived on the outskirts of the polis. Most of the *perioikoi* were farmers, and although they had no political rights within the Spartan state, their communities were internally autonomous. In peacetime, Sparta had little interest in the settlements, but in times of war, the settlements were expected to supply soldiers.

Spartan males were trained from a young age to become soldiers and were banned from engaging in trade or crafts. For this reason, it was the *perioikoi*

who formed the class of traders and craftsmen that exported iron ore, limestone for building, bronze figurines, and painted pottery.

Lycurgus and the constitution

After the final subjugation of the Messenians, a number of changes took place in Spartan society. While the basic administrative and social structure that had existed since the conquest of Laconia continued, it was adapted and systematized in the late seventh and early sixth centuries BCE. These reforms have

Two Greek wrestlers prepare to fight in this relief sculpture. In ancient Sparta, sports such as wrestling were considered an important part of military training.

traditionally been attributed to the great lawgiver Lycurgus, although it is not clear whether any such man ever existed. It is more probable that the reformed constitution was not the work of one man, but rather the result of an evolutionary process. However it was arrived at, the constitution of the revised state is generally referred to as the Lycurgan Constitution, to distinguish it from the earlier society.

Under the Lycurgan Constitution, the joint rule of two kings continued. However, apart from their joint command of the army, most of their functions were purely honorary. The real power lay not with the kings but with three other institutions: the assembly, the council of elders, and the magistrates.

The public assembly, called the *apella*, was an assembly of adult warriors with Spartan civil rights. This assembly had the power to vote on motions presented by the council of elders (the *gerousia*) but could not propose its own motions. Nor could the assembly make amendments to motions laid before it. Voting took place by means of booing or cheering, the outcome being determined by the group that made the most noise.

The most powerful of the governing bodies was the *gerousia*, which consisted of 28 men all aged 60 and above. Each member was either related to one of the kings or came from an aristocratic family, and they were all elected for life. The *gerousia* prepared motions to be debated in the assembly and served as a Supreme Court, with authority to try even the kings if it seemed they had fallen short of their duties.

When motions were voted on in the assembly, the volume of noise was judged by the five *ephors* (overseers), the highest magistrates in the polis. These officials, in whom ultimate authority lay, were elected annually by the assembly and constituted the actual government of Sparta, supervising the entire range of state affairs. The *ephors* held regular meetings with the *gerousia*, influencing the choice of items to be debated at the assembly, and had monthly meetings with the two kings, at which the kings pledged themselves to observe the laws. In return, the *ephors* promised to support the kings, provided the kings did indeed observe the laws. If the kings and the *ephors* had disagreements, the *ephors*, who had the last word, could charge the kings with misconduct, fine them, dethrone them, and even send them into exile.

Military training

In Lycurgan Sparta, the army was of paramount importance, and all Spartan boys had to undergo rigorous training from a very early age for a military life. At birth, infants were inspected by state officials, and any infants deemed to be defective were exposed on the mountains and left to die. At the age of seven, boys were taken from their homes and brought up in "packs," which were supervised by older boys. When they were twelve, the boys were placed in barracks, where they lived on a basic diet of porridge enriched with bits of pork. Their education was primarily physical, consisting mostly of athletics and combat sports practiced naked in all weathers outdoors. Throughout, the emphasis was on learning to obey orders without hesitation and to endure hardships.

At age 20, the warrior graduated and was allotted a plot of land that would provide food to feed himself and his family. He joined a *sussitia* (one of the military messes) to which he would belong

This 19th-century-CE engraving depicts the Spartan lawgiver Lycurgus, who is credited with transforming Sparta's political structure.

for the rest of his life, and he became eligible to vote in the assembly. Spartan males were conditioned to relate primarily to other men. Indeed, part of their youthful training involved being paired with another older boy in what was almost certainly a sexual relationship.

Even when a man and a woman married, they lived in separate male and female quarters, although they were allowed to share a room at night. Marriage was endorsed by the state, since it was necessary to raise another generation of warriors and mothers of warriors. Since it was deemed important that women should be healthy to bear healthy children, great attention was devoted to the physical education of girls. The girls participated—naked, to the amazement of other Greeks—along with boys in the athletics program until the age of 18. To ensure that girls would not embark on pregnancy too young, the marriageable age for girls in Sparta was higher than elsewhere in Greece.

An austere life

From the sixth century BCE, Spartan society became increasingly austere and rigid. Everything was focused on the maintenance of a powerful army, and Sparta became an introverted community where change was seen as undesirable and strangers were not welcome. The Spartan ideology was rooted in the primacy of the state over the needs of the individual. Even today, the word *Spartan* carries a connotation of strict austerity in all aspects of lifestyle.

The settlement of Sparta itself was no more than a collection of villages, not worthy of being called a city. With the exception of a few temples, there were no stone buildings, only mud huts. The art of poetry, which had flourished in the seventh century, died away, and the once famous bronze and pottery work of Laconia also declined.

Music and dance remained important in the religious life of Sparta, but here too creativity was lacking. Only in the military field did Sparta play a prominent role in Greece. During the Persian Wars, Sparta assumed the military leadership almost automatically, and the heroic death of King Leonidas and his followers in the pass of Thermopylae in 480 BCE reinforced Sparta's claim to this leadership.

However, there were some in the ancient world who admired Sparta not only for its military strength, but also for its fine example of virtue, honesty, austerity, and fidelity. The philosopher Plato declared that Sparta came closest to his concept of the ideal state. Many historians, however, would argue that Sparta's rival, Athens, would have a greater claim to the title.

No traces of the ancient city remain on the plains of Sparta. The ruins in the foreground date from a much later period (the 13th to 15th century CE).

Athens

The city-state of Athens consisted of the city of Athens and the region surrounding it—the Attic Peninsula (generally called Attica) on the east coast of mainland Greece. Attica is largely mountainous and dry, but it does have a number of reasonably fertile plains. It is separated from central Greece and the Corinthian isthmus by virtually impassable mountains, but it is enclosed by sea on two sides and has good natural harbors. These harbors allowed the people of Attica to trade by sea and, when necessary, set out by sea for distant lands.

Athens originated as a Mycenaean settlement on and around the Acropolis, a rocky outcrop that lies in the middle of the largest plain of Attica. Legend has it that during the Mycenaean period the Athenian king Theseus united 12 Attican villages into one polis, but whether this has any basis in historical fact is not known. It can, however, be established that the Mycenaean fortress on the Acropolis was never destroyed and that Athens was continuously inhabited from

THE HOPLITE

From around the eight century BCE onward, the key component of the armies of ancient Greece was the hoplite. The hoplite was a heavily armed footsoldier who fought in close formation. The hoplite took his name from the word *hoplon*, meaning a piece of armor. His main weapon was a spear that was around 9 feet (2.7 m) long. He would also carry a short sword for stabbing his enemies at close quarters.

By the fifth century BCE, the hoplite's armor would consist of a large circular shield known as an *aspis*, a breastplate, a pair of greaves (shin protectors), and a helmet. There were various styles of helmet, but one of the most common was the Corinthian, which protected both the bridge of the nose and the cheeks. Early Corinthian helmets also covered the ears, but this design made hearing difficult. Because soldiers needed to hear instructions in the heat of battle, later variations had holes cut out for the ears. In illustrations on Greek vases, helmets are usually topped by a magnificent crest, but historians believe that many helmets did without such decorations. In total, the armor could weigh up to 60 pounds (27 kg), so hoplites needed to be very strong.

In battle, the hoplites fought by marching forward in a dense formation several rows deep. The left-hand side of each soldier's shield covered the right-hand side of the soldier next to him. The spears of the soldiers further back would go over the shoulders of the troops in front of them, presenting the enemy with a wall of spears. Once the two sides engaged, the battle would often degenerate into a brutal pushing contest. As soon as the formation of one side broke apart, the battle was effectively over.

The hoplites were not professional soldiers, but rather an army of citizens who took up arms when the need arose. Because armor was fairly expensive, the hoplites came from the wealthier ranks of society. In the case of most cities, the hoplites had jobs and farms to go back to, so campaigning seasons were short.

The most fearsome hoplites were those from Sparta. Although they were not professional soldiers, in the sense of being a paid, standing army, the fact that all Spartan men trained in military skills from birth meant that Spartan hoplites were fitter, more organized, and more disciplined than those from other cities.

This relief from the fifth century BCE depicts two hoplites following a chariot and carrying the typical round shield (aspis) and long spear.

the late Helladic period, through the Dark Age, to the Archaic period. There is therefore a grain of truth in the claim by the Athenians that they were the original indigenous Greeks whose domain had never been conquered by invaders.

Social groups

As far as its social and political structure was concerned, Athens followed the pattern of many of the other Greek city-states. There were three distinct social groups. Dominating the others were the *hippei*—horsemen or knights. These men were the aristocrats who owned the most

A shoemaker goes about his daily work in this illustration from a Greek vase.

land, which was usually worked by their tenants. In the second rank were the *zeugitai*, men who owned a *zeugos* or yoke for a pair of oxen. These men were farmers who owned enough land to be economically independent. Below both of these groups were the *thetes*, who were small farmers and day laborers. In principle, all these groups, from the aristocrats to the landless, were Athenian citizens. This situation was fairly unusual, because in many city-states, land ownership and civil rights were linked.

From the seventh century BCE, or perhaps earlier, Athens had a board of nine magistrates, called the *archons*, who were elected annually. These *archons* were always drawn from the ranks of the aristocracy. Ex-*archons* became members of the *areopagus*, a council named after the place where it convened, the Areos Pagos, or hill of the god Ares.

Social tension

Athens experienced enormous social tension in the seventh century BCE. Poor small farmers frequently lost their land to richer landholders and were subsequently forced to rent farmland at an exorbitant rate—one sixth of the yield, which was a highly price to pay in the relatively dry and infertile Attica region. Anyone who could not pay the rent was declared a debtor, and creditors were merciless in enforcing their claims against debtors. People who could not pay were often sold into slavery, together with their wives and children. This conflicted greatly with the notion that all Athenians had equal rights in the polis. Growing discontent brought with it the danger of civil unrest, and the constant competition among the aristocrats led to the fear that one of them might take advantage of the situation and seize power for himself.

Solon

One way to deal with the social tension was to reform the law. At the beginning of the sixth century BCE, an aristocrat named Solon, who had been a distinguished general, was appointed chief *archon* with special powers to revise the law and act as an arbitrator to avoid the threat of civil war. Solon was to go down in Greek history as an outstanding example of a wise lawgiver, and many institutions from a later period were also attributed to him.

One of Solon's first decisions was to invite a number of emigrants and exiles to return to Athens. Some of these people had been banished from the country for political reasons, while others had fled due to the huge burden of debt incurred as tenant farmers. To enable people in the latter group to return, Solon negotiated the cancellation of all their debts. He also abolished debt slavery, making it impossible for someone to guarantee a debt with his own person. All the debt slaves who could be traced had their freedoms purchased for them.

Besides being a economic reformer, Solon was also a poet. He recorded his reforms in the following verses: "I gave Athens, divine city, back its sons; men who were sold either lawfully or unlawfully; men who were driven from their native country by poverty; vagrants who had almost forgotten how to speak their own language. I did this by using the laws and powers given to me."

It is not clear whether anything was done to prevent a new buildup of debts.

This sculpture is believed to depict Solon, one of the most important Athenian statesmen of the sixth century BCE.

Poor Athenians probably had to work as agricultural laborers from then on, while some people may have found work in the newly emerging industries.

Political changes

In addition to his efforts in the economic field, Solon was active in political reform. He decreed that all free citizens of Attica be allowed to vote in the public assembly, the *ecclesia*. Other political rights were linked to a division of the citizens into classes. These classes were defined by Solon according to a new criterion based solely on property; previously, birth had been the most important factor. The classification was based on annual income expressed in terms of quantities of grain, and there were four groups. In addition to the *thetes*, *zeugitai*, and *hippeis*, a new group was formed.

ATHENIAN WOMEN

Unlike the women of Sparta, women in Athens had a very low status. Although nominally Athenian citizens, the women were not allowed to vote or to attend the assembly, and their ability to inherit property was very limited.

Most Athenian women were virtually confined to the home, where they spent their days in domestic duties such as looking after the children, spinning and weaving to make clothes for the family, and cleaning. Upper-class women had slaves to perform these duties and needed only to oversee the work. A woman was always in the guardianship of a man, either her husband, her father, or her brother. Only lower-class women worked— perhaps cleaning streets or participating in a menial trade.

Even in the home, women were segregated from the affairs of men and spent most of their time in the women's quarters, where men seldom went. Athenian society was very much a man's society, and a woman's main role was to give birth, particularly to male infants. Fathers had the right to reject an infant of the wrong sex, and it seems that infanticide was a regular occurrence.

A girl was raised in the women's quarters and might see her father only rarely. When she was seven, she might attend school to learn to read and write, and by the time she was 12 or 14, she was considered ready for marriage.

A woman's life expectancy was 36 years, less than that of a man, which was probably because, marrying young, women were worn out by childbearing. However, many women did survive their husbands, who might have been considerably older. If a widow remarried, her inheritance became the property of her new husband.

This painting from the 19th century CE depicts Greek women drawing water from a well. Women in ancient Athens would have spent most of their time performing household tasks.

This new group, the *pentakosiomedimnoi* (five hundred medimners), comprised men with an annual income of more than 500 medimnoi (roughly 1,500 cubic feet or 420 hectoliters) of grain, or the equivalent. This new class was a group of the superrich (distinct from the broader group of *hippeis*) who were granted the honor of performing duties connected with the guardianship of the temple of the goddess Athena, and only they and the *hippeis* could be elected to the position of *archon*.

All Athenians had the opportunity to appeal against decisions made by the *archons*. In order to facilitate this, Solon turned the public assembly into the highest court of justice. A separate "people's court" and a council of 400 members drawn from the upper three classes were also attributed to Solon, though they may have originated at a later date.

Solon's reforms did not please everybody. The rich and privileged had to make sacrifices, while the poorer people were disappointed that Solon had not redistributed enough land. However, his reforms did achieve their goal, which was to make social justice a cornerstone of the Athenian state. Solon described his reforms as follows: "I gave the people the necessary power, without giving them too much honor; and I took away the excess power from the nobility, without offending their noble feelings unnecessarily. In this way the people follow their leaders without the leaders holding the reins too tightly or too loosely."

Solon's measures temporarily endorsed the dominance of the aristocracy while allowing the lower classes to become more involved in politics. The new property criteria made social advancement easier—an important social change that meant it was no longer necessary to be descended from the nobility to enjoy upperclass privileges—high income was sufficient. Some time after Solon, the aristocratic structure was to be replaced by a timocratic structure—one in which political power was in proportion to property ownership.

See also:

The Peloponnesian War (page 138)

The Acropolis lies at the heart of the city of Athens. From the very earliest days of the city, the Acropolis was the site of important temples.

FROM TYRANNY TO DEMOCRACY

TIME LINE

c. 657 BCE

Cypselus drives out rulers of Corinth to establish tyranny in city.

625 BCE

Periander takes over rule of Corinth from his father Cypselus.

582 BCE

Periander's nephew Psammetichus deposed following rebellion; Corinth now ruled by oligarchy.

561 BCE

Peisistratus imposes himself as dictator of Athens for first time; twice driven from city.

546 BCE

Peisistratus returns to Athens at head of army; he establishes tyranny that lasts for 19 years.

510 BCE

Hippias deposed as tyrant of Athens; Cleisthenes later creates new democratic system of government.

In the seventh and sixth centuries BCE, Greece saw the rise of tyranny as a system of government when politicians such as Cypselus in Corinth and Peisistratus in Athens gained power. Later, a new form of democracy arose in Athens.

During the Archaic period (c. 750–500 BCE), there was much social unrest in the burgeoning city-states of Greece. Some of this unrest was relieved by colonization, while attempts were made at home to reduce the gap between rich and poor. For example, in Athens in the sixth century BCE, the lawgiver Solon specifically addressed the rights of the poor by abolishing debt slavery. Another way of dealing with the internal social problems in the Greek communities was the institution of tyranny.

The word *tyrannos* was not originally Greek; it was borrowed from the Lydian language and was used to refer to an absolute ruler who had taken power illegally. Such a ruler was not necessarily a "tyrant" in the modern sense of the word, since an unlawful sovereign was not necessarily a cruel or unjust one. However, the fact that the Greeks adopted a foreign word for this new political phenomenon indicated that they viewed it as alien to the idea of a *polis* (city-state) as a community of citizens.

The age of the tyrants

During the Archaic period, individual aristocrats all over Greece took advantage of infighting among the nobility to seize power. In most cases, the details of how they came to power are not known, but what evidence there is suggests there may have been military coups. The new tyrants had clearly received support from aristocratic friends and followers, and sometimes from another state. They may also have used mercenary troops, which were a new phenomenon at the time. To win the support of the populace, they often promised various rewards, such as grants of land, thereby turning social discontent to their own advantage.

One of the first tyrants was Cypselus. Around 657 BCE, he drove out the ruling aristocracy in Corinth. During the next 150 years, tyranny became the most common form of government in the Greek world; of the more important city-states only Sparta and Aegina appear to have escaped it. Many of these tyrants were quite popular, particularly among the middle-class, mercantile populace who had been denied any social privileges by the previous aristocratic rule. Some tyrants were also popular because they stimulated local patriotism and organized cults and festivals that celebrated the local gods.

The tyrannies followed a similar pattern in each state. Eventually, popular feeling would move against a dictatorship, as councils and tribal meetings were excluded from power and the tyrant placed himself above the law.

Most tyrants decreed their rule hereditary, but the people tended to

This bust depicts the tyrant Periander, who ruled the city of Corinth between 625 and 585 BCE.

unite against the second or third generation. As resistance against a tyrant
increased, he would typically take harsh
measures in an attempt to remain in
power. However, the will of the people
would eventually prevail, and he would
be ousted. One result of the phenomenon of tyranny was that by undermining
the position of the aristocracy, it paved
the way for democracy.

The tyranny in Corinth

After around 750 BCE, Corinth became
the most important port and the most
prosperous city in Greece. Its situation on
the south of the isthmus joining central
Greece to the Peloponnese made
Corinth a crucial trading point. It had
harbors on both sides of the isthmus, and
to avoid the dangerous journey around
the Peloponnese, many traders arranged

THE GREEK WORLD IN THE SIXTH CENTURY BCE

THRACE

The Dardanelles

MACEDON

Aegean Sea

• Mytilene

LYDIA

ATTICA

Thebes •   • Eretria

Corinth •   • Athens   Marathon

• Ephesus

IONIA

• Miletus

SICILY

• Syracuse

• Sparta

Mediterranean Sea

CRETE

KEY

Area of Greek settlement by the sixth century BCE

for their goods to be transferred at Corinth to wagons to be transported to the other side, where they could be shipped again. Trade with states on the eastern shores of the Mediterranean Sea thrived, and after the Greek colonization of southern Italy and Sicily, trade with the west increased as well.

Corinth was also the center of a prosperous export industry in earthenware. Corinthian pottery, painted in exquisite detail, was shipped out to destinations in every direction, outselling any other pottery of the time. Most of this commercial activity was dominated by the Bacchiad family, an aristocratic clan that ruled over Corinth.

Around 657 BCE, the resentment of the mercantile class against the Bacchiads boiled over into revolution, and a new leader called Cypselus was put in place as a tyrant. Cypselus proved himself to be a mild and popular dictator, who needed no bodyguard. According to a popular legend about his birth, Cypselus was a hero favored by the gods. He belonged to the same class as the aristocracy and yet was an outsider.

The rule of Periander

Under Cypselus and, later, his son Periander, the prosperity of Corinth reached new highs. Colonies were founded on the eastern coast of the Adriatic Sea, to develop the trade route to Italy. Periander built a slipway 5 miles (8 km) long across the isthmus so ships could be put on trolleys and dragged

THE LEGEND OF CYPSELUS'S BIRTH

One legend that became popular in Corinth after Cypselus came to power tells the story of his birth.

Cypselus's mother, Labda, was a member of the Bacchiad clan but had been rejected by her family because of a handicap. She married a stranger named Eetion and bore him a son. Oracles prophesied that the child would grow up to destroy the ruling dynasty. When members of the Bacchiad clan heard of this, they arrived at the child's home with the intention of killing him.

However, his mother hid the infant in a wooden chest, called a *kypsele* in Greek, and the child escaped. Taking his name from the word *kypsele*, Cypselus grew up in a village outside Corinth. When he became an adult, another oracle ordered him to return to the city and seize power from the ruling Bacchiads.

This legend is similar to many others in which an infant is hunted but survives, later to become a great ruler. The story of Moses in the Bible is just one such tale.

This ancient road leads from the ruins of the Greek city of Corinth.

This Corinthian tile depicts a potter standing in front of a kiln. Corinth was famous for its pottery in the seventh century BCE.

from one side to the other. The tolls from this facility greatly increased the city's wealth.

Periander ruled from 625 to 585 BCE and showed himself to be a wily statesman. He extended the power of Corinth both by the sword and by diplomacy. When Mytilene and Athens were in dispute over the ownership of a colony in 600 BCE, Periander was asked to adjudicate between them. He came down on the side of Athens, which made the city a valuable ally.

During Periander's reign, Corinth also became a center of culture, where poets and musicians congregated. He inaugurated many public building works, giving rise to the architectural style known as the Doric order.

However, the rule of Periander had a darker side. He was subject to violent mood swings, and he was ruthless in executing anyone he thought threatened his power. His actions, as related by the fifth-century-BCE historian Herodotus, caused his tyranny to deteriorate into a reign of terror.

Periander died in 585 BCE and was succeeded by his nephew Psammetichus, who was deposed following a rebellion in the third year of his reign. The government of Corinth was then taken over by a group of aristocrats, who established an oligarchy (rule by an elite).

The tyranny in Athens

Although the inspired lawgiver Solon had produced a new code of law for Athens in the early sixth century BCE, it was still far from becoming a democracy. Solon had granted civil rights to the poorer Athenians and put an end to debt slavery, but he had done little to secure the economic future of the poor. Rivalry between landed and landless people continued, as did rivalry within the aristoc-

THE DOWNFALL OF PERIANDER

This anecdote from the historian Herodotus describes the downfall of the tyranny in Corinth:

"Periander sent an envoy to the tyrant Thrasybulus of Miletus to ask him the best way to rule without conflict. Thrasybulus took a walk through a cornfield with the envoy, while questioning him about the situation in Corinth. Now and then the tyrant would stop and cut off the largest ears of corn that rose above the others. In this way he destroyed the best of the corn, and he later sent the envoy away without having given him an answer.

"When the envoy returned to Corinth, Periander asked him what Thrasybulus had advised. The envoy replied that he had received no answer, and he also expressed surprise that Periander had sent him to a man who had nothing better to do than destroy the best part of his crop. But Periander understood immediately what Thrasybulus had meant by this action. Believing that this represented the punishment of the most important citizens of Corinth, from that moment he started treating the aristocrats and the rich with extreme cruelty."

The Temple of Apollo is one of the most famous ruins in the ancient Greek city of Corinth. Corinth was one of the most prosperous Greek cities in the seventh century BCE.

The Acropolis in Athens was a focal point of the city during the reign of the tyrant Peisistratus.

racy. Against this unsettled background, a politician called Peisistratus gained the support of the common people and managed to seize power in a coup described by Herodotus:

"At that time [561 BCE] a civil war was raging in Attica between the coastal party and the plains party. Taking advantage of their quarrel, Peisistratus devised a plan to become tyrant of Athens by forming a third party. This was the party from over the hills. He mobilized a group of followers and won victory by means of a clever trick. One day he wounded himself before coming to the market. There, he said that he had miraculously escaped from his enemies, who had tried to kill him. To protect himself from further attacks, he asked for an official bodyguard. The Athenians gave him permission to arm a group of 300 citizens with clubs. With the aid of these people Peisistratus rebelled and succeeded in capturing first the Acropolis and subsequently the seat of government."

The plains party referred to by Herodotus consisted of old, aristocratic families from the region surrounding the city of Athens. The coastal party was more democratic and consisted of several families, the most important of which were the Alcmaeonidae. Their domain lay along the coast to the south of Athens. Peisistratus's party "from over the hills" was probably a splinter group from the coastal party. The phrase "over the hills" may refer to Peisistratus's power base on the east coast of Attica, on the other side (from Athens) of the Hymettos Mountain ridge.

The return of Peisistratus

Soon after Peisistratus had established himself as the tyrant of Athens, however, he was driven out again by the two rival groups of aristocrats. Five years later, he returned from exile and to power with the help of his former rival Megacles. Herodotus described what happened as follows:

"As soon as Peisistratus had left, the two groups who had banished him began to quarrel. Finally Megacles, the leader of the coastal party, sent an envoy to Peisistratus. Peisistratus would be returned to power if he agreed to marry the daughter of Megacles. Peisistratus agreed to the proposal, and together they designed a plan to accomplish the return of the tyrant."

This plan involved dressing up a woman as the goddess Pallas Athena, guardian of the city of Athens, and arranging for her to travel through the city, preceded by heralds who announced that the goddess was leading Peisistratus back to his rightful place. The plan appears to have worked. For a while, Peisistratus resumed his role as tyrant, but the alliance with the coastal party and the marriage to Megacles's daughter soon broke down. Once again, Peisistratus was forced to flee Athens.

During the following decade, Peisistratus first accumulated a great deal of wealth, mainly from the gold and silver mines in Thrace. He then concentrated on building good relations with states and individuals who might be prepared to supply funds and mercenaries to support his planned coup in Athens. In 546 BCE, he landed with an army at Marathon, on the east coast of Attica. Marching towards Athens, he was joined by other disaffected forces. The Athenians sent out an army to meet him, and at the Battle of Pallene, Peisistratus was victorious. He entered Athens as its tyrant and this time remained in power for more than 19 years.

The rule of Peisistratus

Peisistratus was a benign tyrant. He took no revenge against his opponents, and he upheld the laws laid down by Solon. He imposed very moderate taxation on the populace, and, under his rule, trade and industry flourished. In his efforts to make Athens the political center of Attica, Peisistratus organized great "national" religious festivals, such as the Dionysian festivals at which tragedies were performed. The Panathenaea—the celebration of the city goddess Pallas Athena—was also turned into a great festival. The *Iliad* and the *Odyssey*, the two great epic poems of Homer, were recited at this and other events.

An important social institution introduced by Peisistratus was the one of traveling judges, who visited the villages of Attica, listened to cases, and dispensed justice. Peisistratus also initiated a great road-building program, which made communicating and traveling around Attica much easier in general.

Many substantial construction projects were also undertaken to emphasize the great importance of Athens and its ruling family. Poorer Athenians seem to have benefited under his rule from a redistribution of land, as well as from the stimulation of trade and industry. The pottery industry in particular flourished. During Peisistratus's rule, Athenian black-figure pottery came to supersede all other pottery on the Mediterranean markets.

Hippias

Peisistratus was succeeded in 527 BCE by his son Hippias (see box, page 75), who continued his father's policy of making Athens a

This bronze statue depicting the god Zeus dates to the early fifth century BCE. Zeus was king of the Greek gods.

71

cultural center. However, opposition to his rule was growing. The powerful family of the Alcmaeonidae had gathered together a large group of exiles on the Peloponnese. These disaffected Athenians managed to gain the support of the Spartans, who were trying to expand their territory northward. A Spartan army joined in an invasion of Attica in 510 BCE. Hippias and his supporters were trapped on the Acropolis. Hippias was deposed but allowed to go into exile. He subsequently left for a colony in the Dardanelles. His departure brought more than 35 years of Athenian tyranny to an end.

An agricultural economy

Trade and industry flourished in Greece throughout the time of Cypselus and Peisistratus. However, the main economic activity of most people was agriculture. Some 90 percent of the population were farmers, making a living growing olives, figs, grapes, and fruit, as well as cultivating crops such as grain, beans, and green vegetables.

Farming methods were primitive. Plowing was done by means of a wooden plow drawn by oxen, which, rather than turning the earth, merely scratched the surface. At first, farmers had to leave a field fallow every year or so to allow it to regain fertility, but by around 400 BCE, they had learned the art of crop rotation. Most Greek farms were small, although there was the occasional large holding. The work was carried out by individual farmer-landholders or by tenant farmers or serfs.

Olive oil was a major agricultural product. It was an important source of export revenue, and, at home, it was used universally in cooking and for lamp oil. Olive oil also had a significant part to play in religious ceremonies.

Craftsman had a low status in Archaic Greece. Potters, smiths, tanners, and other craftsmen generally worked in small workshops, which were usually run as a family business. Textile production was a domestic industry carried out by women. Only a small handful of people in each polis could have survived by

WAR AND COINAGE

The link between war and the economy is illustrated by the fact that the world's first coins were probably produced to pay mercenaries. These coins were minted at the end of the seventh century BCE by the kings of Lydia in Anatolia. The coins were made from pieces of electrum, a natural alloy of gold and silver, and were stamped on one side with a mark that guaranteed their weight, and thus their value.

Around 600 BCE, Greek cities on the coast of Anatolia, notably Ephesus and Miletus, began to mint their own coins. These coins were made of silver and were marked with the stamp of the polis that issued them. Over the next century, this practice of issuing coins was adopted by Greek states in Europe. Under the Athenian tyrants, Athenian coins were issued stamped with the emblem of an owl, representing the goddess Pallas Athena.

While the use of coinage remained limited in Lydia during the sixth century BCE, it acquired great importance in facilitating trade in Greece, and small bronze coins appeared alongside the silver ones. However, the introduction of coinage did not create a full monetary economy. Barter remained the staple form of exchange.

This illustration from a Greek vase shows a shoemaker at work. Craftsmen such as these were held in low esteem in ancient Greece.

doing non-agricultural work. The low esteem in which craftsmen were held is summed up by the fourth century-BCE author Xenophon in the following words:

"Craftsmanship has a bad name and is quite rightly greatly despised. . . . It makes such demands on a man that he can no longer devote himself to his friends or to the polis. Such people must be bad friends and bad defenders of their nation. . . . The best occupations are farming and the waging of war."

Working at a trade seems to have been equated with a lack of freedom. The work of the farmer was rated more highly than that of the "wage slave," who was dependent on his employer, or the work of the craftsman or small trader, who was dependent on his customers.

Most trade in Greece at this time was on a very small scale. Such trade as there was was either carried on by farmers, who brought their surplus product to the market, or by craftsmen, who sold their goods to customers in the workshops. Professional traders—those who bought the products of others in order to resell them at a profit—were rare. Only rich merchants engaged in this type of overseas trade, and they were wealthy enough to build their own ships and employ others to undertake the trading voyages. Nevertheless, however small-scale or marginal it was, trade in the Archaic period still offered great opportunities for personal enrichment.

War booty was another important source of income in Archaic Greece. The booty taken on military enterprises provided a major source of wealth for aggressive city-states. With wars waged almost constantly among the many Greek states, booty was probably as important a source of income as agricultural production.

A return to democracy

After Hippias was deposed in 510 BCE, the aristocrat Cleisthenes (570–508 BCE) seized the opportunity to establish a new democracy based on the political emancipation of the *demos*, or common people. In the words of the fifth-century BCE historian Herodotus: "Cleisthenes made the *demos* his partners."

Cleisthenes was a member of the Alcmaeonid family, the clan that had opposed the tyrant Peisistratus some 50 years earlier. Cleisthenes was the son of

This Athenian silver coin from the fifth century BCE is stamped with a picture of an owl, the symbol of Pallas Athena, the city's patron goddess.

Megacles, who had been both an ally and an enemy of the tyrant. The Alcmaeonidae had been exiled several times during the late sixth century BCE; Cleisthenes himself was banished from Athens for some 20 years. He returned to take a prominent part in the overthrow of Hippias.

Cleisthenes instigated a program of political reforms between 510 and 507 BCE. His new constitution, under which the political weight in Athens shifted from the aristocrats to the *demos*, took effect around 502 BCE. A crucial part of his reforms was to improve the civil rights of both the *thetes* (the small landless farmers and day workers) and the *zeugitai* (the economically independent farmers). Under Solon, the *zeugitai* had been allowed political office, and during the reign of tyranny, many of them had become prosperous enough to be able to afford the full suit of armor required to be a hoplite. Their role as hoplites had become increasingly significant; their importance to the military security of the polis was almost certainly an influential factor in Cleisthenes's decision to enlist their political support.

The Council of 500

The nucleus of Cleisthenes's reforms was the creation of a new institution, the Council of 500, which may have been an extension of an earlier council established by Solon, but with wider powers. The Council of 500 became the pivotal point of political life in Athens, although the ultimate power of decision making lay with the *ecclesia*, or public assembly.

HIPPIAS, THE LAST ATHENIAN TYRANT

Hippias, the son of Peisistratus, was 40 years old when he succeeded his father in 527 BCE. He ruled with the help of his younger brother, Hipparchus, who was instrumental in bringing two distinguished poets—Anacreon and Simonides—to Athens, strengthening its growing reputation as the cultural center of Greece.

Around 514 BCE, a plot to assassinate both Hippias and Hipparchus was hatched by two young aristocrats, Harmodius and Aristogeiton, who were lovers. The assassi-nation was planned as an act of personal revenge. Hipparchus had apparently made advances to Harmodius but was rejected, spurring Hipparchus to offer a public insult to Harmodius's sister. The assassination plot failed. Only Hipparchus was killed, and in the botched attempt, Harmodius was cut down by Hippias's bodyguard. Aristogeiton was later tortured to death. After this attempt on his life, Hippias ruled with great severity, which accelerated the end of his tyranny. When Hippias was finally deposed, Harmodius and Aristogeiton were hailed as "tyrant killers," and their act was commemorated in an annual religious festival.

After Hippias was forced into exile, he eventually traveled to Persia and obtained an appointment at the royal court as an advisor to Darius I. In 490 BCE, Hippias, approaching 80, returned with the Persian army to Marathon, where he had landed more than 50 years earlier with his father, Peisistratus, and an invading army. The idea was that, after the Persian victory, Hippias would be reinstated as tyrant of Athens, under Persian rule. However, things did not go according to plan—the Athenians defeated the Persians, and Hippias had to flee, along with the remains of the Persian army. Disappointed and disillusioned, the aged tyrant died aboard ship on the return voyage.

This sculpture depicts the "tyrant killers" Harmodius and Aristogeiton. It is a Roman copy of a statue originally made by the Greek sculptor Kritios.

Farmers harvest grapes in this vase illustration from the sixth century BCE.

coastal, and 10 rural districts. Three districts—one urban, one coastal, and one rural—were then selected and combined into one *phyle*. The resulting *phyle* was a completely artificial unit; its urban, coastal, and rural sections often did not even adjoin. The purpose was to thoroughly mix the population of Attica in order to prevent the rise of regional power. The ten *phylae* formed by Cleisthenes were the basis of all the democratic institutions in Athens.

Soon after Cleisthenes initiated his political reforms, ostracism was introduced. This practice was a means to enable the citizens of Athens to banish for 10 years anyone they deemed to be a threat—for instance, anyone suspected of planning to seize power. Every year, the Athenian citizens voted in the public assembly on whether they considered a political banishment was necessary, and if the answer was yes, a quorum of 6,000 citizens assembled at a later date. Each of these citizens had to scratch the name of the political leader he wanted banished on a potsherd (a fragment of broken pottery). Whoever received the most votes had to leave the city for 10 years. The potsherd on which a vote was recorded was called an ostracon, hence the term *ostracism*.

Democracy in practice

The system of government in Athens was a direct democracy. The most important element of government was the *ecclesia*, which was a general assembly of all citizens. Other administrative bodies were composed of either the entire citizenry or a number of representatives, who were sometimes elected but were usually appointed by lot.

Most of the important political decisions were made by the *ecclesia*, which in the fifth century BCE met around 10 or 11 times a year. Extra meetings could be convened if exceptional circumstances

The Council consisted of 10 groups, each with 50 men, selected annually by a complex system that ensured each of the 10 groups represented the total polis. The same principle was applied to the hoplite army, which was also split into 10 subdivisions. The intention behind this system was to avoid a situation where all the citizens living in a particular region could join together to form a section of the Council or a division of the army. A scenario like that might have allowed the most powerful aristocrats in a given region to gain political or military control of Athens.

Under the new system, the entire Athenian citizenry was split into 10 sections, called *phylae*, with each section representing the polis in miniature. To form the *phylae*, the local communities in Attica were divided into 10 urban, 10

made it necessary. However, the agenda for meetings of the *ecclesia* was set by the Council of 500, which therefore exerted a great influence on the assembly. Apart from subjects such as the grain supply, military affairs, and the appointment of magistrates—all of which had to be addressed—the Council determined what would be dealt with at each meeting. The public assembly could accept the Council's agenda but could also add alternative suggestions or new items for discussion. Because the public assembly had the last word, a powerful Council did not necessarily pose a threat to the Athenian democracy.

The preliminary work that was necessary for the Council to draw up the agenda took a great deal of time. Discussions within the smaller body of the Council were more efficient than consulting with the several thousand members of the public assembly. For this reason, the assembly was prepared to delegate less important matters and emergency decisions to the Council.

Membership of the Council

Members of the Council were citizens and 30 years of age or older. They held the position for a period of one year and never served more than twice in a lifetime. The Council members were drawn from all over Attica—50 men from each of the 10 *phylae*. Within each *phyle*, Council members were chosen by lot from a pool of candidates supplied by all the villages and urban districts. In the small communities, every adult male probably had a chance to serve on the Council at least once, which was less likely in the larger communities.

The Council met frequently but was not in permanent session. One of its tasks was to carry out the decisions made by the public assembly. Since this task required an administration that was available all the time, the *prytane* system was created. The *prytane* was a kind of permanent committee of Council members. Each of the 50-man groups taken from the 10 *phylae* served for one of the 10 months of the Athenian year.

This ancient Greek relief depicts athletes training.

The daily administration was formed by the 50 men of the *prytane*. A smaller group selected from the 50 was ready and available 24 hours a day, living together for this purpose in a building on the agora, the open space where the public assembly was sometimes held. The *prytanes* prepared, convened, and recessed meetings of the Council and the assembly and received envoys, messengers, complaints, and a wide range of requests. Because the Greeks liked to introduce a competitive element into everything they did, the various *prytanes* competed for the title of "best *prytane* of the year."

Every 24 hours, the *prytane* had a different chairman, also appointed by lot. A man could hold this chairmanship only once in his lifetime, but an ordinary man from a small village in Attica had a good chance of becoming chairman of the daily administration, an indication that direct democracy really worked.

Each village had to supply a number of Council members each year, and because the number of men who were 30 years of age and older was limited, it was highly probable that every eligible male would be selected at least once. Once chosen, he would belong to the *prytane* administration for a month, and with 35 or 36 days in the Athenian month, he would have a 70 percent chance of being appointed chairman.

Black-figure pottery such as this illustrated vase first emerged in the seventh century BCE.

In the fifth century BCE, the chairman of the *prytane* also acted as chairman of the Council and the public assembly if those bodies happened to meet on that day. He was also in charge of the city seal and the keys to the temples, which also functioned as the city's treasury. These were heavy responsibilities for a farmer from a small village.

Limitations

Athenian democracy had several limitations. All citizens were allowed to participate in direct democracy, regardless of their descent and the amount of property they owned, but not everyone living in the polis was a citizen. First of all, women were excluded. This is not surprising; women were excluded from almost all public life in Greece. Although nominally citizens (if born to citizens), women were considered apolitical beings and had virtually no civil rights.

Other criteria for entitlement to citizenship included being free (slaves had no civil rights whatsoever), being of Athenian descent (immigrants who settled in Attica could not become citizens), and being an adult. Relatively few men were full Athenian citizens; democracy was intended for a small minority of the population.

Also, even though there were tens of thousands of citizens from all over Attica who were eligible to attend the public assembly, it seems unlikely that very many did so. Although it was their right, it was not their obligation. Many lived too far away or were simply unable or unwilling to miss a day's work. Because of these factors, it seems probable that only a minority of the citizens actually attended the assembly, even when important issues were being discussed. Indeed, there was only enough room for around 6,000 men on the Pnyx, the hill in Athens where the assembly usually convened after the end of the sixth century BCE. Although 6,000 men represented only a small proportion of those who were eligible to vote, it was apparently still considered enough to be termed the "entire population of Athens."

However, thanks to Cleisthenes's reforms, a participatory democracy—at least in theory—had been created in Athens by the end of the sixth century BCE. Whether or not they did so, all citizens had the right to participate collectively in the government of the polis.

A threat from the east

As the sixth century BCE drew to a close, a new danger threatened the young Athenian democracy. The Persians in the east were looking to Anatolia to expand their immense empire. Under their king Cambyses II, the Persians had already annexed the Ionian cities on the Anatolian west coast, thereby extending Persian rule from the Indus River right to the Aegean Sea. It was looking increasingly likely that the Persians would try to subdue the small city-states of mainland Greece, which was now on the frontier of the Persian Empire.

See also:

The Persian Wars (page 96) • Sparta and Athens (page 52)

The Erechtheion, a temple found on the Acropolis in Athens, was built in the fourth century BCE.

GREEK RELIGION

TIME LINE

c. 2000 BCE

Indo-European peoples arrive in Greece, bringing worship of a sky god. He later becomes known as Zeus.

c. 1250 BCE

Dorians begin migrations to mainland Greece. Their main god, Apollo, later becomes major deity in Greek pantheon.

c. 800 BCE

Poet Homer believed to have written *Iliad* and *Odyssey* around this time.

c. 750 BCE

Delphi becomes home to cult dedicated to god Apollo; oracle later established at site.

c. 600 BCE

Mystery cult revolving around story of Persephone established at town of Eleusis.

The ancient Greeks worshipped a wide array of gods, many of whom were believed to dwell on Mount Olympus. Worship was usually carried out openly, although more secretive mystery cults were also popular.

Greek religion was polytheistic in nature, meaning that it involved the worship of many gods. The Greeks believed that these deities had a profound influence on life on earth. Most of the gods were believed to have human form and, although they were immortal, they had many mortal defects, being prey to lust, jealousy, anger, and other human failings. In order to propitiate a god, the Greeks offered prayers, sacrifices, and public festivals to win divine approval and help in their human endeavors.

The first Greek gods

The origins of the Greeks' religion lie far back in antiquity. When the first Indo-European tribes reached mainland Greece around 2000 BCE, they brought with them a warlike religion presided over by a patriarchal god. This deity was a universal divine father figure worshipped by Indo-European peoples from India to western Europe. The Greeks knew him as Zeus, the king of the gods who lived on Mount Olympus (see box, page 84). Other deities of Indo-European heritage were Helios, the sun god, and Eos Aurora, the goddess of dawn.

In Minoan Crete, many female deities were worshipped, and they may have been adapted later by the mainland Greeks. The Linear B tablets from the Mycenaean era (c. 1600–1250 BCE)

mention several gods who are later found in the Greek pantheon, such as Zeus, Hera, Dionysus, and Hermes. It is certain that by the time of Archaic Greece (c. 750–500 BCE) multiple influences had contributed to the family of Greek gods; often, they would become merged with similar deities from neighboring regions, a process known as syncretism.

One Greek god whose characteristics were derived from a variety of sources was Apollo. He was the main god of the Dorian people, who invaded mainland Greece around 1250 BCE after the collapse of the Mycenaean civilization. As well as being a sun deity, Apollo was also the god of music and dance. In this aspect of his personality, he may have had Minoan antecedents. Apollo the archer, the god who brought disease with his arrows, may have had Semitic or Hittite connections. In some cases, the influences from the east were very strong. The Greek goddess of love, Aphrodite, shared many similarities with the Phoenician deity Astarte, who in turn was closely related to the Babylonian goddess Ishtar.

In addition to the chief gods and goddesses, the Greeks recognized the existence of heroes (including demigods, or deified mortals) and spirits of various kinds, both good and evil. Greek myths also featured a number of odd creatures that combined the characteristics of

This detail from an Italian fresco depicts the Greek sun god Apollo crossing the sky in his chariot.

different animals. Many were associated with Dionysus, the popular god of wine and pleasure. These creatures included satyrs, which had the legs of a goat or horse and the upper body of a man, and centaurs, which had the head and torso of a man and the body of a horse. There were also various types of nymphs, which were beautiful female spirits associated with natural features such as trees, rivers, and springs.

The temples

Each god had his or her own temple, and one god might have many temples spread throughout Greece. An image of the god was kept in the temple, which at first was a simple wooden construction but was later made of stone. These stone temples were larger than the earlier ones and were surrounded by a colonnade. In the center was a small chamber in which the idol of the god was housed. The temple

This silver coin from around 200 BCE bears the features of Helios, a Greek sun god. Helios predated the better-known sun god Apollo.

Sacrifices were considered the most important element of worship. They were performed before battles, after planting crops, or before any risky enterprise. The object was to placate a god and enlist help. The most usual sacrifice was that of an animal, generally a sheep or goat, which was ritually killed to make an offering of blood to the god. After the animal was sacrificed, it was sometimes totally cremated. However, a god was more often considered to be satisfied with just the aroma of the cremated shanks, and the other meat was eaten during the feast that followed the offering.

Non-blood offerings included the placing or burning of food on the altar, libations (pourings) of wine, milk, olive oil, or aromatics, and the burning of incense. People made these sacrifices in order to express gratitude or to honor a god, or because they sought something from a deity in return. Worshippers often asked a god to give them something first, vowing to bring an offering if the god complied with the request. Offerings made in fulfilment of such a vow included land, slaves, cattle, money, and valuables such as weapons, textiles, jewelry, or objects of art.

also had an altar, which was usually situated outside at the front. The altar was used for sacrifices.

Greek religious life featured a number of rituals and celebrations, which were carried out throughout the year and were often shared by the entire community. Each city had its own patron god or goddess—Athena was the goddess of Athens, for example—with temples dedicated to him or her. The patron was honored with prayers, sacrifices, processions, and festivals of song, dance, poetry, drama, and athletics.

Sacrifices

The Greeks believed that the gods represented vast forces of nature before which humans were helpless and insignificant. However, people could try to influence the actions of the gods through prayer and sacrificial offerings.

Priesthood

Most temples had their own priests or priestesses, but it was not necessary for a member of the priesthood to attend a sacrifice. Priests had no special status, and priests and priestesses were often chosen or drawn by lot to serve for a set period of time. The gods were worshipped at home as well as in public. Every home had altars to the various household gods, such as Hestia, the goddess of the hearth.

RELIGION IN LITERATURE

Two Greek writers in particular provide insights into Greek religion. One of these is Homer, who lived in the ninth or eighth century BCE. In his great poems the *Iliad* and the *Odyssey*, Homer gives a vivid picture of a Greek society in which the gods play a vital part. He is also credited with the authorship of the *Homeric Hymns*, poetic celebrations of the many Greek gods.

Another important writer is the poet Hesiod, who lived around 700 BCE. In his *Theogony*, or *Birth of the Gods*, Hesiod compiled a vast collection of Greek myths and described deities that were not mentioned by Homer. Hesiod also described the creation of the world, the origins of the gods, and related many anecdotes about the gods.

Oracles

In order to gain answers to specific questions, the Greeks consulted oracles. An oracle was a medium who could make a response on behalf of a god. From the eighth century BCE onward, certain sanctuaries associated with oracles became widely honored. Priests, who were sometimes local officials, were present at each of these sites to offer an interpretation of the oracle or prophecy. However, the priests did not have any particular training and were not considered to have any unusual powers. One of the earliest oracles, mentioned in Homer's *Iliad*, was that of Zeus in Dodona, in northern Greece.

The most famous oracle of the ancient Greek world was the one at Delphi, on the top of Mount Parnassus. Supplicants flocked there to put questions to Apollo through the medium of his special priestess, the Pythia. Questions could involve anything from trivial personal matters to important affairs of state. The Pythia fell into a trance in order to give Apollo's answers, which were famous for their vague and confusing

This ancient Greek vase painting depicts two men performing a sacrifice.

THE GODS OF OLYMPUS

The highest mountain in mainland Greece, Mount Olympus, was thought to be the home of the 12 most important gods, who all belonged to the same family. These gods were presided over by Zeus. The others in the Olympian family were Hera, Poseidon, Athena, Apollo, Artemis, Aphrodite, Hermes, Demeter, Dionysus, Hephaestus, and Ares.

As king of the gods, Zeus ruled the skies. He was also a lord of justice and a peacemaker. He had two brothers. One of them, Poseidon, was lord of the waters, while the other brother, Hades, was lord of the underworld and did not belong on Olympus. Hera, both the sister and wife of Zeus, was the goddess of women and marriage. She and Zeus were the parents of Ares and Hephaestus.

Athena was the daughter of Zeus alone—she was born, fully grown, out of his head. Athena was an important goddess, the patron goddess of the city of Athens. She was a virgin and a goddess of war. She was also the protector of women's handicrafts. Apollo and Artemis were the twin children of Zeus by the demigoddess Leto. Apollo, usually depicted as a handsome young man carrying a lyre, was the god of music and poetry and was the leader of the nine Muses. He was also the god of medicine and of oracles. Artemis, another virgin goddess, ruled over hunting, the wilderness, and wild animals.

Aphrodite, the goddess of love and sexuality, was born from the sea. Hermes, the son of Zeus and the demigoddess Maia, was the messenger of the gods and the protector of shepherds, travelers, and heralds. He also guided the souls of the dead to the underworld. The mysterious Demeter, the sister of Zeus, Poseidon, and Hades, was the goddess of agriculture and fertility. She was the mother of Persephone, who was carried away by Hades to the underworld.

Another very important god, Dionysus, was the son of Zeus and the Theban princess Semele. He was the god of wine and ecstasy, and his festivals were very popular with the common people of Greece. Dionysus was, however, also the god of madness and death. Hephaestus, a son of Zeus and Hera, was the smith-god, the patron of all craftsmen. Married to Aphrodite, Hephaestus was considered the outsider of the Olympian family and was always depicted as a cripple.

Ares, also a son of Zeus and Hera, was the god of war and was often Athena's adversary. In myth, Ares was Aphrodite's lover, and one story relates how he killed another of her lovers, Adonis, in a fit of jealousy.

The Ares Borghese, made around the second century CE, is one of the most famous depictions of the Greek war god.

nature. Priests were on hand to transcribe the oracle's pronouncements. In fact, one of the first uses of writing in Greece was to record oracular utterances. Many of the sayings of the oracles, at Delphi and elsewhere, were written down to support certain policies.

Divination was another way of finding answers to questions. Seers were practiced in the interpretation of dreams, of the flights of birds, of the spirals of smoke rising from an altar, and of the arrangement of the entrails of a newly sacrificed animal.

The mysteries

Between the seventh and sixth centuries BCE, mystery religions began to flourish. While the usual religious observances of the polis community were very public,

the mysteries consisted of closely guarded rituals that were only open to worshippers who had been inducted into a secret cult. The purpose of the mysteries was to liberate the initiates from their earthly bonds and to show them the way to a happy life in another world after death. The secrets of the rituals were so closely guarded that there is no way to know what took place in them.

The most famous Greek mysteries were those held in the town of Eleusis, northwest of Athens. For a thousand years, between around 600 BCE and 400 CE, people gathered there to become initiates. The subject of the Eleusian mysteries was the legend of the goddess Persephone, who was abducted by her uncle, Hades, and taken to the underworld. Her disappearance so traumatized her mother, the

The Temple of Poseidon at Cape Sounion is one of the most imposing of the surviving Greek temples.

agriculture goddess Demeter, that the crops ceased to grow. Eventually, an agreement was made that allowed Persephone to spend part of the year with her mother and part in the underworld. The legend was used to explain the seasons.

The initiation ceremonies took place every year on the same date during the autumn. The main public event was a procession from Athens to Eleusis covering some 25 miles (40 km) over the "Holy Road." Then, in a secret ceremony held in Demeter's temple, the initiates underwent the secret rites that admitted them to the mysteries. Those who attended this ceremony had to swear an oath of secrecy, and they left the temple with the expectation of a better life in the hereafter.

The first atheists

Most Greeks took part in community rituals, believed in the supernatural powers of the gods, consulted an oracle occasionally, and possibly were initiated into a mystery cult. However, not everyone could accept all the ideas that were inherent in Greek religion. In particular, the notion that the gods could assume many forms troubled some people. The image of Aphrodite, for example, took different forms in different city-states. In addition, the fact that good was not always rewarded and that evil was not always punished was an important stumbling block for others.

Greek thinkers came up with various theories to address these concerns. One theory was atheism—the idea that there is no god at all. One of the first known atheists was the philosopher Diagoras of Melos, who lived in the fifth century BCE. Diagoras, a stoic and a student of the philosopher Democritus, apparently came up with his theory out of anger at the fact that the gods did not punish wrongdoing—possibly because they did not act against the Athenians, who had slaughtered the citizens of his native city. Diagoras is said to have ridiculed the gods on a number of occasions, most notably when he cut up a statue of the demigod Heracles to provide enough firewood to cook turnips.

See also:

The Great Philosophers (page 122)

Persephone and Hades are shown seated on their thrones in the underworld in this Greek relief sculpture. The story of Persephone was central to several mystery cults.

THE BIRTH OF DRAMA

One of the most important cultural developments to occur in Greece in the sixth and fifth centuries BCE was the growth of drama. Originally part of religious festivals, plays gradually became art forms in their own right.

TIME LINE

c. 550 BCE

Thespis, first known playwright, active around this time.

c. 535 BCE

Great Dionysian festival held for first time in Athens; part of festivities is competition between playwrights.

468 BCE

Sophocles takes part in his first Dionysian festival; he wins competition.

458 BCE

Oresteia trilogy by Aeschylus wins competition at Dionysian festival.

431 BCE

Euripides' great tragic play *Medea* performed for first time.

427 BCE

Revellers, debut play by comic dramatist Aristophanes, first produced.

The drama, and ultimately the theater, grew out of annual festivals held in honor of the god Dionysus, who was the god of wine, intoxication, and ecstasy, a word that implied a way of losing yourself in an alcohol-induced frenzy and becoming one with the god. Dionysus was also regarded as the god of reproduction and of the life force of all living beings. However, because ecstasy also implied a loss of self-control leading to insanity, another view of Dionysus was that he was the god of confusion, destruction, and death. For this reason, he was considered to be the god of the whole of life in all its aspects.

Festivals

Festivals held in honor of Dionysus involved processions of devotees wearing masks and dancing and singing. This type of procession of ordinary citizens was called a *comos* and was usually quite riotous. The words sung by the *comos* revelers were generally satirical and probably involved repartee with onlookers. Comedy seems to have developed from this exchange of backchat.

Tragedy had a different origin. At more solemn festivals for Dionysus a chorus would chant or sing a narrative poem called a *dithyramb*, which told the story of a Greek myth. In time, the leader of the chorus began to step out from the chorus and assume the role of a character in the myth. The person generally credited with this innovation was the chorus master and poet Thespis, who is thought in the sixth century BCE to have introduced an actor wearing a mask to speak lines in between chanting from the chorus. The poet-dramatist Aeschylus (525–456 BCE) later introduced a second actor, which laid the foundation for the development of "drama."

Thespis was a writer, composer, choreographer, director, and actor all in one. Such a person was known as a *tragoidos* (goat bard), probably because the *tragoidoi* took part in a competition that awarded a goat as the prize. The word *tragedy* is supposedly derived from *tragoidos*.

In the middle of the sixth century BCE, performances of tragedy and competitions among poets were the heart of the newly established great Dionysian festival, held every spring in Athens. Each year, a wooden stage and wooden stands for spectators were set up in the agora (the public square where the assembly was held), but one year in the fifth century BCE, the stands collapsed. The accident resulted in the building of a new theater on the south slope of the

Greek drama had its origins in festivals held to honor the god Dionysus, depicted here in a Greek vase illustration.

Acropolis, close to an existing shrine to Dionysus. This theater consisted of a natural auditorium formed by the curve of the hillside and overlooking a circular orchestra at the base of the hill. The orchestra was where the chorus and the actors performed. This plan was followed by all later Greek theaters.

The festival lasted for five days and five nights. On the first day, there was a great procession, and offerings were brought to Dionysus. This was followed by a *dithyramb* competition, an impressive spectacle with 10 boys' choruses and 10 men's choruses of 50 singers each. The day closed with a *comos* procession, usually involving a masquerade and plenty of rough merrymaking.

On the second day, the dramas began, and five comedies by five different authors were performed. Each of the following three days then featured a *tetralogy*—three tragedies and a satyr play—by a single author. The satyr play featured a chorus of clownish satyrs (creatures that were half goat and half man) and was intended to provide comic relief after a long day of tragedy.

The eight authors chosen to challenge each other for the best comedy and tetralogy at the festival were selected by the *archons* (magistrates). The *archons* then looked for *choregi* (literally "chorus leaders") to act as producers. These *choregi* were wealthy people who were obliged to pay most of the costs of the

This carving of a Greek theatrical mask dates to the third century BCE.

event from their own pockets, with the rest being paid for by the state.

After a lengthy pre-festival period of rehearsals, the festival performances were all given. The jury that decided the winners was a committee of 10 people chosen by lot. One *dithyramb* chorus, one comedy, and one *tetralogy* were selected as the winning pieces, and the *choregi* of the winners shared the honors.

The chorus

Greek theater in the fifth century BCE was dominated by the chorus. Comedies had a chorus of 24, tragedies 12 or 15. The chorus recited or sang the text in unison, emphasizing the words with gestures or dance steps. Dance was an integral part of the drama, and the colorful costumes and masks worn by the actors greatly added to the effect of the plays.

To begin with, both the chorus and the actors were located on the orchestra. As it became obvious that a place was needed for the two, and later three, actors to change their costumes, a hut called a skene was erected at the back of the orchestra. It was quickly realized that the skene could be used as a background to the dramatic action, so the drama might be seen to take place in front of a building, such as a temple or palace, rather than in the open countryside as had been the case previously. Later still, a low platform was built at the rear of the orchestra and in front of the skene. Under this new arrangement, the chorus members were located on the orchestra, while the actors were located on the raised platform to declaim and sing the most important parts of the tragedy.

Unlike the members of the chorus, the actors were professionals. Because no more than three actors were allowed on stage in the tragedies, the actors often had double roles. Women were not allowed to act—although they could be members of the chorus—so female roles were played by men, which was made possible by the use of masks. The actors also changed the timbre of their voices when playing women.

In the fifth century BCE, no pieces were performed twice in Athens, which meant that 17 premieres were enacted every year. Only a very few of these plays have survived in their complete state— just 44 pieces out of the thousand or more that must have been performed.

The tragic poets

The oldest dramatist-poet known by name is Thespis, but none of his work survives. A little more is known about Choerilus, whose career began at the same time as that of Thespis in the sixth century BCE. His surviving work includes a couple of small fragments and one title, *Alope*, which may have been a satyr play. Another successful dramatist from this time was Phrynichus (c. 540–475 BCE). He was a winner in the poetic competitions held during the last

The Theater of Dionysus was the largest theater in Athens. Plays by all the great Athenian writers were performed there.

decade of the sixth century BCE. Perhaps his most interesting work is *The Capture of Miletus*. This tragedy is based on a piece of contemporary history—the story of the siege of the Ionian city of Miletus by the Persians in 494 BCE.

Aeschylus

The heyday of Greek tragedy began with Aeschylus, who was born in 525 BCE in Eleusis, northwest of Athens. He wrote around 90 plays, all of them destined to be performed at the annual Dionysian festival. Only seven of them have survived, however. One of his main contributions to Greek drama was to write a part for a second actor, which greatly increased the possibility for dramatic confrontations. Most of the plots for his plays were taken from Greek myths and show how the actions of men on earth bring retribution from the gods.

Aeschylus first took part in the competition of the tragedians in the Dionysia of 499 BCE, but he did not win until 484 BCE. Of his seven surviving tragedies, three formed the trilogy with which he won the Dionysian competition in 458 BCE. The *Oresteia* trilogy was probably his last work and is an outstanding example of Aeschylus's poetic style and mastery of suspense.

The *Oresteia* concerns the fate of the royal family of the Atreides. The action of the first play, *Agamemnon*, takes place in the palace of Mycenae, where Clytemnestra awaits the return after many years of her husband Agamemnon, the leader of the Greeks in the Trojan War. Clytemnestra hates her husband, who sacrificed their daughter Iphigenia to appease the gods. During his absence, Clytemnestra has had an affair with Aegisthus and now, when Agamemnon returns, they plot to kill him. In spite of being warned of his danger by Cassandra, the Trojan princess whom Agamemnon has brought with him from Troy as a slave, Agamemnon is murdered by the lovers soon after his arrival.

This 19th-century-CE drawing depicts the killing of Agamemnon and Cassandra by Clytemnestra and her lover Aegisthus. The story of the murder is told in Aeschylus's play Agamemnon.

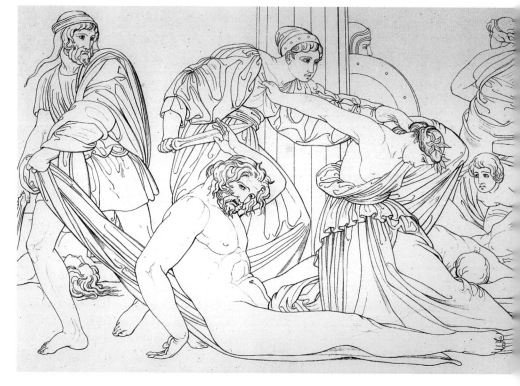

In the second drama of the trilogy, *Libation Bearers*, the murder of Agamemnon is avenged by his son Orestes, who kills his own mother and her lover. In the third part, *Eumenides*, Orestes, pursued by the furies (the goddesses of vengeance), finds no peace until a special court in Athens acquits him of the charge of matricide.

Of the four other remaining works of Aeschylus, *Persians* is based on the story of the Greek victory over the Persians at Salamis, told from the Persian point of view. *Suppliants* tells the story of the Danaides, the 50 daughters of Danaus (the king of Libya), who were promised in marriage to the 50 sons of his brother Aegyptus. *Seven Against Thebes* is about the struggle between the brothers Eteocles and Polyneices for possession of the throne of Thebes, and the battle of the Seven Heroes for possession of the city. *Prometheus Bound* portrays the story of the demigod Prometheus, who gave fire to mankind in defiance of Zeus. Zeus punished him by chaining him to a rock, where an eagle tore out his liver every day. In most of Aeschylus's dramas, the main theme is that man must yield to the jealous power of the gods.

Sophocles

Aeschylus's successor, and for a time his competitor, was Sophocles (c. 496–406 BCE), who was almost 30 years younger than Aeschylus and came from an old, aristocratic Athenian family. As well as being a poet-dramatist, Sophocles served as one of the Athenian *strategoi* (generals) for the year 440 BCE.

Sophocles' literary career began in 468 BCE, when he took part in the Dionysian competition for the first time and defeated Aeschylus. Sophocles won the competition another 18 times. Although Sophocles was the most popular tragedian of Athens, only seven of his estimated 123 tragedies have survived.

Sophocles was an innovator. He was the dramatist who first introduced a third actor on the stage, a convention later taken over by Aeschylus. Sophocles also broke with the tradition that the tragedian must act in his own plays, as Aeschylus still did.

Sophocles was less convinced of the implacability of fate than Aeschylus was and laid greater emphasis on individual human will. However, the consequences of trying to alter one's fate could be tragic. In the plays, this possibility leads to heightened dramatic tension.

None of Sophocles' trilogies remain. The seven surviving tragedies are all independent works in their own right— *Ajax*, *Antigone*, *Electra*, *Oedipus Rex*, *Trachiniai*, *Philoctetes*, and *Oedipus at*

David Oyelowo and Hayley Atwell perform in a modern London production of an English-language adaptation of **Prometheus Bound** *by Aeschylus.*

In this 15th-century-CE manuscript illustration, Jocasta kills herself after realizing that she has married her son Oedipus. The story is contained in **Oedipus Rex** by Sophocles.

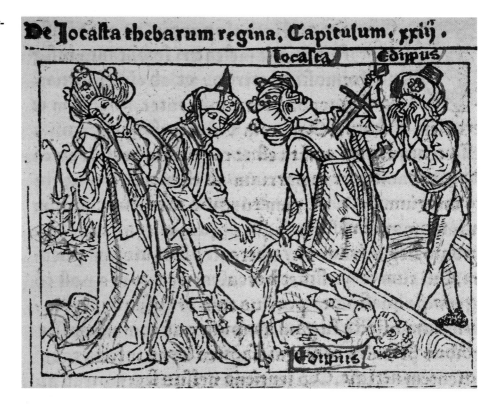

De Jocasta thebarum regina, Capitulum, xxiij.

Colonus. Of all the extant Greek tragedies, *Oedipus Rex* is probably the best known. The play shows a great man brought low through ignorance of his origins. Because he has been raised not knowing who his parents are, Oedipus, the king of Thebes, discovers that he has unknowingly killed his father, Laius, and married his mother, Jocasta. When he realizes that he has committed patricide and incest, Oedipus puts out his own eyes in horror and then goes into exile, where he dies.

In *Antigone*, Sophocles examines the conflict between human laws and divine laws. Antigone is the daughter of Oedipus and goes with him into exile. Her brothers Eteocles and Polyneices fight for the vacant throne of Thebes, and both die in battle before the gates of the city. The throne now falls to their uncle, Creon, and he strictly forbids Antigone to bury the body of her brother Polyneices, whom he regards as a traitor to his country. Creon decrees that the body must lie dishonored on the battlefield, a prey to dogs and vultures.

Antigone, however, knows that she has a moral obligation to give her brother a fitting burial, so his spirit will have rest. By disobeying her uncle, Antigone sets in motion a tragic chain of events that leads not only to her own death but also to that of her lover Haemon.

In this play, Sophocles directs all his attention to the conflict within the human soul. Antigone, Haemon, and even Creon are torn between human and divine laws. Because of this emphasis on human psychological dilemmas, *Antigone* is regarded as one of the greatest of all tragedies.

Euripides

Euripides (c. 485–406 BCE) was the youngest of the three great tragedians. He wrote around 92 plays, of which 18 tragedies and 1 satyr play remain.

Because his characters seem more human and realistic than those of his predecessors, he is seen as the most modern of the Greek tragedians. His play *Medea*, recognized as one of the greatest of the Greek tragedies, tells the story of the enchantress Medea, who helped Jason gain the golden fleece. After the couple settle in Corinth, they have two children, but Jason is unfaithful and threatens to leave Medea. Driven by pathological jealousy, Medea murders her own children as revenge on her husband.

In *Hippolytus*, Euripides paints a sympathetic portrait of a woman in the grip of an obsessive love. To punish the youth Hippolytus, who has angered her, the goddess Aphrodite makes his stepmother Phaedra fall in love with him. When Phaedra declares her love, the chaste youth is horrified. Phaedra commits suicide but leaves a note accusing Hippolytus of lusting after her. When Hippolytus's father, Theseus, hears of this, he banishes his son, at the same time laying a curse on him that swiftly results in his death.

This bust depicts the playwright Euripides. Euripides is seen as one of the three great Athenian tragedians, the other two being Sophocles and Aeschylus.

The comic dramatists

Another group of Greek dramatists wrote comedies, which generally made fun of current politicians and events. The greatest of these dramatists was Aristophanes (c. 450–388 BCE). He was the leading exponent of what is now called Greek "Old Comedy." His first work, entitled *Revellers*, was produced in 427 BCE. That play no longer survives, but of the 30 or so plays he wrote, 11 still do exist.

An enormously popular dramatist in his time, Aristophanes did not hesitate to lampoon leading politicians of the day. His play *Knights*, first performed around 424 BCE, contains a satirical portrait of the ambitious politician Cleon, mocking his attempts to be elected as a *strategos*. In *Frogs*, meanwhile, Aristophanes ridicules his fellow playwrights Euripides and Aeschylus.

In the late fourth century BCE, "New Comedy" emerged. The leading exponent of this style was Menander (c. 341–291 BCE). In this kind of comedy, there was virtually no satire. The plays dealt with social comedy, showing family situations and highlighting individual characters with their various foibles. This form of drama was to have a great influence on the development of comedy in the Roman era.

See also:

The Greek Legacy (page 174) • The Peloponnesian War (page 138)

THE PERSIAN WARS

TIME LINE

499 BCE

Anti-Persian rebellion breaks out in Anatolia.

490 BCE

Darius I sends army into Greece after Sparta and Athens refuse to recognize his sovereignty; Persians are defeated at Battle of Marathon.

480 BCE

Second Persian invasion of Greece led by Darius's son Xerxes. Spartan-led army fails to halt Persian advance at Thermopylae. Greek victory at Battle of Salamis turns tide of war.

479 BCE

Decisive victory for Greeks at Battle of Plataea effectively ends Persian Wars.

449 BCE

Peace treaty finally signed between Greece and Persia.

In the fifth century BCE, the two greatest powers of the Mediterranean world—Greece and Persia—were involved in a titanic military struggle. The great battles of the Persian Wars—Thermopylae, Marathon, and Salamis—are famous to this day.

By the end of the sixth century BCE, the Persian Empire was the greatest the world had ever known. Its rise to power came with stunning rapidity. Only 50 years earlier, the Persians had been just one of several small peoples inhabiting the Iranian plain in the Middle East. They were also subjects of the Medes. In 549 BCE, the Persians' ambitious king Cyrus the Great (ruled 559–529 BCE) led a revolt against the Medes and defeated them. By this victory he became lord of one of western Asia's great kingdoms. He then embarked on a campaign of foreign conquests. First in his sights was Lydia in Anatolia, another great power. He marched into Lydia in 546 BCE and took its capital, Sardis. He then annexed the Greek cities in the western part of Anatolia, which was known as Ionia.

Cyrus seized Babylon in 539 BCE, making him lord of the mighty Babylonian Empire. By the end of the century, the Persian dominions stretched from the Aegean Sea in the west to the Indus Valley in the east and from the Danube River in the north to the Red Sea and Persian Gulf in the south.

After the death of Cyrus, his son, Cambyses II (ruled 529–522 BCE), succeeded in adding Egypt to the Persian Empire. Darius I (ruled 521–486 BCE) was anxious to extend his boundaries to the northwest. By 512 BCE, he had crossed the Bosporus and was actively seeking conquests on the west side of the Black Sea all the way to the mouth of the Danube, but with little success. However, Darius did succeed in conquering Thrace and Macedon, which meant that his empire then bordered the northwest extremity of mainland Greece.

Between the eighth and sixth centuries BCE, Sparta and Athens had become the predominant city-states of Greece. With all of mainland Greece feeling threatened by the presence of the mighty Persian Empire on the border, it seemed that maintaining the balance of power between Persia and Greece would depend on the lead of these two cities.

The Ionian Rebellion

In 499 BCE, a massive rebellion against Persian dominance in Anatolia broke out in the Ionian coastal cities and the neighboring islands. The reasons for the revolt are not clear, but it may be that the Greeks resented the necessity of doing military service in the Persian army (which applied to everyone, of whatever rank), and there was also resentment against the Greek tyrants who served as puppet overlords for the Persians. The rebellion began on Ionian ships that had been engaged in naval operations on behalf of the Persians. Returning home, the seamen and officers mutinied and

arrested the ships' commanders. The leader of this uprising was Aristogoras of Miletus, who went on to mastermind the whole rebellion.

The Ionian cities rose up and deposed their puppet tyrants, replacing them with democracies. The rebels turned to the city-states of mainland Greece for support. Only Athens and Eritria responded, both sending squadrons of warships. With the help of Athenian and Eritrean land forces, the rebels marched on Sardis, where Artaphernes, the brother of Darius I, ruled as a satrap (provincial governor). The Greeks succeeded in occupying the lower town but could not take the citadel. Lacking clear leadership, the Greeks retreated, and the retreat deteriorated into chaos. Artaphernes managed to catch up with the Greeks before they could reach the cost and inflicted a heavy defeat on them near Ephesus.

Despite its failure, the rebellion had inspired other Greek cities—in Cyprus, the Dardanelles, and Byzantium—to rise against their Persian oppressors. The Persians gathered a large navy and army and campaigned throughout the region to bring the Greeks to heel. In 494 BCE, Greeks and Persians met at sea, off Samos, to fight a naval battle, but most of the Greek ships fled, perhaps encouraged to do so by Persian promises of lenient treatment for those who did not fight. The remaining ships were routed. Darius exacted a terrible vengeance on Miletus, the center of the Greek rebellion. The city was sacked, and its inhabitants were either deported to Persia or sold into slavery. Other cities were punished according to their part in the rebellion. However, the episode set the scene for the First Persian War.

This modern stele commemorates the lives of the 192 Greeks who died at the Battle of Marathon.

97

CROESUS OF LYDIA

Croesus, king of Lydia (ruled 560–546 BCE), reigned over an immensely rich and powerful kingdom in Anatolia. The Greek cities of Ionia were conquered by the Lydians in the mid-sixth century BCE, greatly adding to the Lydians' prosperity, but the real basis of Lydian wealth lay in their thriving trade and industries and in the gold and silver mined in their lands.

The first modern coins, minted by the Lydians around 600 BCE, were fat disks stamped with pictures and their specified worth. Up to this time, most trade had been carried on by way of barter—the direct exchange of merchandise—though in some areas, grains of gold and silver, or bars of gold, silver, or bronze, were used to represent the value of goods.

Under Croesus, Lydia achieved the peak of its wealth. As he expanded his empire, he got richer on the booty he took; the expression "as rich as Croesus" dates from this time. There is a story that when the great Athenian legal reformer and philosopher Solon visited him, Croesus claimed to be the happiest man on earth because of his wealth. Solon reputedly replied (prophetically as it turned out), "Call no man happy before his death." Croesus was captured by Cyrus of Persia in 546 BCE and, according to the Greek historian Herodotus, was burned to death on a funeral pyre.

This 17th-century-CE painting depicts King Croesus of Lydia displaying his great wealth to the Athenian statesman Solon.

THE PERSIAN WARS

The First Persian War

The Ionian rebellion led Darius to make some concessions to the Greeks of Anatolia He relaxed his regime slightly and did not require the cities to take their old tyrants back. However, he was determined to subdue mainland Greece. In 491 BCE, he sent messengers to all the Greek city-states, requiring them to send "earth and water" to him as a sign of submission. All the communities on the mainland and islands complied with this request—except for Sparta and Athens. As a sign of their contempt, the Athenians threw the Persian messengers into the pit for condemned criminals. In Sparta, the messengers were thrown into a well where, they were told, there was water and earth in abundance.

Outraged by the death of his messengers, Darius was ready to listen to two Greek exiles in his court who convinced him that they had a number of sympathizers in Greece. These two exiles were Hippias, the ex-tyrant of Athens, and Demaratus, an ex-king of Sparta. Darius formed a plan to take Athens and put Hippias back in power there, under Persian rule.

In 490 BCE, Darius sent an expedition, directed explicitly against Athens, to Greece. On board the Persian fleet was the aged Hippias, convinced that he could regain his position of power. The fleet set sail from the island of Samos, crossed the Aegean Sea, and landed at Eritria, where the Persian forces sacked the city and deported its citizens.

The Battle of Marathon

The Persian army, some 20,000 to 25,000 strong, disembarked at the Bay of Marathon, around 25 miles (40 km) east of Athens. The Persians wanted to make contact with the sympathizers of Hippias, who had his home base on that side of Attica. The Athenians sent to Sparta for assistance, but their request came during a religious festival that the Spartans would not leave. As soon as the Athenians learned of the landing at Marathon, however, they sent a force of 10,000 hoplites, who were joined by 1,000 Plataean soldiers.

This gold Lydian coin was made around 550 BCE.

armor was heavier and provided more protection than that of the Persians, and the Greek hoplites were a formidable fighting force. There was a standoff for several days, with the two armies backing off to sleep in camp at night. Eventually, the Persians decided to sail around to the other side of Attica and launch an attack from there.

Once the Persian cavalry was embarked, one of the Greek generals, Miltiades, convinced the overall commander of the troops, Callimachus, to launch an attack. The Greek hoplites advanced at a run, engaging the Persian infantry with devastating results. After the two Persian wings were crushed, the Greeks and Plataeans wheeled in from the sides to decimate the center. The Persians fled, and many of them were cut down before they could reach the ships. The Persians left 6,400 soldiers dead on the field, while the Greeks lost only 192 men. It was a resounding victory for the Greeks.

The two armies drew up in battle formation on the plain of Marathon. The Persian forces consisted of archers, spearmen, and cavalry, while the Greeks had only foot soldiers. However, the Greeks'

After the unexpected defeat at Marathon, the Persian fleet sailed around Cape Sounion to make a second landing. The Persians planned to march on Athens, which they believed was unprotected. However, the Athenian army quickly returned to the city in a forced march, reaching it within only seven hours. To make matters worse for the Persians, the Spartan army was rapidly approaching Athens. Discouraged, the Persian fleet retreated.

THE MARATHON RACE

After the Athenian victory over the Persians at the Battle of Marathon in 490 BCE, a Greek runner was dispatched to run the 25 miles (40 km) to Athens to bring the good news. Upon arrival, he collapsed from exhaustion and died.

Centuries later, this feat inspired the marathon race. When the Olympic Games were revived in Athens in 1896 CE, they included a long-distance foot race of around that distance. It was called the marathon in honor of the unknown runner. The marathon distance was later standardized at 26 miles, 385 yards (42.2 km).

The story of the athlete who ran from Marathon to Athens has often been intertwined with a separate story, told by Herodotus, of another runner, named Pheidippides, who ran from Athens to Sparta on the eve of the war to ask the Spartans for help. Pheidippides would have run 150 miles (241 km) in two days.

The Second Persian War

The next Persian attack did not come until 10 years later. The delay was caused by Darius's death in 486 BCE. The subsequent domestic disturbances forced his son Xerxes I (ruled 486–465 BCE) to wait until 481 BCE. According to Herodotus, Xerxes was warned by his advisers against the consequences of a new campaign, but the king continued his preparations for what would become the largest military undertaking in history to that date.

Athens had made good use of the 10-year calm. During that time, the city had transformed itself into a naval power. The events of the Ionian rebellion had demonstrated the importance of having a strong fleet. This change of view was largely due to the foresighted statesman Themistocles, who convinced the Athenian assembly to spend the major part of the profits gained from the newly opened silver mines of Laurium on shipbuilding. The number of Athenian triremes (warships; see box, page 109) rose from 70 to 200.

In 481 BCE, when the Persian preparations for war were already under way, a conference of Greek states met in Corinth, probably at Themistocles'

The waters off the Greek island of Samos, shown here, were the site of a naval battle between the Greeks and the Persians in 494 BCE.

instigation, to decide on the tactics to be followed. It was decided to proclaim an overall peace to end ongoing internal conflicts. All states would enter into an alliance against Persia, and none was to consider making a separate peace. The property of traitors would be confiscated and given to the sanctuary in Delphi.

Wooden walls

Despite this friendly gesture, the prophecies of the Delphi oracle were consistently unfavorable. The people of Delphi were so well informed of the formidable Persian war preparations that they dared recommend nothing less than unconditional surrender. The advice of the oracle "to flee to the ends of the earth" was not appreciated by the Athenians. They asked the oracle for less defeatist counsel, and it replied that only "wooden walls" could protect Athens. Themistocles declared that this meant ships; because the ships had already been built, the Athenians were satisfied.

Athens was joined by 30 other Greek states. They decided to meet the Persian attack head on, with Sparta in charge of the entire military operation. The Greek strategy was essentially to avoid battles on the plains, where the Persian superiority in numbers, and in particular their cavalry, would almost certainly overcome smaller Greek forces. Instead, the Greeks planned to try to engage the Persians either in mountain passes or at sea in narrow channels.

On the Persian side, Xerxes was personally in charge of the new expedition. The winter of

481–480 BCE was devoted to preparations in Sardis. The Persian army, the largest that had ever been assembled, was too large to be transported by sea. Equally, the army was too large to live off the land it had to march through, so arrangements had to be made to supply the army with food by sea.

Into Greece

In the spring of 480 BCE, Xerxes led his army north and crossed the Dardanelles by means of a bridge constructed of boats built by his engineers. He then trekked into Europe, following the coast. A large fleet of warships and freight vessels accompanied the army. They were ordered not to lose sight of each other, since the land army could not function without the fleet.

From Thessaly to central Greece, the main road ran through the pass of Thermopylae, between the sea and the mountains. There the Greeks waited for the Persians, and a historic three-day battle was fought, which the Greeks eventually lost.

At the same time that the Battle of Thermopylae was happening on land, the Greeks engaged with the Persians in a naval battle at Artemisium, in a sea channel only 6 miles (9.7 km) wide. Although the Persian fleet had originally numbered around 600 ships, it had lost a number of them in recent storms, so it did not greatly outnumber the 370 triremes of the Greeks. The Persians had the advantage that many of their ships were in fact Phoenician, sailed by Phoenician crews, who were generally acknowledged at that time to be the best sailors in the world. However, in the confined waters at Artemisium, superior

This relief depicts Darius I, the king of Persia at the time of the outbreak of the Persian Wars. Darius insisted that the Greek states should recognize his sovereignty.

This 17th-century-CE engraving depicts the Battle of Marathon, one of the key battles of the Persian Wars.

sailing tactics did not count for much. The Persians' technique was to bring their ships alongside the Greek ships, so that infantrymen could board the enemy ships. The Greeks had their own soldiers aboard their vessels and fought back vigorously. The two fleets inflicted substantial damage on each other, and although the battle was nominally a victory for the Persians, the fact that they had performed so well was a great morale booster for the Greeks. On receiving the news of the defeat at Thermopylae, the Greek ships sailed south.

Campaign in Attica

Following the battles at Marathon and Artemisium, central Greece and Attica lay open to the advancing enemy. On

THE BATTLE OF THERMOPYLAE

The pass at Thermopylae was an obvious place for the Greeks to intercept the Persians. It was hemmed in on one side by tall cliffs and on the other by the sea. A Greek force of 9,000 hoplites, under the command of the Spartan king Leonidas, made camp in the pass to await the Persians.

The 200,000 strong Persian army poured into the pass, but because it was so narrow, only a few could engage with the Greeks at a time. The superior equipment of the Greek hoplites gave them a crucial advantage and they were able to hold the pass for two days. On the third day, a local Greek guide treacherously showed the Persians a mountain path that enabled them to come down behind the Greek lines. Realizing that he was outflanked, Leonidas ordered most of his army to retreat south, and with 300 Spartans and around 1,000 other troops, he made a heroic last stand. The Persians attacked, and the Spartans were all killed.

Themistocles' advice, the population of Athens was evacuated to Salamis, an island in the Gulf of Aegina, and the Peloponnese. This proved to be a wise decision, because Xerxes entered Athens and sacked it. From Salamis, Themistocles was forced to watch the clouds of smoke billowing up from the burning temples on the Acropolis.

The Battle of Salamis

Meanwhile, the Persian fleet had sailed south to Salamis, where the Greek fleet was waiting. According to the poet Aeschylus, who took part in the ensuing battle, the Persian fleet made such an impression that the Spartan leaders were all for retreating from the bay, assembling all land and naval forces by the isthmus of Corinth, and building a wall to block the Persians. Themistocles pointed out that a wall would be useless if the Persian fleet could sail past it. Only "wooden walls" could help.

Before the battle began, Themistocles sent a messenger to Xerxes with false information, claiming that there was dissension among the Greeks, that the Athenians wanted to defect to the enemy, and that the Persians should attack right away if they wanted to take advantage of the situation. The Persians were so confident of victory that Xerxes had a golden throne built on a hill overlooking the harbor of Salamis so he could witness the destruction of the Greek fleet in comfort.

The ruse worked. The Persians, confident that victory would be theirs, sailed into the Salamis narrows by night with the intention of launching an attack at dawn, but first light brought an unwelcome sight. The Greek fleet was drawn up in a semicircular formation, spanning the width of the channel and forming a trap in which the Persian ships were caught. In the ensuing battle, the Greek ships rammed their Persian counterparts, which could not maneuver in the tight situation and, because they were lighter than the Greek triremes, were susceptible to this form of attack. The Persian ships

This 14th-century-CE manuscript illustration depicts the Battle of Salamis, fought between the Greeks and the Persians.

THE HISTORIAN HERODOTUS

The most important source for the history of the Persian Wars is the historian Herodotus, who was born some time around 480 BCE in the Greek city of Halicarnassus in Anatolia. His date of death is also unknown but probably lies sometime between 430 and 420 BCE. Cicero, the Roman statesman and philosopher (106–46 BCE), called Herodotus the father of historiography, that is, the writing of history based on a critical examination of sources. Herodotus attempted to interpret the past, putting a human face on it and infusing it with a moral understanding.

According to Herodotus, his work was the fruit of research and inquiry. He opened his *History*, his account of the Persian Wars, with the following words: "Here follows an explanation of the study that Herodotus of Halicarnassus initiated with the intention that the deeds of the people not be forgotten in time and that the important and amazing feats of the Greeks and non-Greeks be given their due glory, and also to shed light on the reason why they entered into conflict with one another."

Herodotus's *History* is now divided into nine separate books. It does not just tell the story of the Persian Wars themselves; it also attempts to place them into context by giving a history of the Persian Empire. Herodotus's work was based largely on information gathered on his travels throughout Anatolia, Egypt, Palestine, Phoenicia, Mesopotamia, and the Black Sea region. His goal was to collect information, separating what he had seen and heard from other observations. Nevertheless, his work is far from being a dry, historical account. He wrote in an easy-going, engaging style and mixed his accounts of the wars with gossip, descriptions of the personalities involved, and stories of the gods.

This bust from the fourth century BCE is of Herodotus, the "father of historiography."

capsized, littering the sea with wrecks and corpses. By evening, Xerxes could see that his fleet was crushed.

Xerxes returns to Asia

Alarmed by the destruction of his fleet, Xerxes began the long march back to Asia with the bulk of his land forces. However, he left a formidable force of around 60,000 men behind under the command of his brother-in-law Mardonius with instructions to continue the planned subjugation of Greece.

Mardonius spent the winter in Thessaly. In the spring, he sent a delegation to Athens offering to repair all the damage and help in reconstructing the city. He hoped by this means to negotiate a settlement with the Athenians excluding Sparta. All he asked in exchange was that Athens should recognize the sovereignty of the Persian king. The Athenians rejected Mardonius's proposals and hastened to reassure the concerned Spartans that they would stand firm for "the Greek brotherhood, the collective ancestry and language, the altars and the sacrifices in which all Greeks share," as Herodotus put it.

Mardonius responded by ravaging Attica and capturing Athens, but he pulled back his troops when the Spartan main force advanced northward. The Greek forces assembled en masse on the plain of Plataea (a few miles south of Thebes) where the Persian army awaited them. The Battle of Plataea ended in a comprehensive victory for the Greek forces and the death of Mardonius. The Persian hopes of conquering Greece were finally at an end.

Meanwhile, reputedly on the same day that the Battle of Plataea was being fought, another encounter took place that completed the Persians' humiliation at the hands of the Greeks. This battle took place at Cape Mycale in Ionia. Some 4,000 Greek hoplites, under the overall command of the Spartan king Leotychides, landed and confronted a Persian army twice their number. However, the Persian force contained a large contingent of troops from the Greek cities of Lydia. Once the fighting started, a number of the Lydian troops

This vase painting depicts Greek hoplites with prisoners of war.

THE BATTLE OF PLATAEA

On the plain of Plataea in the summer of 479 BCE, a Greek army under the command of Pausanius, the Spartan regent, faced a Persian force under Mardonius. Pausanius had 38,000 heavily armed hoplites from Sparta, Athens, and Corinth, with perhaps an equal number of lightly armed soldiers, but he had no mounted troops. The Persians had the advantage of their formidable cavalry, whose technique against infantry was to charge them, release a hail of javelins and arrows, and then wheel away.

The two armies faced each other across the Asopus River for almost two weeks, with a little daily skirmishing. Each general was reluctant to initiate an attack. Finally, with no access to fresh water, Pausanius decided to withdraw to Plataea. When he saw the Greeks on the move, Mardonius ordered his troops forward to attack.

In the retreat, the Greeks had become separated into several units. One of these units consisted of around 12,000 Spartan hoplites, while another was made up of 8,000 Athenians. At the time of the Persian attack, these units were separated by around 1 mile (1.6 km), so the ensuing battle really took place on two separate fronts. The Spartans turned and formed up in battle order to face the onslaught of the Persian infantry, who were equipped with bows and arrows. Many of the Spartans fell under the rain of arrows, but when the command came to charge, the hoplites proved their superior fighting prowess. In the ensuing chaos, Mardonius was killed, and once their general was dead, the Persians fled. On the other side of the field, the Athenians were engaged with other Persian forces, but once the Persians saw their comrades fleeing, they also ran away. The battle was a resounding victory for the Greeks.

An undated modern illustration shows the Greek and Persian troops fighting at the Battle of Plataea in 479 BCE.

This relief sculpture from the Persian capital of Persepolis dates to the reign of Xerxes I.

changed sides. Leotychides managed to inflict a decisive defeat on the Persian land forces and captured the Persian fleet, which was moored nearby.

The end of the war

Even though the battles of Plataea and Cape Mycale effectively ended the danger that the Persians posed to the Greek mainland, sporadic fighting continued for another 30 years. From this time on, it was the Greeks who were on the offensive. The Athenians attempted to secure a complete dominance of eastern Mediterranean trade by systematically driving the Persians out of Ionia and Cyprus. Eventually, in 449 BCE, a peace treaty was negotiated between Persia and Athens, and the Persian Wars were finally at an end.

This seal depicts the type of Greek warship that would have been used at Salamis.

See also:

Sparta and Athens (page 52)

THE GREEK TRIREME

The main type of warship used by the Greeks during the Persian Wars was the trireme (known to the Greeks as a *trieres*). The triremes derived their name from the fact that they were powered by oarsmen arranged in three separate banks, one above the other. This arrangement came about as the solution to the problem of how to fit as many rowers into a ship as possible. The triple-deck system meant that around 170 oarsmen could be fitted into a ship (as well as a number of foot soldiers). Although triremes also used sails, they were lowered before the ships went into battle; the use of oars gave the ships greater maneuverability.

During a naval engagement, a commander could adopt two different tactics. The ship could try to pull up alongside the adversaries, enabling Greek troops to board the enemy vessel and capture it. Alternatively, a ship could simply try to ram the enemy with the prow, which was specially designed for that purpose. In order to execute this maneuver, one fleet had to outflank the other so the prows of at least some of the ships faced the sides of the enemy vessels. This technique was known as the *periplus*. Various defensive formations could be adopted to offer protection. One was the *kyklos*, which was a simple defensive circle where all of the ships had their prows facing outward.

Greek triremes used ramming tactics to win victory in arguably the most famous naval battle of ancient times—Salamis. The Greek fleet was heavily outnumbered, but the quicker and more maneuverable Greek triremes managed to inflict huge damage in the narrow channel where the battle was fought.

THE AGE
OF PERICLES

During the fifth century BCE, the city of Athens was involved in wars against two major adversaries—Persia and the fellow Greek city of Sparta. However, the period was also a time when democracy and culture flourished.

TIME LINE

c. 495 BCE

Pericles born in Athens.

480 BCE

Greek victory at Battle of Salamis marks start of Athenian naval supremacy.

477 BCE

Delian League formed; Athens becomes alliance's leading state.

447 BCE

Work begins on construction of Parthenon, temple to Athena on Acropolis.

443 BCE

Pericles becomes *strategos* for first time.

431 BCE

Peloponnesian War begins; Spartan force invades Attica, forcing inhabitants to shelter inside walls of Athens.

429 BCE

Pericles dies.

The Athenian statesman Pericles, who lived from around 495 to 429 BCE, was so important to the development of Athens that historians call the time he was in power the Age of Pericles. Under his guidance, Athens reached the pinnacle of its influence. The city also became an unparalleled center of culture and learning, a process that culminated in the construction of the Parthenon on the Acropolis.

The Athenians enjoyed a good life under Pericles, as he himself described it in a speech: "We have feasts and ceremonies throughout the year. Life is pleasant in our homes, and with our noble behavior, we provide ourselves with pleasures that hinder sadness. The fame of our city brings us fruits from the entire Earth, so we can enjoy foreign and exotic products… We are admirers of beauty, but we remain simple."

The upbringing of Pericles

Pericles was the son of Xanthippus, a general who led the Athenian contingent that contributed to the defeat of the Persians at Cape Mycale in 479 BCE. Although he came from an aristocratic family, Pericles made his name in politics as a reformer with left-wing leanings. With the support of the common people, he became leader of the popular party. He was a persuasive orator, and when he spoke in the assembly, he could generally convince his listeners of the merit of his proposals. By 460 BCE, he had virtually become head of state.

The Battle of Salamis, where the Greeks routed the Persians in a sea battle in 480 BCE, marked the beginning of the rise of Athenian sea power. After the final defeat of the Persians at Plataea the following year, Athens emerged as the predominant city-state in Greece.

Up until this time, Sparta had been the greatest military power in Greece. At the end of the wars with Persia, however, the Spartans opted for isolation. They returned to their austere lifestyle on the Peloponnese peninsula, where their lands had remained untouched by the Persian Wars. Although they had ample ability and resources to establish military sovereignty throughout Greece, they preferred to concentrate on domestic affairs.

Athens suffered heavily in the wars with Persia, and it remained fearful of a new invasion. To reduce this threat, the Athenians pursued a policy of offensive, expansionist action. After the battles of Salamis and Cape Mycale, the Athenians had undisputed sea supremacy in the eastern Mediterranean region. However, maintaining a large fleet put a severe strain on the funds of Attica, so Athens needed to form alliances to continue military offensives against Persia.

This bust, created in the second century BCE, is believed to depict the Athenian statesman Pericles, who dominated the politics of Athens for more than 30 years.

The Delian League

In 477 BCE, Athens and most of the Aegean city-states formed an alliance against Persia called the Delian League. It was named for the island of Delos, where the meetings of the league were to be held and the funds of the alliance were to be kept. Athens headed the league, but all the members had an equal vote, in principle at least. As the leading member of the league, Athens commanded a fleet of 200 ships, and every ally was required to pay an annual fee to help maintain the fleet. This fee could consist of ships, men, equipment, or silver talents, all assessed according to the resources of the member state.

Between 476 and 466 BCE, a Greek force, under the joint command of generals Cimon and Aristides, succeeded in liberating the coasts of the Aegean from Persian control. One notable success came in 466 when a force led by Cimon destroyed both the Persian fleet and the Persian army near the mouth of the Eurymedon River in Anatolia.

An Athenian empire

By 466 BCE, most of the members of the league were paying their contributions in silver talents rather than men or goods. This was tantamount to paying tribute. When some of the states started to object, Athens responded ruthlessly. For example, when Naxos objected to paying the tribute and attempted to withdraw from the league, Athens destroyed its forts. Athens then annexed the lands of other recalcitrant allies, distributing the land to its own citizens. The league that had started as a defensive alliance against Persia had become a naval empire run by Athens. It encompassed most of the large islands of the Aegean Sea and many cities to the north, either as equals or as subjected former allies.

Following his famous success at the Eurymedon River, Cimon had become a

Women draw water from a well in the illustration on this vase from the fifth century BCE.

treaty with the Persians, which put an end to the Persian Wars. To celebrate the end of hostilities, Pericles embarked on an ambitious building program that resulted in the construction of the group of buildings that are still seen on the Acropolis today. With the Persian threat gone, and Athens obviously in the ascendancy, other city-states on the Greek mainland lined up to join the league. In the long run, however, the result was that the members of the Delian League simply became the vassals of Athens.

The Peloponnesian War

The Peloponnesian War that was to devastate Greece between the years 431 and 404 BCE was sparked off by growing tension between Athens and the cities of Corinth and Sparta. Corinth had developed from an ancient settlement near the isthmus of Corinth to become a thriving trading city by 1000 BCE. Benefiting from two harbors, one on the Corinthian Gulf and one on the Saronic Gulf, Corinth became the major center of commerce in Greece by 650 BCE. As Athens increased both its naval and commercial activity under Pericles, the older city felt threatened.

The years leading up to 431 BCE also saw relations between Athens and Sparta deteriorate; Sparta saw the growing Delian League as a threat to the stability of the Greek mainland. In 431 BCE, Corinth joined with Sparta in forming the Spartan Confederacy to counteract the rising power of the Delian League. Other members of the confederacy were Thebes, Macedon, and Ambracia on the Ionian coast. These allies faced the might

leading politician. However, his reputation was severely damaged when he took an Athenian contingent to assist Sparta in quelling a slave rebellion. The Athenian expedition ended badly when the Spartans rejected the offer of help. Cimon was ostracized and banished from Athens in 461 BCE. His exit left the stage clear for Pericles to become the city's leading statesman.

In 449 BCE, an Athenian diplomat named Callias succeeded in negotiating a

The House of the Poseidoniasts stands on the Greek island of Delos. Delos was the meeting place of the Delian League, an association of city-states dominated by Athens.

of Athens, which was concentrated along the northern and eastern coasts of the Aegean Sea, on most of the large Aegean islands, and in Byzantium. Before long, the rivalry between Sparta and Athens finally erupted into the Peloponnesian War.

In 431 BCE, the Spartans launched the first of a number of raids against the countryside surrounding Athens. As the army of the Spartan Confederacy pillaged unimpeded through the rural regions of Attica, Pericles gathered the residents of Attica inside the city walls of Athens for safety. In the following year, 430 BCE, plague decimated the overcrowded city. The angry and dying Athenians removed Pericles from office, and he was tried and fined for misuse of public funds. After a brief reinstatement, he died in 429 BCE. The Age of Pericles was at an end.

Golden age of Athens

During the time of Athenian ascendancy under Pericles, the government of Athens and its culture can both be said to have enjoyed a golden age. In particular, the constitution was modified to extend the principles of democracy, further weakening the power of the aristocracy.

The main body of the Athenian political system was the public assembly (the *ecclesia*). In theory, all Athenians could attend the assembly, but in practice, although there were something like 30,000 to 40,000 citizens, only around 6,000 actually attended meetings. The meetings were held around once a month in a natural amphitheater on a

This statue from the fifth century BCE depicts Athens' patron goddess Athena.

hillside, where the citizens would debate and vote on motions prepared by the Council in advance. The Council consisted of 500 members who were elected each year, usually from families of the middle and upper classes.

In earlier centuries, one of the most important political offices was that of archon, or magistrate. In 487 BCE, a change had been made in the way the archons were selected. From that point onward, the archons were appointed by lot, rather than elected. The change meant that the magistracy lost much of its importance, as did the Areopagus, the old council of the nobility to which ex-archons belonged. In 462 BCE, the judicial function of the Areopagus was largely taken over by jury tribunals, and its supervision of polis administrators was relegated to the Council of 500.

Farmers and politicians

Around the middle of the fifth century BCE, it became possible for archons to be drawn from the *zeugitai* (farmers who owned land). A system of attendance fees, payable to magistrates and council and jury members so they did not lose financially because of their services, was introduced. At the beginning of the fourth century BCE, the payment was extended to cover attendance at the public assembly, which meant that all citizens could exercise their political rights without the worry of financial loss. The change was of particular benefit to the *thetes* (small landless farmers and day laborers).

The selection of magistrates by lot carried risks, because some aspects of the role required a degree of specialized knowledge not available to the ordinary man. In an effort to deal with this problem, the Athenians created 10 elected

The ruins of the ancient city of Corinth can still be seen to this day. Corinth was a major rival of Athens in the fifth century BCE.

strategoi (commanders-in-chief), who were appointed for one-year terms. They could be reelected but were subject to monitoring by their fellow *strategoi*. If necessary, they could be removed from office by popular vote in the assembly, which meant there was little chance of a *strategos* becoming a tyrant. Pericles served as a *strategos* continuously from 443 to 430 BCE.

The assembly

Given the size of the assembly, there was only time for a few of those present to speak. Because the issues discussed were often complicated, not everyone could be expected to speak with equal authority. To address several thousand people and convince them to vote the way the speaker wanted demanded special skills in public speaking. In response to these demands, a new class of orator-politicians, called rhetors, developed. These rhetors were generally wealthy people, and they played an essential role in political decision making. Pericles was the most famous of the rhetors, and the most important.

Rhetors spoke either on their own behalf or on behalf of special interest groups. They were not politicians representing specific political parties; political parties did not exist in the modern sense. Athenian democracy allowed everyone, from all classes and walks of life, to participate in political life, but it was not until the second half of the fifth century BCE that nonaristocrats were called on as designated speakers in the public assembly.

Pericles on democracy

A speech attributed to Pericles and believed to have been given around 431 BCE encapsulates his beliefs on the benefits of democracy. The speech praises Athens for its power, strength, prosperity, openness, and freedom, as well as the equality of its citizens. He says: "Our government is no imitation of our neighbors'. On the contrary, we serve as an example for them. We are a democracy, because the government is in the hands of the people and not in the hands of a small group. Our law states that every citizen has equal rights. We Athenians recognize the supremacy of intelligence, and when a fellow citizen distinguishes himself from the others, the people appoint him to the highest positions. This is not the right of a gifted man, but the reward for his great merits. Lack of money is no obstacle to fulfilling high office: any citizen can serve the state. There are no privileges in our political life, nor in our personal relationships; we trust one another."

He goes on to say: "Although there are few among us who are extraordinary enough to formulate proposals, we are all good enough to make decisions. It is our conviction that danger does not lie in discussion, but in ignorance. We have the special characteristic that we can think before we act, even in the middle of action. Others, however, are brave in ignorance, yet hesitate as soon as they begin to think!"

In other parts of the speech, Pericles talks about the glorious history of Athens, the great Athenian Empire, and the courage of Athenian soldiers. He

This depiction of Artemis, the Greek goddess of hunting, is part of a frieze that decorated the Parthenon in Athens. The Parthenon was a temple to another goddess, Athena. It stood on the Acropolis, the fortified hill at the heart of the city.

paints an ideal picture of Athenian democracy. There is no mention of slavery. Slaves were an accepted fact of life in the Athenian state. Their lack of rights was an issue ignored by all Greeks, including Pericles.

The perils of democracy

Not everyone was in favor of the idea of democracy. An anonymous political pamphlet from the Age of Pericles summarizes a number of arguments against democracy that were widespread in Athens at the time. Although the pamphleteer argues against these opinions, he nevertheless offers a good impression of the anti-democratic viewpoint.

Against equal participation in government for all citizens, he writes: "One can argue that not everyone should be allowed to speak and sit on the council, but only the best and most intelligent citizens … how can such a low person decide what is good for himself or for the entire populace?" The main objection of the critics of democracy was that effective government was impossible when left to the less educated members of society.

This was certainly the view of the Athenian philosopher Plato (c. 428–348 BCE). In his dialogue *The Republic*, he called democracy anarchy. He wrote: "Whenever a meeting must be held concerning matters of state, the one to stand up and offer advice can be a carpenter, a smith, a shoemaker, a merchant, a shipowner, a rich man, a poor man, of good family, or of no family at all, and no one thinks of telling him that his

The Temple of Athena Nike was just one of several magnificent temples erected on the Acropolis in the fifth century BCE.

117

meddling is not justified by any knowledge of matters, nor by the instruction of a teacher."

There were certainly other citizens in democratic Athens who held such opinions, and who favored an oligarchy (government by the few), even if they played no significant political role. They were admirers of Sparta, a state where, it was said, everyone knew his place. Only in the last quarter of the fifth century BCE, when Athens was at war with Sparta, did the supporters of oligarchy have the opportunity to attempt to change Athenian democracy. Their efforts came to nothing, however.

The culture of the golden age

During its golden age, Athens was both powerful and prosperous. The city's wealth came from the silver mines of Attica and the harbor dues of Piraeus, which was now the most important port in the eastern Mediterranean region.

The Athenian golden age saw an explosion of creativity in philosophy, art, architecture, and science. For the first time, Athens became an important center for philosophy and science. Philosophers gathered there from all corners of the world, finding a warm welcome among the richer citizens. Among the leading figures who congregated in Athens were Anaxagoras, Socrates, and Plato.

Athens was also visited by sophists—traveling teachers who specialized in teaching intellectual skills, particularly rhetoric and disputation. One of these sophists was Damon, who was also a master of music. He had a special influence on Pericles, as did the Ionian philosopher Anaxagoras. Throughout his life, Pericles was noted for his eloquence, wisdom, and patriotism, which won him recognition from the majority of the citizens of Athens. Although he remained aloof from most Athenians, he had a number of distinguished friends, includ-

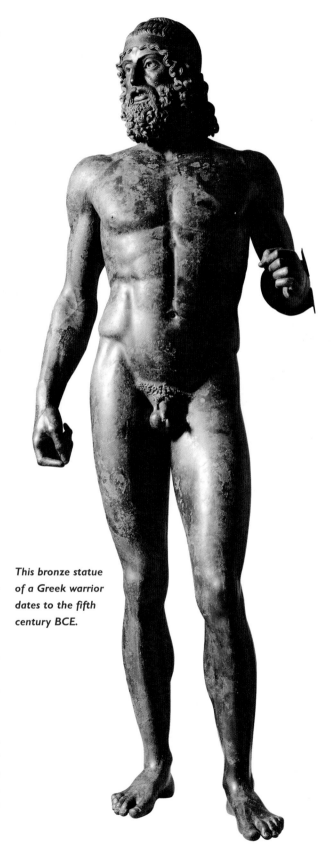

This bronze statue of a Greek warrior dates to the fifth century BCE.

the colony of Thurii on the Gulf of Tarentum in southern Italy. Thurii was intended to be a model colony, taking in emigrants from all over Greece, the Aegean islands, and Ionia and molding them into an ideal community. Many famous figures became involved. The philosopher Protagoras of Abdera is said to have written its laws, while the famous architect and urban designer Hippodamus of Miletus drew up city plans for the colony. Hippodamus had designed Piraeus, which featured a street plan of straight streets crossing each other to flank rectangular blocks of buildings. Because of this connection, some historians believe that Thurii may have had a similar plan, but this has not yet been confirmed by archaeological excavation.

The literary arts flourished in Athens under Pericles. In the theater, Greek tragedy reached its peak, with the plays of Aeschylus, Sophocles, and Euripides being performed. The great comedy writer Aristophanes was also working at this time.

Architecture

After the destruction of the Acropolis by the Persians in 480 BCE, the Athenians had vowed never to build there again. As they regained confidence and power during the fifth century BCE, this viewpoint gradually changed. To mark the peace with Persia of 449 BCE, Pericles initiated a great building program on the Acropolis, both to restore the temples destroyed by the Persians and to construct new buildings.

The years between 447 and 406 BCE saw the completion of some of the most outstanding examples of Greek architecture. Among the buildings constructed during that period were the Propylaea, the Erechtheum, and the Temple of Athena Nike. The most famous product of this construction program, however, was the Parthenon.

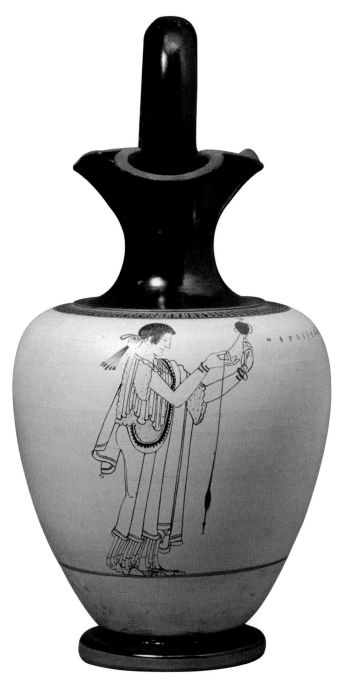

This jug, made in Athens in the fifth century BCE, is illustrated with a picture of a woman spinning thread.

ing the playwright Sophocles, the historian Herodotus, the sculptor Phidias, and the sophist Protagoras. Pericles never married, but he had a mistress, Aspasia. She was a *hetaira*, a sophisticated, highly educated type of prostitute.

One project that had personal interest for Pericles was the development of

MARRIAGE IN ANCIENT ATHENS

In ancient Athens, marriage was seen as a practical rather than a romantic arrangement; citizens were expected to marry and to procreate. Usually, the fathers of the bride and groom made a contractual agreement for a dowry to be paid by the bride's family to the groom, although the agreement could occasionally be between the groom himself and the bride's father.

The main purpose of a marriage was to produce legitimate children, who would be citizens of Athens. So, an Athenian citizen had to marry another Athenian citizen; otherwise, the children of the marriage would not be deemed citizens. The wedding was celebrated by a wedding feast, held in the house of the bride's family. After the feast, the bridegroom led his veiled wife to his own house, followed by well-wishers who usually sang outside the bridal chamber.

The bride was generally much younger than her bridegroom. In classical Athens, she would typically be around 14, and he might be in his late twenties. Greek society was strictly patriarchal, and the young wife had a subordinate position. Her place was in the home, and in theory, she would leave it only rarely to attend funerals and religious celebrations. In practice, however, there were many religious events in which women played an important role.

In Greek society, women were generally thought to be inferior beings. Men viewed women largely in terms of their bodies—

they were categorized into four groups by their ability to bear children. These groups were the young, sexually immature girl; the marriageable virgin; the sexually active, fertile wife and mother; and the elderly, infertile woman. Outside of this classification, and essentially outside of society, fell unmarried women who had lost their virginity, infertile women, and prostitutes.

A marriage could be ended by divorce. For the husband, this was a simple matter of just banishing his wife from the house. The wife could also leave, but she would probably be unable to obtain the return of her dowry. For this, she would have to go to the courts, which, like so many other things in Greece, were dominated by men and would be unlikely to find in her favor.

A man is shown leading his bride in this illustration of a wedding scene on a Greek pyxis (jewelry box). In ancient Athens, women married when they were very young.

A marble temple dedicated to Athena, the Parthenon took its name from one of the goddess's titles, Athena Parthenos, meaning Athena the Virgin. Work began on the building in 447 BCE, yet it was not completed until 438 BCE. The building works were carried out under the direction of the sculptor Phidias. He was also responsible for one of the most imposing features of the temple, a statue of the goddess that stood 40 feet (12 m) high. Made of gold and ivory, it was one of the most admired pieces of art of the ancient world. It is believed to have been destroyed by fire.

The Athenian building program provided employment for many of the city's poorer citizens, while making Athens the most magnificent city of the ancient world. This blossoming of culture, art, and architecture in the fifth century BCE is evidence of the preeminent position Athens held in Greece at that time.

See also:

The Birth of Drama (page 88) • From Tyranny to Democracy (page 64) • The Peloponnesian War (page 138) • The Persian Wars (page 96) • Sparta and Athens (page 52)

The Parthenon is the most famous of all the temples built during the Age of Pericles.

THE GREAT PHILOSOPHERS

TIME LINE

c. 575 BCE

Thales establishes school of philosophy in Miletus. He is first of three great philosophers of School of Miletus, other two being Anaximander and Anaximenes.

c. 530 BCE

Pythagoras sets up school in Croton. He establishes number of mathematical principles, including famous theorem.

399 BCE

Socrates charged with heresy; found guilty and sentenced to death.

387 BCE

Plato establishes Academy in Athens. Among greatest works are *Laws* and *Republic*.

c. 335 BCE

Aristotle, student of Plato, establishes Lyceum.

From the sixth century BCE, Greece was home to a number of famous philosophers. Men such as Socrates, Plato, Aristotle, Pythagoras, and Diogenes came up with ideas that were to shape the history of Western thought.

Like most ancient peoples, the Greeks worshipped a variety of gods, who they believed could influence human affairs. However, from the sixth century BCE onward, there was also a general growth of secular thinking. The fifth-century-BCE physician Hippocrates searched for a natural, rather than a supernatural, explanation for disease, while the historian Thucydides made no allowance for the actions of the gods in his account of events of the past. The philosopher Protagoras, also of the fifth century BCE, claimed that there was no absolute "right" and "wrong"—only what human opinion determined was so. This idea was expressed in his famous saying "Man is the measure of all things."

Some thinkers, such as Diagoras of Melos (c. fifth century BCE), went so far as to doubt the existence of the gods. However, even for people who did not possess such extreme views, the relationship between the gods, fate, and man's own responsibility became increasingly a matter for debate in the fifth and fourth centuries BCE, which contributed to the growth of Greek philosophy.

Ionian philosophy

Greek philosophy had its origins in the sixth century BCE in Ionia. Ionia was a region in western Anatolia that had been occupied by Greeks since around 1000 BCE. People who lived there were more open to influences from other lands and cultures than the citizens of the city-states of mainland Greece. They would have been aware of intellectual accomplishments such as the discoveries of the Babylonian astronomers. These new ideas opened the way for discussions about natural phenomena and gave rise to the birth of philosophy and science.

These new "natural philosophers" tried to describe and explain the origin and existence of heaven and earth in a rational manner, rather than through myths involving the various gods. The philosophers were searching for basic rational principles that could explain the entire universe.

The School of Miletus

The center of the explosion of new ideas was Miletus, a city on the southwest coast of Ionia. The first of these thinkers (now considered to be the founder of Greek philosophy) was Thales of Miletus, who lived from around 610 to 540 BCE. In the first half of the sixth century BCE, Thales rejected a mytho-

The School of Athens, *painted by Raphael in 1510 CE, depicts some of ancient Greece's greatest philosophers, including Plato (center left), Aristotle (center right), and Diogenes (bottom right).*

Thales of Miletus, shown in this undated modern illustration, is considered to be the father of Greek philosophy.

the east and possibly also from Egypt in the south. Thales is said to have visited Egypt, where he calculated the height of a pyramid. He subsequently introduced geometry to the Greek world, using Egyptian examples and applications. Because of his practice of making careful observations in order to draw conclusions about the physical nature of the world, Thales has sometimes been called the first scientist. He formulated a theory that the original principle matter of the cosmos was water, from which everything proceeds and into which everything is eventually resolved.

Anaximander

Anaximander of Miletus (c. 611–546 BCE) was, if anything, even more brilliant than Thales, his teacher, was. Anaximander recorded his theories about the nature of the cosmos in a treatise called *About Nature*. Much of this work is now lost, although the substance of it is referred to by later writers.

According to Anaximander, the entire cosmos was created and derived from something that he called the *apeiron*, which can be translated as "the indeterminate" or "the unlimited." Everything originated from the *apeiron*, which he defined as the first element, and everything would return to it. Anaximander is credited with having produced a sundial and the first Greek map of the world. He is also believed to have introduced a number of hypotheses about astronomy. According to Roman writers of the third century CE, Anaximander also came up with a remarkable theory about the development of life on earth. He believed that humans developed from embryos that were once found inside of fish, a theory that predated the evolutionary theories of Charles Darwin by more than 2,300 years.

Anaximenes of Miletus, a student of Anaximander, was active in the second

logical explanation of the universe and attempted to explain it in rational terms. Thales left no writings of his own, but his beliefs are discussed in Aristotle's *Metaphysics*, a work written in the fourth century BCE. Thales was noted for his knowledge of astronomy. He is reputed to have predicted the solar eclipse of May 28, 585 BCE. To make this calculation, Thales would have used mathematical techniques borrowed from Babylon in half of the sixth century BCE. The last of the three great scholars of the School of Miletus, Anaximenes proposed a system of philosophy based on the idea that a primary element was the origin of all things and beings, including the gods. This primary element was air. Air, he argued, could be transformed into water, earth, and fire. This theory explained the origins of the four elements that were seen as being basic to nature—earth, water, air, and fire. A saying of his sums up his concept: "As the soul, which is breath, holds us together, so does air hold the whole world together."

Xenophanes

Two other main thinkers who contributed to Ionian natural philosophy were Xenophanes and Heraclitus. Xenophanes was a poet–philosopher who lived from around 580 to 480 BCE. He was born in Colophon, not far from Miletus, but left his place of birth when it came under Persian rule. He settled in the Greek city of Elea in southern Italy, where he is believed to have founded the school of philosophy that was later made famous by Parmenides.

Xenophanes roamed through southern Italy, Sicily, and probably the Greek mainland until old age, reciting his poetry, through which he criticized the opinions of his contemporaries. He was particularly scathing about the accepted mythical explanations of the world and the fact that people believed the gods resembled humans. In attacking how human beings worshiped gods that looked like themselves, he suggested that if cows or horses could draw, they would portray their gods as cows or horses. He also spoke out against wealth, soothsaying, the drinking parties of the nobility, and the idolization of the winners of the Olympic Games. In the last case, he emphasized that it was better to honor a scholar than an athlete because, he said, a

This 15th-century-CE illustration depicts Anaximenes, one of the three great philosophers from the School of Miletus.

learned man could be of benefit in the managing of the polis, and wise counsel could even bring money. Xenophanes' criticisms were based on his conviction that sensory perceptions were always deceptive and, consequently, could not lead to sure knowledge. Sure knowledge could only reside in the divine—an invisible and omnipresent god.

Heraclitus

Heraclitus of Ephesus, who probably lived from around 560 to 480 BCE, expressed his ideas in a series of proverbs. His main theory was that the entire cosmos is organized and directed by a single principle, called the Logos in Greek. The material embodiment of this Logos was fire, which Heraclitus considered to be the essential form of matter. The logos is the directing force that ensures equilibrium in the world by balancing change in one area with an equivalent and opposite change elsewhere. One of Heraclitus's best-known sayings, attributed to him by the later philosopher Plato (c. 428–348 BCE), was that "all things are in flux."

Anaxagoras

One result of the Persian drive into Anatolia in the fifth century BCE was the emigration of Ionian scholars to the Greek mainland and its colonies. Anaxagoras (c. 500–428 BCE), who was born in Clazomenae in Ionia, moved to Athens around 480 BCE. In contrast to earlier thinkers who looked to earth, air, fire, and water for the origin of ultimate reality, Anaxagoras formulated the doctrine of nous (meaning eternal intelligence, from the Greek for "mind" or "reason"). In a work entitled *On Nature*, only portions of which survive, he suggested that all matter existed in a state of chaos as infinitely numerous and small particles called "seeds." These seeds were brought into order by the animating force of nous.

Anaxagoras taught in Athens for 30 years, during which time his students included the dramatist Euripides and possibly also the philosopher Socrates (469–399 BCE). He was also friends with Pericles, but the Athenian statesman was unable to help Anaxagoras when he was charged with impiety for insisting that the stars, including the sun, were glowing masses of red hot stone and that the moon received its light from the sun. For these ideas—far ahead of their time—Anaxagoras was sentenced to death, but he managed to escape to Lampsacus in Anatolia.

Pythagoras

Thinkers leaving Ionia set up schools of philosophy in southern Italy and Sicily as well as in Athens. One of these thinkers was Pythagoras (c. 580–500 BCE), who was born on the island of Samos off the coast of Anatolia. In his late twenties, apparently unhappy with the policies of the Samian tyrant Polycrates, Pythagoras left Samos for Croton, a Greek colony in southern Italy, where he settled around 530 BCE.

In Croton, Pythagoras established a philosophical sect that had two main

In ancient Greece, solar eclipses were mysterious events. Thales of Miletus is believed to be the first person to predict one successfully.

Helios the sun god rides across the sky in his chariot in this vase painting. The philosopher Xenophanes ridiculed people who believed that the gods looked like humans.

teachings. One idea was that the study of mathematics and numbers could reveal the hidden order of the universe. The other idea was the doctrine of metempsychosis, which stated that at death the soul passes into another body, either that of a human or that of an animal.

The fact that the Pythagorean movement was a sect was important. It was the first time in the history of Greek religion that a group had distinguished itself in this way. At first, the Pythagoreans had great influence in Croton, but the residents of the city came to distrust the sect so much that around 500 BCE they set fire to the Pythagorean building. The embittered Pythagoras left the city for another Greek colony close by called Metapontion, where he died within a short time.

An important part of Pythagoras's teaching was the concept of purity and *ascesis* (training or exercise). He asserted that anyone who does not succeed in keeping his body pure by following the rules of life also contaminates his soul.

Unjust behavior also pollutes the soul, which is then not capable of achieving *sophia* (wisdom or insight).

According to Pythagoras's followers, someone's conduct in life could affect his or her eternal fate. An immoral life could lead to reincarnation as an animal. Pythagoreans believed that the main goal in life is to attain as much *sophia* as possible, so the soul rises toward a better body in the next life.

Music and mathematics

After Pythagoras's death, his disciples continued to develop his ideas. In mathematics, they searched for patterns, believing that the essence of all things lay in numbers and that all relationships could be expressed numerically. Music, in particular, could be explained by mathematical formulas. Pythagoras's followers discovered that if a string of a stringed instrument is stopped halfway along its length, it will produce a note one octave higher than the note of the whole string.

Anaxagoras, shown in this 15th-century-CE illustration, was one of the first astronomers to believe that the moon received its light from the sun.

whom was Parmenides of Elea. Elea was a small Greek colony on the southwest coast of Italy, and it was there that Parmenides was born in 515 BCE. Growing up in a wealthy and powerful family, he became a politician before founding a school of philosophy in his home town.

An ideal world

The heart of the philosophy of Parmenides was that the material world is unreal; reality only subsists in a timeless "ideal world," an idea that may have owed something to the Pythagoreans. Parmenides expressed his ideas in a poem, large parts of which have survived. He believed that all movement is nothing other than outward appearance. Only "being" exists; there is no "not being." The "being" is like a sphere—perfect and indivisible.

In geometry, the Pythagoreans established the famous theorem that the square of the hypotenuse (the longest side) of a right-angled triangle is equal to the sum of the squares of the other two sides. This theorem is still taught in schools today.

The Pythagoreans were among the first to teach that the Earth is a spherical planet that revolves around a fixed point. They also saw a numerical scheme behind the arrangement of the heavenly bodies. Pythagoras's followers believed that these bodies were separated from each other by intervals corresponding to the harmonic length of strings. The very movement of the heavenly bodies, they contended, produced music—the "harmony of the spheres."

The teachings of Pythagoras had a considerable influence on many Greek thinkers of the fifth century BCE, one of

The radical nature of Parmenides' philosophy is evident when compared to that of the great Ionian philosophers of the seventh and sixth centuries BCE. They supposed that all things were derived from a basic element—whether water, fire, air, or earth—and assumed that the contraction of that element brought about changes in nature. When an element assumes a material form, however, it must necessarily occupy a place that was originally empty—a vacuum. This vacuum is what Parmenides called "not being." Because he believed that such a vacuum could not exist, he considered the entire philosophy of the Ionian school invalid.

Pythagoras, shown in this 17th-century-CE illustration, is identified with the theorem about the lengths of the sides of a right-angled triangle.

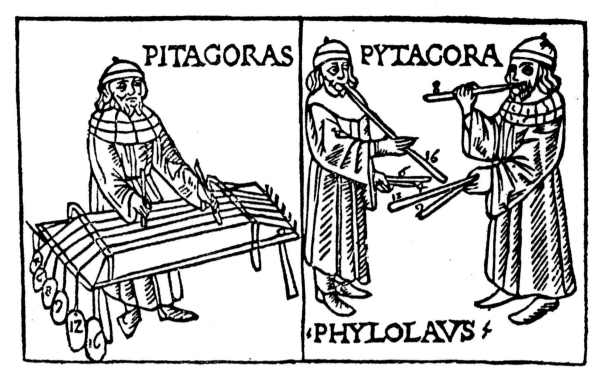

In this 15th-century-CE woodcut, Pythagoras demonstrates the relationship between music and mathematics.

ACHILLES AND THE TURTLE

One of Zeno's famous paradoxes is the story of Achilles and the turtle. Achilles, the fastest runner among the Greeks, challenges a turtle, the slowest of animals, to a race. Achilles gives the turtle a head start of a certain distance, and then they start to run at the same time. When Achilles comes to the place where the turtle started, the turtle has run a certain distance and is ahead of Achilles. Achilles keeps running, but every time he arrives at the place where the turtle was, the turtle has also run a certain distance farther. As fast as Achilles runs, and as slow as the turtle crawls, there will always be a distance for Achilles yet to cover. In other words, Achilles can never catch up with the turtle. This paradox rests on the assumption of infinite divisibility. On the basis of such clever absurdities, which appealed enormously to the Greeks, Zeno attempted to demonstrate the truth of the "indivisibility of being"—and thus that Parmenides was right.

Parmenides also believed it was impossible to explain motion in a philosophical manner. When an object moves from one place to another, he believed, something must be moved that was there before, or the object has to move to a place where there was nothing. Even when the object is initially moved to a place where it replaces another object, there must come a time when the moved object comes to a stop on a place where there was nothing—a vacuum. A vacuum (a "not being") cannot exist, so consequently, neither can motion, from Parmenides' viewpoint.

Zeno (c. 495–430 BCE), a student of Parmenides, tried to prove his teacher's theory of the "indivisibility of being" by means of a number of paradoxes, the most famous of which is that of Achilles and the turtle. In spite of all their logic, these stories led their readers to conclusions that seemed totally absurd. For this reason, the stories exercised the minds of Greek thinkers for lengthy periods of time.

Atomic theory

Another of Parmenides' students was Leucippus (c. fifth century BCE), the founder of the theory of atoms. In Greek, the word *atomos* means "something that is not divisible." Leucippus argued that all matter consists of countless tiny particles, or atoms, and that the diversity of matter depends on the way in which these atoms are combined. The point over which Leucippus stumbled was that he had to allow for empty space, or a vacuum, between the atoms, which brought him into conflict with the ideas of his master.

The work commenced by Leucippus was continued by his student Democritus of Abdera, who perfected the theory of atoms. Democritus maintained that visible reality is made up of atoms, which are in eternal motion in endless space. Atoms are unchangeable but infinitely varied, and by joining together, they form all living and non-living matter.

Greek thinkers of the sixth and fifth centuries BCE were obsessed with questions that were actually unsolvable by philosophers. However, while seeking answers to these questions, some of the philosophers discovered mathematical and scientific truths that were way ahead of their time.

The sophists

In spite of their importance in the development of Western thought, the early philosophers did not have the same social influence as the fifth-century sophists. The sophists were teachers who traveled from city to city, offering to tutor young men in intellectual skills such as public speaking. The Greek word *sophistes* originally meant "expert" or "man of wisdom," but it gradually acquired a different connotation.

The negative image of the sophists arose because they excelled at rhetoric and taught would-be public speakers how to look at a question from both sides and defend both viewpoints. Consequently, a sophist came to be regarded as someone who was very clever with words and could convince an unsuspecting listener of just about anything. Good or bad, the sophist could make a good argument for it.

Initially, the sophists were quite popular in Athens, but they eventually drew fire from Socrates, Plato, and Aristotle, as well as the state itself, for their indifference to morality. Plato and Aristotle also criticized the sophists for taking money, even though, as itinerant educators, that was how they earned their living.

The term *sophist* came to acquire a derogatory meaning, and the word *sophistry* was defined as "deceptive or false reasoning." On one occasion, Socrates compared the sophist to a fisherman: Both try to fish—one to catch his meal, the other to catch people to cheat them out of their money in exchange for false teachings.

An artist's impression of the inside of an atom. The Greek philosopher Leucippus was responsible for one of the world's earliest atomic theories.

Socrates

The philosopher Socrates was of seminal importance to the development of Western thought. Unlike most Greek philosophers, he came from humble origins, being the son of Sophroniscus, a sculptor, and Phaenarete, a midwife. It is

Socrates, shown in this 20th-century-CE illustration, is considered to be one of the greatest philosophers of all time. His teachings survive through the work of his pupil Plato.

From a relatively early age, Socrates wanted to be a philosopher and to guide the moral and intellectual improvement of Athens. In order to do so, he turned an otherwise normal life into one of public dialogue in the marketplaces and squares of Athens. However, Socrates wrote no books and established no formal school of philosophy. What is known about him and his thinking comes primarily from the works of his student Plato and, to a lesser extent, from the historian Xenophon. It is through the writings of these two men that Socrates has been able to exert his profound influence on all later Western thinking.

A matter of ethics

Socrates rejected the conflicting ideas of the "one," the "indivisible," and the "eternally changeable." He also refused to become involved in the search for the "core of things" or "basic matter." His interest was in ethics and in the objective definition of love, justice, and virtue, achieved through rational argument. He argued that all vice is the result of ignorance and that no one is intentionally wicked. Because those who know what is right will act rightly, virtue is the result of knowledge.

Sophocles despised rhetoric and long-winded arguments about nothing. Consequently, he ridiculed the sophists and rhetoricians. He was relentless in employing logic as a weapon in his philosophical duels. In these "battles," clarity and simplicity had the highest priority, and in his arguments, he used expressions and terms derived from daily life. Plato recorded how Socrates managed to embarrass Gorgias, one of the most famous sophists of Athens, simply by plying him with question after question.

Plato also recorded an encounter between Socrates and the two great philosophers of Elea, Parmenides and Zeno. The two Elean philosophers had

not known who his teachers were, but he seems to have been acquainted with the doctrines of Parmenides, Heraclitus, and Anaxagoras. However, far from pursuing their ideas, he was more interested in ethical matters, such as how a man should conduct himself in life.

There is no clear indication as to how Socrates supported himself. He apparently worked as a sculptor for a while; his statue of the Three Graces stood near the entrance to the Acropolis until the second century CE. It is also known that he fought as a hoplite for Athens in the Peloponnesian War, serving with distinction in the campaign of Potidaea in 432–430 BCE.

traveled to Athens to attend the Panathenaea and were staying at the home of Plato's stepbrother. One morning, Socrates visited the famous guests and subjected them to his relentless questioning. Parmenides kindly attempted to answer Socrates' questions, while Zeno did his best to get the troublesome visitor out of the door.

Socrates then summed up his impressions of the two philosophers: "I understand that Zeno is actually a second Parmenides, even though he says things in a totally different manner. You, Parmenides, want to convince us that everything is one, and Zeno says, on the other hand, that diversity cannot exist. So you argue in two different manners to express the same truth: one of you claims something, and the other repudiates the opposite. Something like this demands a mental effort that far exceeds my moderate abilities."

Socrates' attitude toward the two philosophers from Elea illustrates his manner of disputation. He typically presented himself as someone who needed things explained to him. This profession of ignorance, given his brilliance and extraordinary sharpness of mind, is called Socratic irony. By constantly questioning his interlocutor and forcing him to define his terms, Socrates' aim was to encourage people to think for themselves and seek eternal truths.

The pursuit of knowledge

Socrates started from the basic principle that only the good can guide the behavior of man, and man must strive toward knowing that good. When man has found that out, he will pursue it—no one will ever go deliberately against the good. Socrates' philosophical enquiries took the form of a conversation or dialogue—starting from the specific, he

The Death of Socrates *was painted by Jacques-Louis David in 1787 CE. Socrates was condemned to death for heresy and died by taking hemlock.*

sought general truths through an endless game of question and answer. Even though his method was based on logic and rationality, Socrates also accepted that there was something like "the voice of one's own conscience"—an instinctive, nonrational sense of higher values that could keep a man from committing wrongful actions.

Unlike the sophists, Socrates refused to gather paying students around him. Instead, he would present questions to anyone who talked to him at any time. He elicited answers that, after subjecting them to acute analysis mixed with mild derision, he rejected as inadequate or incorrect. He then attempted to reach a logical and correct conclusion, encouraging his "victim" to formulate clear-cut definitions. This goal was hardly ever achieved, but the value of the discussion lay in the enlightenment of both people involved.

By the end of the fifth century BCE, Socrates had made a lot of enemies in Athens. His criticism of the sophists and of the institution of democracy did not endear him to the general public. In the drama *The Clouds*, Aristophanes made fun of him as the director of a "thinking shop." Eventually, Socrates' enemies managed to get their revenge. In 399 BCE, he was charged with religious heresies and corrupting the morals of Athenian youths.

The trial of Socrates

In accordance with Athenian law, the accused had to defend himself by means of a public speech. Plato's *Apology* gives an account of Socrates' defending arguments, which exhibited both his ironic style and his simple dialectic. Socrates disputed the Athenian judges' authority to sentence him to death, as his accusers wished, and pointed out great gaps in the official accusation. However, he had clearly determined that if the jury took offense at his life and work, then they had to condemn him. He refused to deny what he had asserted for so many years.

It is possible that Socrates could have avoided his heavy sentence by using a different defense, based less deeply on principle. Had he done so, he might have got off with a fine; there were plenty of

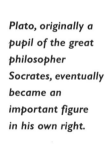

Plato, originally a pupil of the great philosopher Socrates, eventually became an important figure in his own right.

his students who would have been happy to pay it for him. Instead, he was sentenced to death, although at first only by a small majority. As allowed by Athenian law, Socrates replied to the sentence—with an ironic proposition that it should be changed to a small fine because his importance to the state was also small. Enraged by his stance, the jury voted again. The result was an increased majority for the death penalty.

Socrates could easily have fled the city; his friends even planned his escape. However, he preferred to comply with the verdict. Plato's *Phaedo* describes the final day of Socrates' life. In the evening, in accordance with the usual method of execution, he drank a fatal cup of the poisonous herb hemlock.

Plato's Academy

Socrates' student Plato (c. 428–348 BCE) went on to become a distinguished philosopher in his own right. He came from a noble, wealthy family and grew up during the time of the Peloponnesian War. Plato contemplated a political career when he was young, but he became disillusioned with politics, and it was then that he became a follower of Socrates. Plato was greatly influenced by Socrates' method of question and answer in the pursuit of truth.

In 387 BCE, Plato founded his Academy, a school devoted to the pursuit of philosophical knowledge, and it was there that he refined his own philosophical ideas. He considered that only "the idea" was real and rejected the view that

In this 19th-century-CE illustration, Alexander the Great visits the philosopher Diogenes in his tub. As part of his austere lifestyle, Diogenes lived in a tub in the streets of Athens.

THE CYNICS

Some students of Socrates attempted to carry on the work of their master, in particular by practicing asceticism (giving up material pleasures). One of those students was Antisthenes, who founded the movement that was later known as the Cynics. Antisthenes had been a sophist until he came under the influence of Socrates, after which he started to protest against the material interests of established society. He contended that any form of luxury or pleasure made people slaves, and therefore unhappy. Instead, people should free themselves from all needs and strive toward the good; only that approach could offer a happy life.

These ideas were carried to the extreme by Diogenes (c. 400–325 BCE), who was born in Sinope on the coast of the Black Sea. In middle age, he went to Athens, where he became a student of Antisthenes. Diogenes rejected all social conventions and completely embraced poverty and austerity. Homeless and sleeping outdoors, he traveled from city to city expounding his belief in the simple life to all who would listen. His brutish lifestyle earned him the abusive name of *kuon* ("dog"), and from this, his followers came to be called *kunikoi*, or Cynics. Diogenes welcomed the nickname, arguing that if humans lived like dogs, they would be far happier.

DIOGENES.

B. Kilian sculp.

Diogenes was famous for his austere lifestyle. He believed that human society was hypocritical and that it was better to live like a dog with no material possessions. This engraving is based on a 17th-century-CE drawing by Joachim von Sandrart.

knowledge was based on sensory experience. The object of knowledge (the idea) had to be something fixed, permanent, and unchangeable—it was based on reason, not sensory perception. This approach countered the ideas of most previous philosophers, who had sought to explain reality in terms of the material world. Plato maintained that reality did not reside in the material world but in another world of eternal phenomena that he called Forms. All objects in the material world are merely representations of the eternal Forms.

Applying his theory of knowledge to social philosophy, Plato wrote the *Republic* and the *Laws*. These described an ideal city-state, which could serve as a blueprint for a state on earth. In this state, the philosopher-rulers would exercise control over the two lower classes—peasant-artisans and soldiers. Because the leaders would have true knowledge, there would be no room for dissent. In 367 BCE, Plato tried to persuade the tyrant Dionysius II of Syracuse to put his ideas into practice but did not succeed.

Aristotle

Aristotle (384–322 BCE) was Plato's most important student. He spent 20 years at Plato's Academy, but while he was strongly influenced by Plato's ideas, his own philosophy developed in a different direction. Aristotle preferred an experimental and deductive approach based on the reasoning of the mind, insisting that the observation of visible reality was of prime importance. His major contribution to philosophy was to establish a system of logic that was to influence philosophical reasoning for more than two thousand years.

In 335 BCE, Aristotle established his own school in Athens, called the Lyceum, where scientific subjects such as biology and physics were studied in addition to philosophy and logic. Aristotle taught at the school but also had time to pursue his own research. He wrote major works on zoology, geography, history, mathematics, and astronomy, which were to be highly influential in medieval times. He also drew up an inventory of all political systems of the time and described an ideal polis that would combine the best elements of existing systems.

See also:

The Age of Pericles (page 110) • The Greek Legacy (page 174) • Greek Religion (page 80)

This bust depicts the Greek philosopher Aristotle, a former pupil of Plato.

THE PELOPONNESIAN WAR

TIME LINE

446 BCE

Athens and Sparta sign pact known as Thirty Years' Peace.

431 BCE

War breaks out between Athens and Sparta; Spartan forces invade Attica and lay waste to farmland.

430 BCE

Plague breaks out in Athens.

421 BCE

Peace of Nicias signed; lasts for three years only.

415 BCE

Athenians launch naval attack on city of Syracuse in Sicily; campaign ends in failure.

404 BCE

Peloponnesian War ends with defeat of Athens, which surrenders after long siege.

371 BCE

Thebes defeats Sparta at Battle of Leuctra.

The Peloponnesian War was a mammoth struggle between Sparta and Athens that took place toward the end of the fifth century BCE. The war lasted for 27 years, from 431 to 404 BCE, and tore the Greek world apart.

The roots of the conflict between Athens and Sparta lay in their cultural differences. By the middle of the fifth century BCE, Athens had become the undisputed artistic and intellectual center of Greece. It was an "open" society, engaging in many commercial transactions with the outside world and depending on large-scale imports of food to feed its population. Athens was a progressive and democratic state, and an expansive naval power. Sparta, on the other hand, was an isolated, agrarian, and largely self-sufficient closed society with an oligarchic government (one dominated by a small elite). While the militaristic Sparta experienced only stagnation, Athens became increasingly self-confident and more aggressive in its foreign affairs.

Alliances

Both Athens and Sparta had many allies. Athens was backed by the member states of the Delian League, an alliance that had been set up in 477 BCE to protect the Greek cities of Ionia (an area of southwestern Anatolia) and the nearby islands against possible Persian attack. As the Greeks defeated the Persians in successive battles, Athens, with its powerful navy, gradually came to dominate the league, which soon became more of an Athenian empire than a voluntary confederation of independent city-states. On Sparta's side was the Peloponnesian League, a group of city-states located in the Peloponnese (the southern part of mainland Greece).

In the middle of the fifth century BCE, there were occasional skirmishes between Athens and Sparta. The skirmishes ended in 446 BCE, when the two parties signed a peace agreement. The pact was supposed to hold for three decades. In fact, the Thirty Years' Peace lasted only until 431 BCE, when full-scale war broke out.

The origins of the war

The immediate cause of the war was the fact that Athens assisted the island of Corcyra (present-day Corfu) in its conflict with Corinth, an ally of Sparta. Corcyra had long been a colony of Corinth and, in turn, had founded its own colony, called Epidamnus, on the Adriatic coast of what is now Albania. When a dispute erupted between Epidamnus and Corcyra, Epidamnus called on Corinth for help. Corcyra, feeling threatened by Corinth, decided to join the powerful Delian League. Athens was happy to welcome the island into the coalition, particularly because the addi-

This vase painting depicts a Greek hoplite of the fifth century BCE. He is armed with the long spear that was typical of the period.

tion of Corcyra's fleet of 120 war vessels to its own fleet would greatly strengthen the naval power of Athens. A joint force of Athenian and Corcyrean ships clashed with the Corinthian fleet in 433 BCE. The following year, Athens laid siege to Potidaea, a Corinthian colony. Incensed, the Corinthians demanded that Sparta should declare war on Athens.

Archidamus II, king of Sparta, made a final attempt to avoid a confrontation with Athens. As commander-in-chief of the Peloponnesian League, he urged its members to review the situation before acting precipitously. His urging was in vain, however. In 432 BCE, the League voted for war. The following year, Athens in turn declared war on Sparta.

The leading Athenian statesman, Pericles, was confident that Athens was the stronger power. Money collected from the Delian League meant that any campaign would not be short of finance, while the Long Walls gave the Athenians a secure route to the vital port of Piraeus, where there lay a fleet of 200 warships.

Pericles made the decision not to defend Attica on land; his plan was to defeat Sparta at sea. In 431 BCE, the Spartans invaded unopposed, destroying the harvest, cutting down olive trees and grapevines, and demolishing buildings. The raid lasted perhaps a month—historically campaigning seasons were short because soldiers had to return home to tend to their farms. However, the raids became an annual occurrence over the following five years. Pericles retaliated with attacks on Megara and Epidaurus.

Plague

In 430 BCE, a deadly epidemic broke out in Athens, which was overcrowded with refugees from Attica. The historian

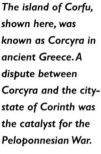

The island of Corfu, shown here, was known as Corcyra in ancient Greece. A dispute between Corcyra and the city-state of Corinth was the catalyst for the Peloponnesian War.

This vase painting depicts a Greek warship. Naval power was a major factor in the Peloponnesian War.

Thucydides provided a very graphic account of the illness (see box, page 142), which killed around 50,000 people. The psychological effects of this sudden mass death were as serious as the physical consequences of the epidemic. Believing they might be struck down and die within days, people began to live for the moment, squandering their wealth and committing many acts without regard for the law. According to Thucydides, "they did not believe they would live long enough to be prosecuted and punished by the judiciary."

A change of leadership

When Pericles fell victim to the epidemic in 429 BCE, the leadership of Athens fell to Cleon, the major representative of the pro-war party. Together with the general Demosthenes, Cleon spearheaded several victories, notably the crushing of Spartan forces at the Battle of Pylos in 425 BCE. However, in 422 BCE, Cleon's luck changed abruptly. In a battle to recapture the Athenian colony of Amphipolis, which had fallen to the

THE LONG WALLS

Some 30 years before the outbreak of the Peloponnesian War, the Athenian statesman Pericles initiated the building of two walls to safeguard the route between Athens and its port Piraeus. Between 461 and 456 BCE, two great walls were constructed, enclosing a roadway around 600 feet (183 m) wide. The Long Walls turned the whole Athens-Piraeus complex into a single fortress, ensuring that Athens had unrestricted access to the fleet at Piraeus. When Attica was invaded by the Spartans during the Peloponnesian War, its citizens took refuge in Athens, and many were crammed between the Long Walls. The difficult and unsanitary conditions greatly contributed to the catastrophic outbreak of the plague in 430 BCE.

THUCYDIDES' ACCOUNT OF THE PLAGUE

When the plague broke out in Athens in 430 BCE, the historian Thucydides was living in the city. He wrote extensively about the plague, noting that it claimed more victims than all of Sparta's campaigns combined. He went on: "I want to discuss this illness so that able physicians may determine whence this evil came and which causes may have produced such a calamity. If this illness returns, everyone shall be warned and take measures. I speak of this epidemic as someone who knows it intimately, for I too was affected and I saw many fall ill and die.

"That year had been extraordinarily healthy and free of all other disease. But if someone sustained a wound or became ill, it immediately turned into this pestilence. The healthy were suddenly afflicted, without there being any evident reason for their illness. First they felt a severe headache; their eyes turned red, their throat became inflamed and their breathing became labored. Hoarseness, pain in the chest, and a mucous cough were followed by painful contractions and convulsions, which lasted longer with some than with others. The skin swelled up and turned red and became covered with small blisters of pus. Some died after seven or nine days as a result of a burning pain in their intestines. Those still living after this time were struck with stomach pains. After severe diarrhea and cramps, most succumbed from total exhaustion.

"Generally, the contagion appeared first on the head and subsequently spread over the entire body. Some were blinded or paralyzed; others went mad and did not recognize friends or relatives. Although there were many unburied corpses lying out in the open, the vultures and other scavengers did not come near them, and when they did eat the diseased human flesh, they also died."

Still a bustling commercial center today, Piraeus has been the port of Athens since ancient times. During the Peloponnesian War, Athens and the port were connected by fortified walls.

Spartan general Brasidas, Cleon was killed. Brasidas also died.

With the leading proponent for war on either side dead, the stage was clear for peace negotiations. On Cleon's death, the Athenian general Nicias became the leading Athenian politician, and he negotiated a peace agreement with Sparta and the Peloponnesian League. The Peace of Nicias was intended to last for 50 years. In fact, it broke down in less than three.

Alcibiades

Alcibiades (c. 450–404 BCE) was a young, ambitious nobleman who, having lost his father at an early age, had been reared by his uncle, Pericles. Spoiled but handsome, Alcibiades used his charm to secure great personal popularity. Contemporary sources describe his great appetite for power as well as his sexual and other excesses.

In 420 BCE, when he was around 30 years old, Alcibiades was called on by the Athenian people to act as one of the ten *strategoi* (chief military commanders). It was not a good decision. Alcibiades was keen to win honors on the battlefield, even though the Peace of Nicias had only just been negotiated. Alcibiades was a staunch political opponent of the

treaty, and he sought to stir up some trouble for Sparta by playing on the dissatisfaction that some members of the Peloponnesian League felt with the conditions set forth in the recent peace agreement. He persuaded Athens to join with the disaffected cities of Argos, Mantinea, and Elis in confronting Sparta at the Battle of Mantinea in 418 BCE. The result was a resounding victory for the Spartans.

Undaunted by this setback, Alcibiades sought to revive the policies of Pericles, who had aspired to found an empire in the west with Thurii, in southern Italy, as its center. The Athenian fleet already controlled the Aegean Sea, the Dardanelles, and the Bosporus, so Alcibiades argued that if Athens could extend its dominion to the western basin of the Mediterranean, Sparta would be completely isolated on the Peloponnese.

Sicilian campaign

The primary objective of Alcibiades' plan was to gain control of Sicily, which he considered a bridgehead to both southern Italy and Africa. A large number of Athenians enthusiastically supported this scheme, but several cautious men, including Nicias and Socrates, opposed the enterprise. A decision in favor of war was made after a delegation from Sicily visited Athens. The party consisted of representatives of several Sicilian cities, who claimed that they felt threatened by the powerful Dorian city of Syracuse, an ally of Sparta, that dominated

This statue depicts the Athenian nobleman Alcibiades, who defected to Sparta when he was accused of sacrilege.

143

In this undated modern illustration, the Greek military commander Alcibiades returns to Athens after a military defeat.

the island. Alcibiades' plan encountered little further resistance from the Athenian assembly. Nicias, Lamachus, and Alcibiades were appointed leaders of a military expedition to Sicily to capture Syracuse. A fleet of around 260 ships was fitted out. On board were more than 5,000 heavily armed hoplites, in addition to thousands of support troops.

Disaster in Sicily

From the moment the fleet reached Sicily in 415 BCE, everything went wrong. The island's Greek colonies were not willing to participate in the campaign against Syracuse. Nor did they want to bear the heavy cost of provisioning the Athenian troops, which forced the expedition's leaders to look outside the city walls, where makeshift markets sold supplies at monstrously inflated prices. The cities of Tarentum and Locris even refused to supply fresh water.

In spite of such setbacks, the Athenians succeeded in taking the city of Catana, which was strategically important because it lay between Syracuse and Messina and could be used to command the strait between Sicily and southern Italy. The aim was to isolate Syracuse and enable the Athenians to find allies among the discontented cities on the other side of the strait.

By this point, Alcibiades was no longer involved in the campaign, however, because he had been recalled to

The Temple to Apollo in Syracuse. The Athenians unsuccessfully tried to capture the city in the Peloponnesian War.

Athens on a charge of sacrilege. The accusation was that he had "mocked the goddesses of Eleusis and ridiculed their mysteries." On the return voyage to Athens, he escaped his captors and fled to Sparta, where he became a counselor to the enemies of his native city.

Syracuse

In the spring of 414 BCE, the aging Nicias took command of the Athenian troops on Sicily and started a siege of Syracuse. The Athenians attempted to isolate the city by building a siege wall on land while their fleet kept the Syracuse warships confined to the harbor. However, the arrival of a Spartan general, Gylippus, with a Peloponnesian force put an end to Athenian hopes of a swift victory. Suddenly, the Athenians were on the defensive. Nicias was forced to send a desperate message to Athens for more troops. Athens responded with a second army and support fleet, but neither was able to salvage the expedition.

When, in September of 413 BCE, Nicias finally decided to abandon the siege of Syracuse, the retreat degenerated into a debacle. The Athenian troops were surrounded and either massacred or taken prisoner. The commanders, including Nicias, were summarily executed. The other prisoners either became forced laborers in the mines of Syracuse, where they died slow deaths, or were sold into slavery.

The Sicilian campaign was a disaster for Athens. The campaign had been immensely expensive, and the whole expeditionary force of both

This Greek sculpture from the sixth century BCE depicts a hoplite. Hoplites still formed the backbone of Greek armies 200 years later.

men and warships was wiped out. The Athenian spirit was undaunted, however. The war on the Greek mainland, in the Aegean, and in Ionia was to continue for another nine years.

The end of Alcibiades

Alcibiades established a niche for himself in Sparta as a strategic advisor on the Syracuse campaign. However, his position there became much less secure once the Athenian expeditionary force was destroyed. He fled to Anatolia and settled in the court of the Persian governor, where he tried to persuade the Persians to conclude an alliance with Athens against Sparta. This plan failed, driving the distrustful Persians into the arms of Sparta instead. In 411 BCE, following some political unrest in Athens, Alcibiades was reinstated as an Athenian army commander and won some victories for Athens in the Aegean. Toward the end of the war, however, he lost the trust of the Athenian people for a second time. He once again fled to the Persians, who killed him.

The defeat of Athens

After the disastrous Sicilian campaign, the war continued, being mainly fought in the Aegean and Ionia. Because so many Athenian ships had been destroyed at Syracuse, Sparta's sea power now more than equaled that of Athens. To make matters worse for Athens, Persia lent financial support to Sparta and helped it to build a new fleet. In 404 BCE, the beleaguered

THUCYDIDES

Much of what is known about the Peloponnesian War is derived from the work of the historian Thucydides (c. 460–400 BCE). Born into a wealthy Athenian family, Thucydides lived through the war, and from its beginning, he set out to document it as objectively as possible. Unlike his predecessor Herodotus, Thucydides recorded events in chronological order without reference to the work of fate or the meddling of the gods.

Thucydides took the view that events were the result of both the circumstances of the time and the characters of the leading personalities involved. He had the advantage of firsthand knowledge of many of the events, and indeed took part in the war himself at one point. In 424 BCE, he was elected as a *strategos*, given the command of the Athenian fleet, and ordered to go to the assistance of Amphipolis, which was under siege by the Spartans. However, he arrived too late to save the city from being taken, and for this blunder, he was banished from Athens. He spent the next 20 years in exile, but he used the time to travel extensively around the Greek region, gathering material for his great *History of the Peloponnesian War*.

Thucydides visited Sparta, which he compared unfavorably with Athens in the following words: "If the city of Sparta were to be depopulated so that only the temples and public buildings remained, then I believe that in due course someone visiting the city would not be able to believe that Sparta had been as powerful a state as it currently is. But if the city of Athens were to have the same fate, a person visiting it later would think that it had been even greater and more powerful than it actually is today—just from seeing the ruins and the enormous space they occupy."

Thucydides' comparison was prophetic. Anyone traveling to Sparta today will find an insignificant rural town without many monuments. Athens, on the other hand, still boasts numerous ruins of temples, theaters, marketplaces, and other great monuments, despite its eventful and sometimes violent history.

This bust depicts the Greek historian Thucydides. His History of the Peloponnesian War *is the main source of knowledge about the military struggles between Athens and Sparta in the fifth century BCE.*

and isolated Athens was forced to surrender. The Delian League was dissolved, the Athenian fleet was destroyed, and the walls of Athens were razed.

The aftermath of the war

At the end of the war, Athens was occupied by the Spartan general Lysander, who proposed that in place of the former democracy, the city should be ruled by an oligarchy. Thirty Athenians were appointed to govern the city. With Lysander's approval, they proceeded to seize absolute power. Backed by Spartan troops, the Thirty Tyrants immediately set about settling accounts with their former political opponents. All democratic institutions were abolished, and with the help of their own police force, the tyrants confiscated property, arrested

ARISTOPHANES AND THE WAR

The atmosphere of war appears to have no detrimental effect on the art of theater in Athens. With the city under siege, Attica in flames, and the Athenian fleet threatened with destruction, dramatists such as Euripides and Aristophanes (c. 450–388 BCE) continued to produce tragedies and comedies.

Aristophanes' plays enjoyed great popularity. They were biting satirical comedies in which he mocked both politicians and society. As a comedy writer, his goals were to entertain his audience and to win the annual prize at the festival of Dionysus. His plays about the war describe the atmosphere of the time—firewood is scarce and olive oil expensive, while traitors, defectors, defeatists, and war profiteers abound.

In *Acharnians* (425 BCE), Aristophanes mocks the war and makes a plea for peace, portraying a peasant concluding his own peace with the

Spartans. In *Knights* (424 BCE), he attacks Cleon, the radical democrat, who is portrayed as a scheming slave outwitted by a sausage seller. The warlike Cleon was a frequent target of ridicule in Aristophanes' plays. *Clouds* (423 BCE) is an attack on the sophists and Socrates, while *Wasps* (422 BCE) satirizes the Athenian love of litigation. *Peace* (produced shortly before the Peace of Nicias was signed in 421 BCE) sees a farmer flying to heaven to find the goddess of the title, while the farcical *Lysistrata* (413 BCE) depicts the women of Athens going on sex strike, declaring they will withhold their favors from their husbands until the men end the war and make peace.

In all, 11 of Aristophanes' plays have survived. It is clear from their content that he enjoyed great freedom of speech to mock whatever he disliked in Athenian society and politics, even in a time of war.

This 19th-century-CE colored lithograph shows the Spartan general Lysander outside the walls of Athens.

citizens on flimsy charges, and carried out summary executions.

The rule of the Thirty Tyrants was so unbearable that, after only one year, the Athenians rebelled. Opponents of the regime who had fled the city gathered under the exiled Athenian soldier Thrasybulus, and this makeshift army met the forces of the Tyrants and defeat-ed them. The triumphant Athenians then entered the city and executed most of the remaining Thirty, after which, democracy was restored. Surprisingly, Sparta did nothing to stop this turn of events. It seems that the Spartan king, Pausanias, disagreed with Lysander's ruthless treatment of the Athenians and, rather than send out an army to reverse

This 18th-century-CE drawing of an ancient Greek bust depicts the Athenian orator Lysias. He was an adversary of the Thirty Tyrants, who ruled Athens after the end of the Peloponnesian War.

logographers are counted among Attica's best-known orators, even though they never spoke during Athenian legal sessions; not being citizens of Athens, they were not allowed to do so. One of the most famous litigators of the late fifth century BCE was Lysias (c. 459–380 BCE), who was a *metic*, or foreigner residing in Athens.

Lysias was a native of Syracuse. His father acquired such fame as a manufacturer of armor and shields that Pericles invited him to settle in Athens. After their father's death, Lysias and his elder brother moved to Thurii, the Athenian colony in southern Italy, where Lysias learned the art of rhetoric and eloquence from a distinguished orator. After the failure of the Athenian campaign in Sicily, the brothers returned to Athens, where they earned a fortune from the sale of weapons before the end of the Peloponnesian War.

Following the defeat of Athens and the installation of the Thirty Tyrants, the new government instituted a ruthless purge of anyone suspected of democratic sympathies. Scores of people were sent into exile or condemned to death. Lysias's brother was executed, but Lysias himself managed to escape from the city and join the conspirators who were planning to restore democracy. After the Thirty Tyrants were defeated, Lysias returned to Athens. In a major trial, he prosecuted Eratosthenes, one of the Thirty who had survived, for the murder of his brother. Due to the trial's political background, it attracted a large audience.

In his speech, Lysias outlined the crimes that Eratosthenes had committed, together with his role in the Thirty Tyrants' reign of terror. Lysias's words touched on matters that were fresh in the memory of everyone. His indictment of the oligarchs' crimes aided the recovery process that saw democracy reestablish itself in Athens.

the situation, preferred to recognize the new government.

The orators

After democracy was restored in Athens in 403 BCE, the city saw a period in which great orators became highly influential in meetings of the public assembly. These orators were for the most part legal experts who were accustomed to arguing a case in the law courts. Because, in theory, anyone accused of a crime in Athens had to argue his own defense, many orators made money by writing speeches for their clients to read in court.

Orators who wrote speeches for other public speakers were known as logographers or storywriters. Several

Spartan imperialism

Although Athens had won back its freedom, Sparta remained the overlord of all Greece, which had some catastrophic consequences. Sparta's victory in the Peloponnesian War had been achieved with the help of Persian financial aid, and in return, the Ionian Greek cities in Anatolia had to cede their autonomy to Persia once more. Sparta made other cities protectorates and forced them to pay large sums of money in tribute. In effect, this meant that Athenian imperialism, as manifested in its domination of the Delian League and its demands for annual tribute, had simply been replaced by Spartan imperialism.

In 399 BCE, a new king was chosen in Sparta. Agesilaus II (c. 444–360 BCE) distinguished himself by his forthrightness and piety and proved to be a major statesman and general. One of his first projects after becoming king was to go to the aid of the pro-Sparta Greek cities

Agesilaus II, shown on the right in this 18th-century-CE illustration, was king of Sparta in the fourth century BCE. He conducted several successful campaigns against the Persians.

In 387 BCE, Persia switched sides and signed its own peace treaty with Sparta. Under the terms of this settlement, which was called the Peace of Antalcidas (or the King's Peace), all the Greek cities in Anatolia were ceded to Persia, while the city-states of mainland Greece and the Aegean islands became autonomous. This treaty put an end to Spartan imperialist ambitions and left Athens free to develop its position as a commercial and cultural center.

The rise of Thebes

The early fourth century BCE saw a new power arise. Thebes, a large city on the plain of Boeotia in central Greece, was known for the excellence of its army. Under the strong leadership of the charismatic and ambitious Epaminondas (c. 410–362 BCE), Thebes was to achieve preeminence in Greece for at least a short time.

In 382 BCE, despite the terms of the King's Peace, Sparta attacked and occupied Thebes. Thebes sought and received the support of Athens, and in 379 BCE, the Spartans were driven out. However, a full-scale war had started. Epaminondas was appointed army commander in 371 BCE. He introduced new infantry tactics that brought spectacular results at the Battle of Leuctra, fought the same year. It was traditional for hoplite commanders to put their strongest and most experienced soldiers on the right of their formations (to stop phalanxes from drifting to the right as soldiers sought protection behind their comrades' shields). At Leuctra, Epaminondas attacked in mass on the left. This surprise move allowed him to overwhelm the opposition.

After annihilating the Spartans at Leuctra, Epaminondas invaded the Peloponnese and annexed the regions of

The Athenian orator Demosthenes, depicted in this bust, warned his fellow Athenians of the threat posed by Philip II.

in Anatolia. They were being harassed by Persian forces, so in 396 BCE, he took a large force to the coast of Anatolia to halt Persian raids. He campaigned around the Bosporus and the Meander River for the following two years. His success on the battlefield was an indication of the decline of the Persian Empire.

The Corinthian War

On the mainland, a new threat to Sparta's dominance was looming. In 395 BCE, the cities of Athens, Argos, Corinth, and Thebes formed, with Persian support, an alliance against Sparta. Several battles were fought between Sparta and the coalition before Agesilaus was recalled from Anatolia to help deal with the situation. The conflict, called the Corinthian War, lasted eight years.

Arcadia and Messenia, freeing them from the yoke of Sparta. At a stroke, Thebes ended Sparta's dominance in Greece and took first place among the Greek city-states. However, the time of triumph for Thebes was short-lived. Alarmed by the emergence of this new rival, Sparta and Athens joined forces against the common enemy in 369 BCE. The new alliance engaged with the Theban army at the Battle of Mantinea in 362 BCE. Although the battle was indecisive, Epaminondas was killed, which put an end to the decade of glory enjoyed by Thebes.

This coin bears the features of the Macedonian king Philip II. Philip's victory over a combined Greek army at Chaeronea changed the Mediterranean world.

Macedonia

During the decade of Theban dominance (371–362 BCE), two Macedonian princes had been held as hostages in Thebes. In 359 BCE, one of these princes became Philip II, king of Macedon. Macedon lay just to the north of Thessaly, and during Philip's reign, it became a powerful state. The great Athenian orator Demosthenes understood that there was great danger lurking in the kingdom of Macedon and the wild surrounding region, and he incessantly warned the Athenian people of the threat of Philip. According to Demosthenes, Philip "was willing to sacrifice everything to gain fame and glory."

In his now famous oratories against Philip of Macedon (called the *Philippics*), Demosthenes spoke out with increasing vehemence against the danger posed by this military usurper from the north. When a rumor spread in Athens that Philip was seriously ill, Demosthenes railed at his fellow citizens: "Did Philip die? No, he is merely ill. And his illness is of no account, because even if Philip should die, your sluggishness would cause another Philip to rise up." In spite of the fact that the advancing Macedonian armies were uncomfortably close to the borders of Attica, the Greek city-states did not react.

Demosthenes' opponent was the orator Aeschines, who was acting as the spokesman for the pro-Macedonian party in the assembly. This party was in favor of a negotiated settlement with Philip. However, although Aeschines twice visited the Macedonian court, he had no success. In the end, Demosthenes succeeded in marginalizing the pro-Macedonian movement and then pushed for an alliance with Thebes. However, the alliance came too late, and it was not strong enough to stop Philip and the Macedonian army.

Chaeronea

On August 7, 338 BCE, Philip of Macedon, with an army of 30,000 foot soldiers and 2,000 cavalry, defeated the smaller army of the Greek allies near Chaeronea on the plain of Boeotia. This battle gave Macedonia complete hegemony in Greece. Philip's young son Alexander played a key role in the Macedonians' victory. As Alexander the Great, he would later change the Greek world beyond all recognition.

See also:

The Age of Pericles (page 110) • The Birth of Drama (page 88) • Macedon and Alexander the Great (page 154) • Sparta and Athens (page 52)

MACEDON AND ALEXANDER THE GREAT

TIME LINE

356 BCE

Alexander the Great born in Pella, Macedonia.

336 BCE

Alexander ascends to throne of Macedonia following assassination of father, Philip II.

334 BCE

Alexander crosses Dardanelles to begin campaign of conquest in Anatolia; defeats Persian army at Granicus River.

332 BCE

City of Tyre finally seized by Alexander after seven-month siege; later that year, Alexander founds city of Alexandria near Nile Delta in Egypt.

326 BCE

Macedonian army defeats Indian force at Hydaspes to expand Alexander's empire to Indus Valley.

323 BCE

Alexander dies from fever.

Alexander the Great was one of the greatest military leaders that the world has ever known. Building on the great military successes of his father, Philip II, Alexander created an empire that covered the entire eastern Mediterranean world.

The young Macedonian king Alexander crossed the Dardanelles in 334 BCE. He was scarcely 22 years old, and his aim was to conquer Persia and the whole of Asia. By the time he succumbed to fever at age 33, he had succeeded in moving the frontier of his empire 3,000 miles (4,800 km) east to the borders of India, subduing tens of millions of people along the way. However, his empire was to be short-lived—within a few years of his death, his generals had divided the vast territory among themselves.

Early life

Alexander was born in 356 BCE in Pella, the capital of Macedonia. He was the son of Macedonia's king Philip II (ruled 359–336 BCE) and Olympias, a princess of Epirus, whom Philip had met when he was being initiated into the local religious mysteries of the island of Samothrace. When Alexander reached his teens, Philip sent for the Athenian philosopher Aristotle to teach his son rhetoric, philosophy, literature, and science. Alexander seems to have been an attentive student, and he remained in touch with Aristotle for the rest of his life.

According to the Greek biographer Plutarch, Alexander inherited a love of medicine from his tutor. The king would prescribe treatment and medication to his friends when they were ill. Plutarch goes on to describe how Alexander was an avid reader and would go to bed with a copy of the *Iliad*, which he would place next to his dagger under his headrest. On his Asian campaign, he ordered his treasurer Harpalus to send him books. Among the works that he received were Philistus's history of Sicily and the plays of Euripides, Sophocles, and Aeschylus.

Alexander was only 14 years old when he got his first taste of power and command. When his father went away on campaign and left him in charge of Macedon, Alexander successfully fought off an attack by a tribe of Thracians. Two years later, at the age of 16, he was given a command at the Battle of Chaeronea, where the Macedonians defeated the Greek forces.

Ascent to the throne

Philip II was assassinated in the summer of 336 BCE. The reason has never been clearly established. The Persians may have been behind it, or even Alexander himself, who was not on the best of terms with his father. Whatever the truth of the matter, Alexander ascended the throne and had the alleged conspirators summarily executed.

Before his assassination, Philip had been preparing to invade Anatolia (present-day Turkey) via the Dardanelles. Alexander was anxious to continue this

mission against the region's Persian-held cities, but before he could embark on the campaign, he had to deal with troubles closer to home. In Thessaly, leaders of an independence movement had taken over the government. Alexander threw them out and reasserted Macedonian rule. By the end of the summer, Alexander had been elected leader of the Corinthian League (a military alliance created by his father), although he could not count on the support of the Greek city-states south of Thermopylae.

The following year, Alexander crossed the northern border to quell rebellious Thracians. The successful campaign lasted for five months and took him as far as the Danube River. On his return, he took only a week to subdue yet another rebellion, this time by the Illyrians.

This statue depicts Alexander the Great on horseback. Alexander's Companion cavalry was a key component of his army.

After he put down the Illyrian rebellion, Alexander was forced to confront yet another insurrection, one by the city of Thebes, located on the plain of Boeotia. The revolt, supported by a number of other Greek cities, was incited by the orator Demosthenes and funded by Persian gold. The rebels spread the rumor that Alexander was dead and then attacked the Macedonian garrison occupying the citadel. Hearing this news, Alexander moved his army rapidly southward in forced marches. One morning, the Thebans were alarmed to see that the king they had presumed dead was outside their walls. The Macedonians took the city by storm, razing it and spar–

PHILIP OF MACEDON

Philip of Macedon, the father of Alexander, was born around 382 BCE, the third son of King Amyntas of Macedonia. When his brother Perdiccas was killed in a battle against the Illyrians in 359 BCE, Philip became king at around the age of 23. Philip was a shrewd diplomat and an inspired military commander who was to transform his hitherto insignificant kingdom into the most powerful Greek state.

At that time, Macedon was beset by enemies, and one of Philip's priorities on acceding to the throne was to reorganize his army into a more efficient fighting force. He introduced rigorous new training and refined the phalanx formation. Under Philip, the soldiers that made up the phalanx were armed with metal-tipped pikes around 16 feet (4.9 m) long. He also incorporated equipment for siege warfare, such as catapults and siege towers.

With his revitalized army, Philip embarked on a 20-year campaign of warfare and diplomacy that was to make him master of the Greek world. In 357 BCE, he married Olympias, a princess of Epirus, and a year later, she bore him a son whom they named Alexander. In 338 BCE, having subjugated all his non-Greek neighbors, Philip invaded mainland Greece and defeated the combined forces of Athens and Thebes at the Battle of Chaeronea. Once Greece was his, Philip planned to invade Anatolia and conquer the Persian-held cities. However, before his preparations were much advanced, Philip was assassinated, leaving the throne of Macedon and the conquest of Persia to his son, Alexander.

THE PHALANX

Much of the deadly efficiency of Alexander's army depended on the phalanx, which had been restyled by his father, Philip II of Macedon. The phalanx was made up of around 9,000 infantrymen, often drawn up in 256-man squares, 16 men wide and 16 men deep. The weapon of the phalanx was the *sarissa*, a long, heavy pike that measured around 16 feet (4.9 m). These weapons were held horizontally by the first few rows, making a wall of sharp points that stretched 10 feet (3 m) or more ahead of the advancing phalanx. Because the infantry of opposing armies tended to be armed with spears no more than 8 feet (2.4 m) long, the Macedonian phalanx had an immediate advantage.

An advancing phalanx presented a deadly wall of metal spikes and was a formidable fighting force. While the *sarissas* of the leading rows were inflicting damage on their opponents, casualties within the phalanx were immediately replaced by men from the rear. However, a moving phalanx was effective only on level ground and was vulnerable on its flanks, which had to be protected by cavalry or light infantry such as slingers. For this reason, the usual function of the phalanx was defensive—while it stood its ground as the enemy attacked, the cavalry could harass their adversaries on the flanks.

The phalanx was a flexible unit that could, if necessary, assume different shapes—such as a square, a rectangle, or even a wedge or arrowhead shape. Because the *sarissa* required both hands to hold it, each soldier wore his circular shield on a neckstrap. When in battle, the shield was brought around to the front of the body. Each soldier also wore a helmet and greaves.

This artist's illustration depicts a Macedonian phalanx about to engage with the enemy. The front three rows of the square hold their pikes horizontally. The soldiers in the rows farther back hold them at an angle, ready to replace any fallen comrades.

THE EMPIRE OF ALEXANDER THE GREAT

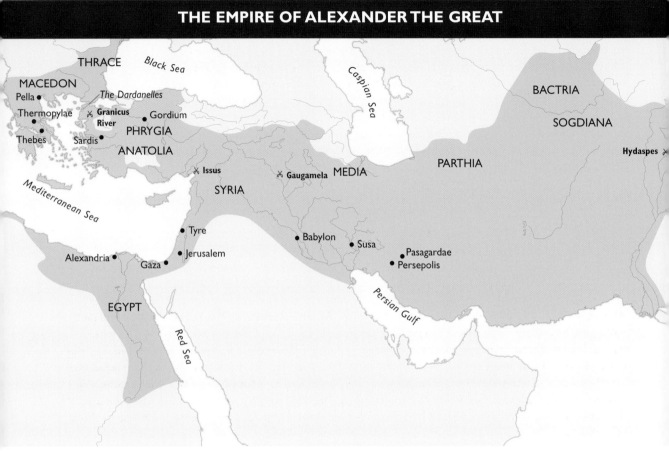

KEY

Empire of Alexander at its greatest extent

✗ Major battle

ing only the temples and the house of the famous Greek poet Pindar. Of the surviving inhabitants, some 8,000 were sold into slavery. The speed and severity of this retaliation left such an impression on the other rebellious Greek cities that they surrendered almost immediately and were treated with comparative leniency by Alexander.

Into Asia

Leaving his general Antipater as regent of Macedonia and Greece, Alexander was free to embark on the long-delayed Asian campaign. He set out with a formidable army that comprised 30,000 foot soldiers and some 5,000 horsemen. These cavalry units were the core units of the force and were composed mainly of Macedonians and Thessalians. There were also many

Macedonians among the infantry, but at least half of the footsoldiers were mercenaries drawn from the rest of the Greek world, from Thrace, and from regions farther north.

Alexander was also surrounded by his personal retinue, called the *hetairoi*, or Companions. This *hetairoi* squadron of 1,500 men was mainly drawn from the Macedonian aristocracy. They answered directly to Alexander and, wherever he was and whatever he did, his *hetairoi* were always near. The king regarded the members as his friends and allowed them liberties not granted to others.

Alexander did not have much difficulty in assembling his army. Since the peace forged by him and his father in Greece, there had been a much reduced demand for mercenaries. Serving as a mercenary was a popular occupation. Although the soldier had to provide his own equipment, military service provided pay and a share of any booty won. Mercenaries were accustomed to serving on the side that offered the greatest reward. Many Greek soldiers had already crossed the Aegean Sea to join Persian troop contingents. In every one of his battles against the Persians, Alexander faced opposing Greek mercenaries. Many of them defected to his army—not through patriotism, but because they expected higher earnings.

Alexander's Companions, the army's elite horsemen, were highly skilled riders and were armed with lances and short swords. They trained intensively so their horses would be manageable in battle. Alexander almost invariably led the charge of his Companion cavalry himself, and these attacks generally inflicted great damage on the enemy.

The main foot soldiers were used in a phalanx (see box, page 157), a formation that had been in use long before the time of Philip and Alexander. However, the Macedonians adapted it by using far longer spears than their predecessors. If the formation became confused, all was lost; it was impossible to restore the original order in the heat of battle. Generally, the phalanx was able to resist a frontal attack by cavalry but not one from the side. For this reason, the phalanx was always placed at the center of the battle formation, with the cavalry and more mobile infantry at its flanks. Alexander exploited the flexibility of this army to great advantage, and it brought him victory after victory.

The Battle of Granicus River

In the spring of 334 BCE, Alexander led his army of 35,000 Macedonians and Greeks across the Dardanelles and into Anatolia. At the Granicus River in northwestern Anatolia, he attacked an army of 40,000 Persians and Greeks. Alexander won the battle and reputedly lost only 110 soldiers of his own. The road to Anatolia lay open.

The victory at Granicus River had a serious effect on Persian morale. When

Alexander (left, on horseback) leads his forces against those of Darius III (in chariot) at the Battle of Issus. This Roman mosaic was found in the city of Pompeii and dates to the fourth century BCE.

Alexander's army approached the Persian government center of Sardis, which had long been able to withstand attack, the governor walked out through the gate to surrender. One by one, the Greek colonies of Ionia fell to Macedonian hands, and it took Alexander barely a year to subdue the whole of Anatolia.

After the Persian king Xerxes died in 424 BCE, the kingdom of Persia had gone into decline. Under a succession of ineffective kings, the provincial governors had divided Persia into a large number of semi-independent principalities. Artaxerxes, king of Persia from 358 to 338 BCE, had restored his authority in the cities of Susa and Persepolis with brutal force, so it is possible that many Persians regarded Alexander's arrival as a liberation.

The Gordian knot

On his route of conquest, Alexander passed through Gordium (the capital of Phrygia), which was home to an ancient legend. According to Greek mythology, Gordius, a Phrygian peasant, had been made king because he fulfilled a prophecy that said that the first person to enter the town driving a wagon must be made ruler. The grateful king dedicated his wagon to Zeus, tying it with a complex knot in a grove in the god's temple. The knot was so difficult that no one could undo it—it was said that anyone who could untie it would rule all of Asia. When he was told this story, Alexander unsheathed his sword and simply sliced through the knot. This act gave rise to the expression "cutting the Gordian knot," meaning to find a swift and imaginative solution to a difficult problem. For this act, Alexander was rewarded with enough booty to cover his campaign expenses.

Carrying on south to Syria, the Macedonians encountered a large Persian army, commanded by King Darius III himself. At the ensuing Battle of Issus, the Persians outnumbered the

Macedonians by almost two to one, yet the result was a catastrophic defeat for the Persians. When Alexander and his cavalry penetrated the Persian infantry, Darius turned and fled, with much of his army following. Alexander captured Darius's wife, mother, and children, who had been left behind in the Persian army's camp. However, Alexander ordered that they be treated with the respect normally accorded to royalty. He was already beginning to make efforts to placate conquered peoples in order to build a socially integrated empire.

Phoenicia

After the Battle of Issus, Alexander carried on down the coast of Syria and Phoenicia. His object was to capture all of the ports of the eastern Mediterranean, thereby cutting the Persians off from their naval bases. Alexander encountered little resistance; only the well-fortified Phoenician seaport of Tyre put up a fight. Although its rulers were willing to acknowledge Alexander as king, they were not prepared to let him and his army enter the island on which the city lay. A prolonged siege of seven months followed, but finally, in 332 BCE, Alexander seized the city and razed it in a bloodbath. Any surviving citizens, including all the women and children, were sold into slavery.

After the fall of Tyre, Darius offered all his lands up to the Euphrates River, his daughter in marriage, and a large dowry in exchange for peace with Alexander. As a guarantee of his good intentions, Darius offered to send his son as a hostage. However, Alexander replied

This silver coin, which bears a portrait of Alexander, was issued during the reign of Seleucus I, several decades after the death of Alexander.

that he already had whatever Darius could offer and that he would marry his daughter regardless of her father's permission. Alexander also said that he would come to take what he considered his, but not immediately.

Alexander continued down the Mediterranean coast to the fortress at Gaza, which also offered resistance. It took a long siege before the city was taken, and because Alexander was injured in the course of the siege, he exacted a terrible revenge. Jerusalem, however, surrendered without a single blow being exchanged—the high priest came out in full regalia to welcome the conqueror and his army.

Egypt

Later that same year, 332 BCE, Alexander led his army across the Sinai Peninsula and into Egypt, where the Persian governor surrendered without a fight. Alexander was welcomed everywhere as a liberator, and he was installed as the new pharaoh. Alexander founded a new city on the coast next to the mouth of the Nile River. Named Alexandria, the city was destined to become the commercial and cultural center of the Greek world (see box, page 162).

During the summer of 331 BCE, Alexander made a pilgrimage to the oracle of Amon-Re, the Egyptian god of the sun, at the Siwa Oasis in the Libyan desert. Around this time, Alexander had begun to entertain the notion that he was descended from the gods, and the Egyptians, who had made him their pharaoh, did not attempt to dissuade him from the idea; all Egyptian pharaohs were considered to be the sons of Amon-Re. The oracle apparently confirmed his

THE CITY OF ALEXANDRIA

Founded by Alexander the Great in 332 BCE, Alexandria was designed to be a model city that would reflect the splendor of its founder. It was probably originally conceived as a military stronghold and naval base, but it rapidly became the trading and administrative center of Egypt under the Greeks. Situated on the Mediterranean coast just west of the Nile Delta, it extended for around 4 miles (6.5 km) along the coast and around 1 to 2 miles (2–3 km) inland. Its streets were laid out in a grid pattern, with two wide main avenues where many of the most important commercial and cultural buildings were found. At its southern end, an isthmus projected into the Mediterranean Sea and separated two great harbors. In 280 BCE, a lighthouse around 460 feet (140 m) high was built at the mouth of one of the harbors. It has since disappeared, but in its time, the lighthouse was counted as one of the seven wonders of the world.

After Alexander's death in 323 BCE, the city came under the control of the Egyptian Ptolemaic dynasty and continued to flourish. Its two big harbors made it an important center for Mediterranean trade. Alexandria exported various products manufactured by Alexandrian craftspeople, including linen, papyrus, and precious metalwork. It was also an important transit port for Egyptian grain and wares from India, Arabia, and even more distant countries. These wares arrived by way of the Red Sea and the caravan routes.

Within 100 years of its founding, Alexandria had become the leading city of the world and the center of Greek cultural life. Its great library housed hundreds of thousands of books and attracted many scholars and poets, including Theocritus, Apollonius, and Callimachus. Another great center of learning and research was the Museum, next to the royal palace of the Ptolemies. The Museum was both a temple of the Muses and a research institute where scholars and artists could devote themselves to learning at the ruler's expense.

Alexandria, shown in this undated modern illustration, was perfectly situated for trade.

divine lineage, and because the Greeks identified Amon-Re with Zeus, Alexander proclaimed himself to be a son of Zeus. The Greeks had no difficulty with this concept, involving as it did a young king with military achievements so remarkable as to appear superhuman. Divine or not, Alexander was a great man, and most Greeks and Egyptians were happy to treat him as a god.

The Battle of Gaugamela

Once he had secured the Mediterranean coast (he had also captured Cyrene, capital of the kingdom of Cyrenaica on the north African coast), Alexander turned his attention north and east. In the late summer of 331 BCE, he retraced his steps across the Sinai Peninsula and then proceeded up through Palestine to Babylon. He had with him an army of 40,000 infantry and 7,000 cavalry, and after crossing the Euphrates and Tigris rivers, Alexander found Darius waiting for him with a far larger army.

The two forces engaged near the town of Gaugamela in northern Mesopotamia on October 1, 331 BCE. In spite of the disparity in numbers, and the fact that the Persian army included an Indian contingent with elephants, the Macedonians were again victorious, although they suffered heavy losses. Once again, Darius fled from the battlefield, taking refuge in the mountains to the northeast.

Alexander turned south and entered Babylon, which surrendered without a fight. From there, he continued eastward into Persia, conquering the royal city of

This relief sculpture depicts the Persian king Darius I. Darius's great palace at Persepolis was destroyed by Alexander.

Susa (which held the treasury of the Persian Empire), the capital Persepolis, and Pasagardae. The splendid palace at Persepolis, built by Darius I as a symbol of the might and wealth of the Persian Empire, was looted by the army and set on fire by Alexander, possibly in a fit of drunkenness. It burned to the ground.

Alexander was lord of all Persia—Darius had essentially forfeited the

A PORTRAIT OF ALEXANDER

Alexander was of medium height, with fair hair and a pale complexion. He grew up believing he would achieve greatness (his mother encouraged him to believe he was not actually Philip's son but a son of the god Zeus), and from an early age, he yearned to explore the world. He excelled at all martial skills but was not keen on any other sports apart from hunting. He became a heavy drinker and was capable of ungovernable rages and great cruelty. He had a lifelong passionate relationship with Hephaestion, a young Macedonian aristocrat, and when Hephaestion died of a fever in 324 BCE, Alexander was prostrated with grief. He organized a stunningly expensive royal funeral in Babylon for his friend and built an extravagant monument to him.

throne. In the summer of 330 BCE, Darius was murdered at the instigation of a group of satraps (local governors). One of them—Bessus—then proclaimed himself king. Alexander branded the satraps as regicides and usurpers, but Bessus unleashed a popular war, forcing the Macedonians and the Persians into yet another conflict. Bessus was eventually betrayed, taken by Alexander, and executed as a traitor.

Central Asia and India

In 329 BCE, Alexander set out on a new campaign to complete his conquest of the eastern Persian Empire, including the provinces of western India. Over the following two years, he broke the last traces of resistance in central Asia, extending his realm to encompass Media and Parthia (present-day Iran, Afghanistan, and Baluchistan) and Bactria and Sogdiana (present-day Turkmenistan).

In 327 BCE, Alexander led his army over the dangerous pass through the Hindu Kush mountains to reach the Indus Valley. There, in 326 BCE, he encountered the Indian king Porus, whose considerable army contained a mighty contingent of elephants. The Battle of Hydaspes was fought in torrential monsoon rains, and Alexander was once again victorious. He captured Porus and made him the local governor under Macedonian rule.

Despite their successes, Alexander's troops had begun to grow unhappy with their lot. It was rumored that they still had far to go, even that Alexander's aim was to conquer the whole world. In the fall of 326 BCE, the troops mutinied and refused to proceed any further. They had been on campaign for eight years and wanted to go home. Alexander was forced to compromise; he could not continue without an army. He abandoned the idea of conquering the rest of India. Instead, he had a fleet built and sailed down the Indus River

Alexander reached the mouth of the river in 325 BCE. From there, the fleet continued by sea to the Persian Gulf, while Alexander and the army marched west by land along the arid coastline. The fleet was supposed to sail parallel to the army's line of travel, to keep it supplied with food and water, but because the ships were unable to sail close to land against the prevailing winds, the army was forced to forage for supplies. Because

Alexander the Great and Hephaestion hunt a lion in this contemporary mosaic from the Macedonian palace at Pella. Hephaestion was a boyhood friend of Alexander's who served with him on many of his campaigns; he was also possibly his lover.

the army needed a daily supply of 190,000 gallons (720,000 l) of water and 250 tons (225 tonnes) of cereals to survive, many troops perished. Alexander lost more men on this march than in he did in all his battles combined.

Uniting the empire

In 324 BCE, Alexander returned to Susa to attend to affairs of state. In an effort to reconcile the conquered and the conquerors, he organized a funeral for Darius (the last of the Achaemenids) so that he was buried with his forefathers with due ceremony. Alexander adopted Persian customs, wearing the vestments and insignia of the "king of kings" on all ceremonial occasions. He arranged a mass marriage ceremony of Macedonian men with Persian wives, at which he himself married Barsine, the daughter of Darius. He also appointed Persians to important offices and drafted thousands of young Persians into his army.

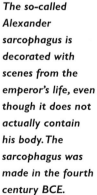

These actions showed that Alexander intended to create a mixed Macedonian-Persian elite that would hold his empire together, but they resulted in considerable tension between Alexander and his Macedonian entourage, particularly his *hetairoi*. When the new Persian troops were called up at the same time that Macedonian veterans were dismissed, the veterans mutinied. However, Alexander still had enough influence to effect a reconciliation with the rebels. At a celebratory banquet for the entire army, he openly prayed to the gods for "unity and equally shared rule" between Macedonians and Persians.

The so-called Alexander sarcophagus is decorated with scenes from the emperor's life, even though it does not actually contain his body. The sarcophagus was made in the fourth century BCE.

Final days

In the spring of 323 BCE, Alexander transferred to Babylon, where he took up his quarters in the palace of Nebuchadnezzar. Soon after his arrival, Alexander came down with a fever, an illness that was probably aggravated by heavy drinking. He died ten days later, on June 10. He was 33 years old. Alexander bequeathed his empire "to the strongest," thereby setting off a power struggle that was to last for 50 years.

See also:

After Alexander (page 166) • The Greek Legacy (page 174)

AFTER ALEXANDER

TIME LINE

323 BCE

Alexander the Great dies, leaving power vacuum.

322 BCE

Antipater crushes Aetolian rebels at Battle of Crannon.

306 BCE

Antigonus and son Demetrius Poliorcetes declare themselves joint kings and successors of Alexander.

305 BCE

Ptolemy proclaims himself king of Egypt.

281 BCE

Seleucus's victory at Battle of Corupedium secures him Anatolia.

235 BCE

Cleomenes III becomes king of Sparta.

165 BCE

Having recaptured Jerusalem from Seleucids, Judas Maccabaeus restores Jewish rites to temple.

After the death of Alexander in 323 BCE, several empires rose to prominence. The Ptolemaic dynasty took control of Egypt, the Antigonids rose to power in Macedonia, and the Seleucids took over the area that had formerly belonged to the Persians.

When Alexander the Great died at age 33 in 323 BCE, he left behind a power vacuum. The ensuing struggle among his generals was to result in the eventual breakup of his mighty empire into three main kingdoms.

The age of the diadochs

Alexander's first wife, Roxana, did not give birth to their son, also called Alexander, until four weeks after the king's death. The only other person with any claim to the throne was the 35-year-old Aridaeus, an illegitimate son of Philip II, who was rumored to suffer from both physical and mental illness. Nevertheless, both the newborn Alexander and his uncle Aridaeus were immediately invested with imperial titles—Alexander IV and Philip III. Since neither of them was in a position to exercise power, it fell into the hands of the imperial regent, Perdiccas, who divided the empire among the commanders of Alexander's army. These commanders are known as the *diadochoi* (successors), or diadochs.

For a time, while each diadoch attempted to secure for himself as much land and wealth as possible, a precarious unity was preserved in the empire, but the diadochs soon fell into open conflict. Years of war ensued, many of them marked by the formation of fresh coalitions. In 317 BCE, Aridaeus was mur-dered. After the 13-year-old Alexander met a similar fate in 310 BCE, there was no longer any lawful successor to stand in the way of the diadochs' ambitions.

Ptolemy and Egypt

One of the kingdoms that was to emerge from the breakup of Alexander's empire was a new, Greek-influenced Egypt, ruled by the diadoch Ptolemy (c. 367–283 BCE). Ptolemy came from an aristocratic Macedonian family and had grown up in the court of Philip II, becoming a friend of the king's young son, Alexander. When Alexander embarked on his Asian campaign, Ptolemy accompanied him as a general in his army. Ptolemy was later appointed satrap (governor) of Egypt.

After Alexander's death, Ptolemy was confirmed as diadoch in charge of Egypt and Libya, and he used the position as a power base. For almost 20 years, he battled the other diadochs, consolidating and expanding his realm. He successfully fended off invasions of Egypt and the island of Rhodes and annexed Cyprus, Palestine, and Cyrenaica. In 305 BCE, he proclaimed himself king of Egypt, taking the title Ptolemy I.

This Roman wall painting depicts Antigonus Gonatas, who helped establish the Antigonid dynasty in Macedonia.

This coin bears the portrait of Ptolemy I. A former general in Alexander's army, Ptolemy crowned himself king of Egypt in 305 BCE.

culture. The new king built a famous library and museum that attracted and supported Greek scholars and artists from all over the Greek world.

Ptolemy I died around 283 BCE, having established a dynasty that was to rule Egypt until the arrival of the Romans in 32 BCE.

Antigonus and son

Antigonus was another important general in Alexander's army. He was nicknamed Monophthalmos (One-Eye), the result of his having lost an eye in battle. Antigonus was already an old man—almost 60 years old—at the time of Alexander's death. For the previous 10 years, he had been governor of the recently conquered Phrygia, ruling the territory while the king went on to other conquests.

In 321 BCE, having been made commander in chief in Asia, Antigonus joined forces with his son Demetrius Poliorcetes (Taker of Cities), so-called for his skill in laying sieges. Together they hoped to preserve the unity of the empire, but they almost immediately found themselves in conflict with the other diadochs. Initially, they were very successful in battle, and in 306 BCE, they proclaimed themselves joint kings as Alexander's successors, ruling a huge region centered around western Asia

Five years later, in 301 BCE, Antigonus and Demetrius were forced to defend their territory against a coalition of the other diadochs (now also calling themselves kings) at the Battle of Ipsus. Antigonus, now 80, was killed, but Demetrius escaped to Greece. There, he succeeded in conquering Macedonia and much of mainland Greece, but in 286 BCE, while on a campaign in Anatolia, he was captured and imprisoned by the diadoch Seleucus. Demetrius died in prison in 283 BCE.

Taking up residence in his capital city, Alexandria, Ptolemy set about expanding the might and wealth of his kingdom. He improved the administrative system and established a system of land registration to simplify the collection of taxes. He also expanded Alexandria itself, making it the largest Greek settlement in the known world.

Ptolemy succeeded in having his friend Alexander's body brought to Egypt. Although it was known that Alexander would have preferred the Siwa Oasis as his final resting place, the funeral took place in Alexandria. The body was placed in a golden coffin and given divine honors.

In 285 BCE, Ptolemy abdicated in favor of his son, Ptolemy II. It was Ptolemy II who was to make Alexandria an unparalleled center of learning and

THE HELLENISTIC WORLD IN 270 BCE

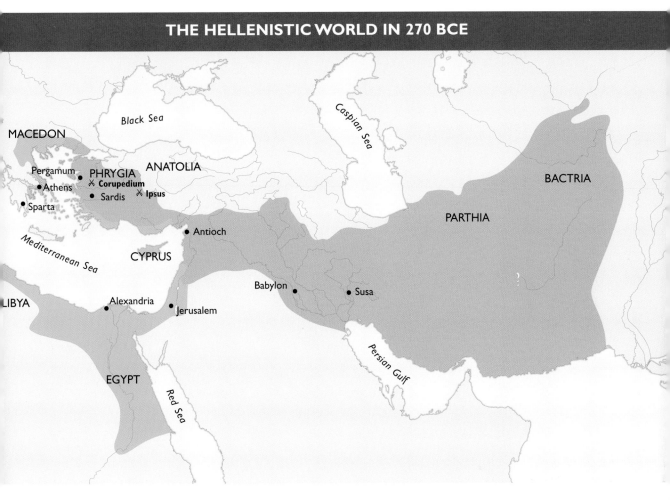

MACEDON

Black Sea

Caspian Sea

Pergamum
PHRYGIA
ANATOLIA
BACTRIA

Athens
✕ Corupedium
Sardis
✕ Ipsus

Sparta

PARTHIA

Mediterranean Sea

CYPRUS

Antioch

LIBYA

Babylon

Susa

Alexandria

Jerusalem

Persian Gulf

EGYPT

Red Sea

Demetrius's son, Antigonus Gonatas, regained possession of the Macedonian throne around 272 BCE, and his descendants—the Antigonids—remained in power until the Romans put an end to their dynasty.

The Seleucids

The Seleucid Empire was the largest of the kingdoms that resulted from the division of Alexander's domains. It was founded by Seleucus, one of the diadochs who rose to power after Alexander's death. Born around 358 BCE, Seleucus was, like Ptolemy, the son of a Macedonian aristocrat. He was roughly the same age as Alexander and probably his friend. He accompanied the young king on his Persian campaign and, after Alexander's death, was appointed governor of Babylon.

Having secured Babylon and the regions farther east, Seleucus gradually expanded his influence to the west. In Syria, he built himself a new capital city, Antioch, which was to become the most important metropolis in Asia. In 281 BCE, Seleucus met the diadoch Lysimachus at the Battle of Corupedium near Sardis and defeated him, thereby securing Anatolia for himself. Because Lysimachus (who was killed in the fighting) had been the king of Macedonia, Seleucus tried to secure that territory. However, before he could achieve this aim, he was assassinated.

KEY

Seleucid kingdom

Ptolemaic kingdom

Macedonian kingdom

✕ Major battle

Pompey's Pillar, built in the third century CE, is one of the most famous monuments in Alexandria. Alexandria was the capital of Egypt during the Ptolemaic period.

JUDAS MACCABAEUS

The most famous opponent of the Seleucids is probably the Jewish guerrilla fighter Judas Maccabaeus. Palestine was seized from the Ptolemies by the Seleucid king Antiochus III in 198 BCE. In 168 BCE, Antiochus IV outlawed Judaism, ordering the worship of Greek gods and persecuting anyone who remained true to the Jewish religion and culture.

Mattathias, patriarch of the priestly Hasmonaean family, objected to this edict and killed both a government official and a Jew who had complied with the order. In 167 BCE, Mattathias fled to the mountains with a loyal band of Jews, initiating a lengthy revolt against the Seleucids. After he died, his son Judas Maccabaeus (The Hammer) took command of the rebellion, defeating much larger Syrian armies in 166 and 165 BCE and capturing Jerusalem. He restored Jewish rites to the temple in Jerusalem in December 165 BCE, an event that is commemorated by the Jewish festival of Hanukkah. For the next 80 years, the Jews in Syria were virtually an independent nation.

Seleucus had carved out an enormous empire, one that almost rivaled Alexander's in size. He was succeeded by his son, Antiochus I. The Seleucid dynasty was to survive for more than two hundred years.

The people who lived within the boundaries of the Seleucid Empire spoke many languages and adhered to many different ways of life. The empire never became truly integrated, and under Seleucus's successors, it gradually crumbled away. In central Asia, Bactria made itself virtually independent, while in northern Persia, the warlike Parthians roamed at will, ultimately conquering many of the eastern provinces. Other usurpers set up their own kingdoms in imperial territory. One such state was Pergamum, on the Aegean coast, which rebelled against Seleucid rule to become the leading city of Anatolia and an important hub of Greek culture.

Antipater and the Lamian War

Antipater (c. 397–319 BCE) was a trusted friend of Philip II and Alexander the Great. When Alexander embarked on his Persian campaign, Antipater was left behind to act as his regent in Macedonia and Greece. As soon as news of Alexander's death reached Greece in 323 BCE, Athens and several other states rebelled. The insurrection was spurred on by the oratory of Demosthenes, who had long led Athenian opposition to Macedonia. Antipater acted promptly to put down the revolt.

The conflict between Antipater and the Greek states was called the Lamian War. The Athenians were backed by the Aetolian League, an alliance based in the mountainous region of Aetolia. At first, the rebels were successful, but Antipater eventually crushed them at the Battle of Crannon in 322 BCE.

Antipater demanded that the Athenians hand over the rebel leaders, including

This bust depicts the diadoch Seleucus I. In the decades following Alexander the Great's death, Seleucus gained control of much of the eastern part of Alexander's empire.

Demosthenes, and the Athenian assembly condemned the rebels to death. Demosthenes managed to escape to the island of Calauria, where he took poison rather than surrender.

Antipater's next battle was with his own countryman, the Macedonian general Partakes, who challenged his authority. Antipater won this struggle easily—Partakes was killed in 321 BCE. Antipater was then confirmed as supreme regent of Macedonia and charged with the care of Alexander's children. On Antipater's death in 319 BCE, the regency passed to Polypechon, but he was swiftly replaced by Antipater's son Cassander, who seized control. Continued infighting between the diadochs led eventually to Antigonus

Gonatas becoming the king of Macedon in 272 BCE. He established a dynasty that was to last for more than a hundred years.

By the early third century BCE, therefore, Alexander's entire empire had been broadly divided into three much smaller empires. Macedonia was ruled by the Antigonid dynasty, solidly established in their homeland. Outside Macedonia, their position was less strong, but their sphere of influence extended from present-day Bulgaria to the Peloponnese. Egypt was ruled by the Ptolemies, who gradually relinquished their possessions beyond its borders. The Seleucid dynasty held the region that had originally stretched from the Aegean Sea in the west to the Indus River in the east. However, over the years, the eastern boundary was gradually eroded and receded westward. Although the diadoch dynasties lived in continual conflict, no one empire was able to achieve dominance. The division of power remained unsettled until the advent of the Rome Empire.

Hellenism

The campaigns of Alexander the Great had far-reaching consequences that were not only political but also social and cultural. In his epic progress of conquest across Asia, he had established many new cities and populated them with Greek veterans from his army. Those cities became oases of Greek language and culture in the middle of an Oriental culture, which gave rise to the concept of Hellenism, a term used to describe the unprecedented spread of Greek culture

Judas Maccabaeus led a Jewish rebellion against the Seleucid Empire, capturing the city of Jerusalem.

in the east in the period between the death of Alexander and the beginning of the Christian era.

Alexander had founded cities as far away as Uzbekistan and Kashmir, leaving the new cities as small, isolated islands of Greek civilization in an enormous sea of local culture. However, the new Greek cities were not modeled on the old idea of a city-state ruled by its citizens. That concept had no place in Alexander's empire; these cities were ruled by a distant king. Greek was generally used as the common language in large parts of the Hellenistic empires, without wholly replacing Aramaic, which had played a similar role in the Persian Empire. In spite of this unity of language, Greek culture had little effect on the indigenous population. In most cases, the Greeks and the native inhabitants existed side by side, with little interaction between them.

Although the old Greek gods were worshipped in the new Greek cities, they faced fierce competition from the non-Greek gods that surrounded them. Many of these other gods were messianic (saviors or deliverers) with cults of an ecstatic nature. Similar Greek cults, especially Dionysiac cults, also flourished at this time. The cult of the ruler derived strength from the popularity of the messianic gods: often, he too was regarded as a savior or messiah.

The Greeks did not automatically adopt foreign gods—the gods first had to be adapted to Greek tastes, which was done through a process of syncretism. Syncretism occurs when deities merge by assuming one another's characteristics. In this way, the Egyptian god Amon-Re and the Syrian god Baal became identified with Zeus.

Cleomenes

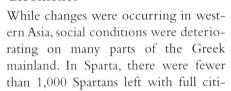

This statue depicts the god Dionysus, who was widely worshipped in the Hellenistic empires.

While changes were occurring in western Asia, social conditions were deteriorating on many parts of the Greek mainland. In Sparta, there were fewer than 1,000 Spartans left with full citizenship rights, and most of them were living below subsistence level. All the wealth was in the hands of a select few. In the last half of the third century BCE, when the situation was ripe for revolution, a reforming leader emerged: Cleomenes.

Cleomenes III became one of the two kings of Sparta in 235 BCE. He was determined to introduce new policies to redress the inequalities in Spartan society. After ridding himself of his political enemies, he took the radical course of canceling all debts and dividing the land into equal parcels, which he distributed among the citizens. At the same time, he granted full citizenship to several thousand of the *perioikoi* (original inhabitants). The revolutionary ideas of Cleomenes spread, and in many Greek states, a cry arose for debts to be canceled and land to be redistributed.

Cleomenes also attempted to restore Sparta's military prestige by going to war with the Achaean League, an alliance of city-states under the leadership of Aratus of Sicyon. Aratus was deeply opposed to the revolutionary ideas fanned by Cleomenes, and in order to ensure his success in battle against the Spartans, he called on the help of Macedon. Cleomenes was defeated, and his reforms were dismantled. The king fled to Alexandria, where he died in 219 BCE.

Roughly 20 years later, the radical ideas of Cleomenes resurfaced during the brutal reign of the Spartan tyrant Nabis (ruled 207-192 BCE). Nabis reintroduced Cleomenes' system, even going so far as to free the slaves, but his rule came to an end when he was betrayed by his allies during a war against Rome. His death marked the end of Sparta's days as a major power.

See also:

Macedon and Alexander the Great (page 154)
• Sparta and Athens (page 52)

THE GREEK LEGACY

TIME LINE

332 BCE
Alexander the Great founds city of Alexandria.

c. 308 BCE
Zeno of Cyprus begins giving lectures in Athens; his teachings form basis of school of philosophy known as Stoicism.

c. 300 BCE
Ptolemy I expands Temple of the Muses in Alexandria to establish center for arts and sciences; Euclid writes *Elements*.

c. 275 BCE
Aristarchus of Samos suggests Earth orbits around sun, instead of sun orbiting around Earth; radical theory rejected.

c. 250 BCE
Aristotle studies at Museum in Alexandria before returning to native Syracuse; he formulates concept of specific gravity.

The ancient Greeks made profound and far-reaching contributions to the worlds of literature, science, and philosophy. Their discoveries and achievements became the building blocks for generations of later scholars and artists.

Many of the cultural achievements associated with ancient Greece took place not in Greece itself but in the Greek outpost of Alexandria in Egypt. The city was founded by Alexander the Great in 332 BCE. When he left Egypt to go on a campaign, Alexander left one of his generals, Ptolemy, in charge of the province. On Alexander's death in 323 BCE, Ptolemy effectively became the ruler of Egypt. He crowned himself king of the country in 305 BCE.

From the very beginning of his reign, Ptolemy encouraged Greek scholars and philosophers to congregate at his court in Alexandria. When Demetrius of Phaleron was banished from Athens, he took refuge in Alexandria and suggested that Ptolemy should establish a center of study dedicated to the Muses (see box, page 182). The center would allow scholars to pursue their studies in all the arts and sciences. Ptolemy happily agreed to the idea.

The first museum

The Temple of the Muses was expanded to make it a true academy of literature and the sciences. The Greeks knew the temple as the Mouseion, although it is now known as the Museum—the origin of the word used today. Those who were appointed to work there became well-paid servants of the state and lived in the building. They were overseen by the director and chief priest.

Under Ptolemy's son, Ptolemy II (ruled 285–246 BCE), Alexandria became renowned as a center of arts and a magnet for scholars and poets, whom Ptolemy welcomed to his court. He increased his financial support for the Museum, which became a research center for the natural sciences and mathematics as well as an academy for more literary pursuits.

Most of the writers working at the Museum did not produce original work. Instead, they focused on collecting and preserving the literary works of the past. The versions of Homer's epic poems the *Iliad* and the *Odyssey* that exist today are essentially the work of Alexandrian scholars. The Museum's archivists collected manuscripts of literary texts attributed to Homer and then compiled them to produce new editions. Copies of these texts were widely sold and greatly prized for their authenticity.

The scholars also did invaluable work in the area of textual criticism, a discipline that had its beginnings in Alexandria. After scrutinizing all available manuscripts of a text, the scholars would

This 15th-century-CE painting by Joos Van Gent depicts the astronomer Ptolemy of Alexandria.

publish their own version of an ancient work, together with annotation. Crucial to this process of textual criticism were the resources provided by the great Library of Alexandria, which contained many thousands of handwritten scrolls—a unique collection during that period of history.

Theocritus

The Museum also supported original writers producing new works. One of these poets was the Greek Theocritus (born c. 300 BCE), who became famous in the third century BCE for his sophisticated verses that extolled the pleasures of an idealized pastoral life. The Arcadian landscape depicted by Theocritus was filled with amorous shepherds and shepherdesses who frolicked to the sound of melodious music. This view of the countryside was in complete contrast to the archaic tradition of Arcadia, in which the countryside was rugged and inhabited by fearsome mythological beasts. This new view of Arcadia found favor with the citizens of Alexandria who, oppressed by the stench, noise, and crowds of city life, began to idealize life in the countryside. It is a view of Arcadia that was to be handed down from Theocritus to the Roman poet Virgil, and from him to the

This vase illustration shows the Greek hero Odysseus with the blind soothsayer Tiresias. The existing version of Homer's Odyssey was written down by scholars working in Alexandria.

poets of the Renaissance period, including William Shakespeare.

Theocritus also wrote comedies, one of the very few genres in which the Hellenistic writers were noted for their originality. The ancient comedy of Attica had been a kind of satirical revue, often politically based, and covered contemporary issues. The comedies of the Alexandrian poets, on the other hand, had tightly structured plots that owed nothing to the current political scene. Instead, they told stories of real life, albeit with highly stereotypical characters.

One famous contemporary of these Alexandrian comic writers was the playwright Menander (c. 341–291 BCE). He was very popular in Egypt, and several of his plays have been discovered there on papyrus scrolls. Many attempts were made to persuade him to join the Museum in Alexandria, but Menander preferred to stay in his native Athens.

The pure sciences

Study of the sciences also came into their own at Ptolemy's academy. The Library of Alexandria was filled with the output of the Museum's scientists as well as its writers. One of the foremost mathematicians in Alexandria around 300 BCE was Euclid, who produced a major work—the *Elements*, which was a compilation of all mathematical knowledge that existed at the time. The work was assembled in 13 books and had a particular emphasis on geometry. This synthesis of everything that had gone before was a typical product of Hellenistic science. Euclid's book was an essential basis for all later mathematical studies. The sections on plane geometry were turned into a school textbook that was used as late as the end of the 19th century CE.

The discoveries of the Greek mathematicians were not always original—many had already been made by the Egyptians or Babylonians. What the

The playwright Menander was popular in Egypt in the late fourth and early third centuries BCE.

Greeks did realize, however, was that theorems could be linked, and that geometry was an integrated system that could be studied through the use of logic.

Mathematics was put to little practical use. Only those with something to construct, such as temple architects, knew how to use mathematics to help them in their work. One reason that applied mathematics was ignored was that technology was still in its infancy, and there was little incentive to develop it. Since the sheer brute strength of animals and slaves was enough to construct buildings and turn mill wheels, society could keep going without it. Another factor that worked against the development of technology was the dismissive attitude usually displayed by the Greek elite toward practical matters. It was felt that anything to do with manual labor—and that included technology—was not worthy of the attention of the learned.

One invention in particular could have had a huge effect on the course of history if its implications had been recognized. The scientist Hero of Alexandria discovered the principle of the steam turbine in the first century CE and used it to construct an amusing little steam toy to entertain his friends. The principle was never put to further use, however.

Archimedes

One ancient Greek citizen who did not ignore the opportunities offered by putting the sciences to practical use was the mathematician and inventor Archimedes (c. 287–212 BCE). Archimedes studied at the Museum in Alexandria before returning to his native Syracuse. He made a particular study of the characteristics of force. It was already known that heavy loads were easier to lift with the help of pulleys and levers, but Archimedes discovered that even the heaviest weight could be lifted easily by using a long lever that moved around a fixed point, or fulcrum.

Archimedes applied this knowledge to many applications, including military catapults. He is also said to have single-handedly launched a massive ship with the help of levers and pulleys. Legend has it that he once boasted: "Give me a solid place to stand in space, and I will move the Earth."

This relief sculpture depicts the mathematician Euclid. His book, the Elements, *was one of the most important works produced in Alexandria.*

Eureka!

Another famous myth tells the story of one of Archimedes' most famous discoveries, that of specific gravity. The king of Syracuse had asked him to find out whether a supposedly golden crown was in fact pure gold. As water slopped out of the overfull bath when Archimedes got in, it came to him that the amount of water displaced by objects of different volumes would also be different. For this reason, the amount of water displaced by the crown (if it was adulterated) would be different from the amount of water displaced by a lump of pure gold that weighed the same as the crown. Archimedes is reputed to have jumped out of the bath and run down the street naked crying "Eureka!" ("I have found it!").

Astronomy

Rather than thinking that the stars were controlled by the gods, as earlier civilizations had believed, the Greeks adopted a scientific approach to astronomical study. They employed mathematics, particularly geometry, to help explain the movements of the heavenly bodies. The Greeks were pioneers in making careful observations of the heavens, and they noted that the stars remained in approximately the same place in relation to each other throughout the year, while the moon and five other bodies (Mercury, Venus, Mars, Jupiter, and Saturn) seemed to move around the sky. The Greeks called these heavenly bodies *planates*, after the Greek word meaning "wanderer."

In order to explain the movement of the planets, Greek astronomers put forward the theory that the cosmos was divided into concentric spheres, each one the path of a planet. They usually assumed Earth to be at the center of these spheres (a geocentric view of the universe), which was an error that made the calculations very complicated. One astronomer, Aristarchus of Samos (flourished c. 275 BCE), suggested that everything would be easier to explain if it was assumed that the sun was the central point of the universe, but his ideas were too revolutionary for their time; they were dismissed in favor of the more popular geocentric model.

The geocentric view of the universe was refined in the second century CE by Claudius Ptolemaeus (also known as Ptolemy of Alexandria), who lived from 90 to 168 CE. He used geometric calculations to show that the sun, the moon, and the planets moved in small circular orbits (which he called epicycles) around larger circles, like rings strung on a bracelet. To support his contention that Earth was at the center of these circles, he provided mathematical calculations that were accepted by other astronomers up to the 16th century CE. The calculations were then rejected by Polish

In this 19th-century-CE woodcut, Hero of Alexandria shows his steam engine, the aeolipile, to his friends. Hero lived in the first century CE. The first truly practical steam engine was not invented until 1,600 years later.

great work *Geography*, he drew maps of the known world that incorporated lines of latitude and longitude. In spite of being based on incomplete data, these maps were used for centuries. He built a device to study light and presented a mathematical theory of its properties in his treatise *Optics*. In *Harmonica*, he offered an outline of music theory, while in *Tetrabiblos*, he used his knowledge of astronomy and astrology to make predictions about the future.

Another Greek mathematician who contributed a great deal to the knowledge of astronomy was Eratosthenes of Cyrene, who was director of the Library of Alexandria from around 240 to 196 BCE. After distinguishing himself by cataloging 675 stars, Eratosthenes set about trying to calculate the circumference of Earth. He discovered that at the summer solstice a stick placed vertically in the ground in Syene (now Aswan) in Egypt would cast no shadow at noon, while a similar stick in Alexandria would cast a shadow one-fifth of its length. Using this data, Eratosthenes calculated the Earth's circumference, with only 3.5 percent error.

Medical science

Great advances were made in medical science in Alexandria in the fourth century BCE. They were based on the rational approach to medicine pioneered by Hippocrates of Kos (c. 460–377 BCE), who is called the father of medicine. Previously, the practice of medicine had been bound up with religion and magic. However, Hippocrates believed that disease had natural causes. He considered medicine to be an art that people could learn, diagnosing disease through an examination of the patient.

Hippocrates was born on the Greek island of Kos, where he eventually established a school of medicine. His method of clinical observation was to influence

The mathematician Archimedes is famous for discovering the concept of specific gravity while in the bath. This drawing is based on a 16th-century-CE engraving.

astronomer Nicolaus Copernicus, who postulated a heliocentric (sun-centered) view of the cosmos that retained Ptolemy's system of epicycles.

Ptolemy also contributed to several other fields of knowledge. He added to the understanding of trigonometry, using this knowledge to make astrolabes (instruments used for measuring the altitude of the stars) and sundials. In his all succeeding generations of doctors, while his *Regimen in Acute Diseases* introduced the concept of preventive medicine through healthy diet and lifestyle. Hippocrates also suggested that the weather and drinking water can have an effect on public health.

The 70 works generally known as the Hippocratic Collection may not have been written by Hippocrates himself, but they originated from his school of medicine. Similarly, he probably was not the author of the Hippocratic Oath—the oath to act ethically that is taken by all doctors today on graduation.

Herophilus, the personal physician to Ptolemy I in the fourth century BCE, is considered the father of the study of human anatomy. Born in Chalcedon in Anatolia around 335 BCE, he spent most of his life in Alexandria. By dissecting dead bodies, he discovered that the brain is the center of the nervous system. He also identified the separate functions of the motor and sensory nerves. He studied the liver, genitalia, eyes, pancreas, and salivary glands and pioneered research on the blood vessels, learning that they carried blood and not air, as even Hippocrates had believed. Erasistratus (born c. 275 BCE) also carried out many dissections at his school of anatomy in Alexandria and identified the pumping function of the heart, even though he did not understand the concept of the circulation of the blood.

Philosophy

In addition to advances in literature, the sciences, and medicine, the fourth and third centuries BCE saw the development of several new philosophical movements, including Skepticism, Stoicism, and Epicureanism.

By the fourth century BCE, a number of Greek philosophical schools of thought had been established, including that of Sophism. Traveling teachers of philosophy, politics, and rhetoric, the Sophists thought it was more important to be able to argue on either side of a question than to be morally right.

The Dance of Apollo with the Muses, *by Baldassare Peruzzi, was painted in the early 16th century CE. The Temple of the Muses in Alexandria was one of the most important centers of the arts and sciences in the ancient world.*

Plato (428–348 BCE) and his student Aristotle (384–322 BCE) objected to the Sophists' view that truth and morality were matters of opinion and countered that view with the concept of idealism. Plato maintained that the object of knowledge (the "idea") was fixed, permanent, and unchangeable. He considered that only this "idea" was real and rejected the view that knowledge was based on the experience of the senses.

The Skeptics countered by saying that all knowledge is questionable and that inquiry itself is a process of doubting. A philosophical school based on these ideas was founded by Pyrrhon of Elis (c. 363– 272 BCE). The essence of its philosophy was the impossibility of obtaining certain knowledge. Pyrrhon assumed that mankind primarily strives for happiness, and this is the sole reason for the practice of philosophy. He said that no human could ever know the real nature of things; therefore, the wise person would suspend judgment. Pyrrhon never took sides, believing solely in the value of observation—*skepsis* in Greek. His followers were called Skeptics, and their questioning of everything, based on the example of the questions and answers of Socrates, gave rise to the modern connotation of the word *skeptic*.

Epicureanism

Epicureanism was founded by the Greek philosopher Epicurus (341–270 BCE), who was born on the island of Samos. When he was 18, he had to go to Athens to do his military service. When his service was completed, he traveled for 10 years, studying and developing his own philosophical ideas. Around 311 BCE, he established a school of philosophy at Mytilene on the island of Lesbos. Later, in 306 BCE, he settled in Athens, where he bought a house with a garden. He set up a school in the garden, and many of his followers from his travels in Anatolia flocked there.

Epicurus's philosophy was based on a system of ethics and the belief that good and evil were to be perceived through the senses. To achieve a happy life, one should seek pleasure and avoid pain. However, he also taught that a simple life was best, because any attempt to satisfy all desires would itself bring pain. So, although the goal of life was pleasure (and intellectual pleasure was to be preferred to sensual pleasure), moderation was the path to true happiness. He described justice, honesty, and friendship as virtues, while politics was to be avoided because it produced only misery.

Epicurus subscribed to the atomic theory refined by Democritus in the fifth century BCE. According to this theory, everything is composed of tiny unchangeable atoms, which join together to form material objects. Epicurus maintained that the soul and the body

THE MUSES

In Greek mythology, the Muses were nine goddesses thought to inspire artists of all kinds, including philosophers, poets, and musicians. The Muses were all born of a union between Zeus, king of the gods, and Mnemosyne, the goddess of memory. Each Muse presided over a different art or science. Poetry was so important that it had four separate Muses: Polyhymnia for sacred poetry, Calliope for epic poetry, Erato for love poetry, and Euterpe for lyric poetry. Terpsichore was the Muse in charge of choral singing and dance, while Thalia was the Muse for comedy, and Melpomene was the Muse of tragedy. Clio presided over history, and Urania presided over astronomy.

The companions to the Muses were Apollo, the god of music, and the Graces, who were the three goddesses of beauty, joy, and charm. The Graces were also daughters of Zeus, but by the nymph Eurynome. Thalia was associated with good cheer, Aglaia with splendor, and Euphrosyne with mirth.

are composed of material atoms, and when the body dies, the soul is also dissipated and no longer exists. Consequently, there can be no afterlife, and there is nothing to fear from death.

Epicurus did not deny the existence of the gods, but he considered them irrelevant to human affairs. He viewed them as existing in empty space outside the cosmos and believed that they were too caught up in their own affairs to be interested in the material world of mortals. To fear or venerate them was as pointless as fearing life after death.

Followers of Epicurus lived a comparatively austere life in his school. They consumed little other than bread and water and enjoyed few pleasures beyond those of friendship and intellectual pursuits. This modest lifestyle, withdrawn from the world, is in direct contrast to the modern understanding of the word *epicurean*, which has come to mean the pursuit of pleasure; an epicure is someone who indulges freely in the pleasures of food and wine.

Stoicism

Around 308 BCE, the philosopher Zeno of Cyprus began giving public lectures in Athens under the painted colonnade next to the agora. The colonnade was known as the Stoa Poikile in Greek, which gave the name Stoicism to his teachings. Zeno had studied with the Cynics, at Plato's Academy, and at Aristotle's Lyceum, but he developed his own view of life and the universe.

The Stoics believed that everything in the universe, including mankind, was

This bust depicts the Greek philosopher Epicurus, who gave his name to a school of philosophy—Epicureanism.

linked by a divine force (Logos), which they also called reason. Zeno considered that by living in conformity with nature, mankind would live in conformity with the Logos, and this was the only way to attain happiness. By calmly accepting everything that life deals out, mankind can be freed from passion, grief, and joy.

Zeno believed that information received through the senses is based on correct perceptions. If mistakes are made, they are due to inaccurate observation or faulty processing of the information. The person who uses his reason to digest information will come to a correct conception of things. Once one has a correct conception of virtue, one can then gain virtue.

Equality for all

The Stoics believed that because all mankind is animated by the Logos, all men and women, rich or poor, free or slave, should be treated as equals. This was a revolutionary idea in the third century BCE.

The Stoics considered possessions and wealth unimportant in human relationships and believed that people had a responsibility to help one another. For this reason, they encouraged people to enter public life because it allowed them to improve the lot of their fellow citizens. Stoicism, as first taught by Zeno and later refined by his follower Cleanthes and his successor Chrysippus, was destined to become a major influence in the Roman world.

See also:

After Alexander (page 166) • The Great Philosophers (page 122)

GLOSSARY

Achaemenids Persian 27th dynasty of Egypt (525–404 BCE); founded by Cambyses II of Persia and named after his family, the Achaemenids. Darius I was a member of this dynasty.

acropolis fortified part of an ancient Greek city. The most famous such fortress is the Acropolis in Athens, where various large temples were built, including the Parthenon.

Adonis in Greek mythology, a young mortal man of outstanding beauty; favorite of Aphrodite.

Aegean Sea part of the Mediterranean Sea that separates mainland Greece from Asia Minor (part of modern Turkey).

Alcmaeonidae influential Athenian political family during the lifetime of Peisistratus.

Alexandria greatest city of the ancient world. It lies on the Mediterranean Sea on the western edge of the delta of the Nile River and was founded in 332 BCE by Alexander the Great.

Anatolia another name for Asia Minor (part of modern Turkey).

Antigonids descendants of Demetrius Poliorcetes; ruling dynasty of Macedonia from 306 to 168 BCE.

Apollo Greek god of the sun, oracles, music, poetry, and justice; son of Zeus. The god of medicine, Apollo could also choose to inflict disease as punishment.

Aramaic Semitic language that was widely spoken in western Asia until displaced by Greek after the conquests of Alexander the Great.

Arcadia mountainous region of the central Peloponnese, Greece.

archons magistrates in Athens, beginning around the seventh century BCE. Elected annually, their duties comprised legislation, the dispensation of justice, the conduct of religion, and military affairs.

Artemisium, Battle of Persian naval victory over the Greeks in 480 BCE.

Athens preeminent city-state of ancient Greece.

Attica region of central Greece. Its chief city was Athens.

Babylon city in southern Meso-potamia that was the center of an Amorite empire under Hammurabi. Later, Babylon continued as the cultural and political capital of the region. From 612 to 539 BCE, Babylon was the capital of the Neo-Babylonian Empire.

Bacchiads aristocratic family that ruled the city-state of Corinth in the seventh century BCE.

Bosporus strait, 19 miles (30 km) long, that joins the Black Sea and the Sea of Marmara.

Byzantium ancient Greek city on the shore of the Bosporus; later known as Constantinople; modern Istanbul.

Chaeronea, Battle of conflict in which Philip II of Macedon defeated Thebes and Athens in 338 BCE.

Chalcedon ancient port on the Bosporus; overshadowed by its proximity to Byzantium.

choregi Greek sponsors of theatrical productions and competitions.

comedy originally, any play or literary composition with a nontragic ending.

comos procession of Greek citizens during which they wore masks and danced and sang; often part of festivals in honor of Dionysus.

Corcyra ancient name for the Greek island of Corfu.

Corinth city of the Peloponnese, around 50 miles (80 km) west of Athens.

Corinthian War conflict that lasted from 395 to 387 BCE between Sparta and an alliance among Thebes, Athens, Corinth, and Argos, initially supported by Persia.

Corupedium, Battle of fought in 281 BCE, the decisive final confrontation between the rival successors to Alexander the Great.

Council of 500 originally conceived by Cleisthenes and fully realized by Solon, a political decision-making body in Athens consisting of 10 groups, each of 50 men, chosen by lot.

Crannon, Battle of military confrontation in 322 BCE in which Macedonian forces under Antipater defeated rebellious Greek forces led by the Athenians.

crop rotation farming system in which fields are divided into groups (typically of three) in which a different one is left fallow every year so that it may regenerate.

Croton Greek colony in southern Italy in which Pythagoras settled around 530 BCE.

Cynics from the Greek *kunikoi*. Followers of Diogenes and

Antisthenes, they protested the material interests of established society. Holding virtue to be the only good, they stressed independence from worldly needs and pleasures and led austere lives.

Cyrenaica coastal district of southern Mediterranean Sea; former Greek colony; now part of Libya.

Delian League military alliance set up in 477 BCE to protect the Greek cities of Ionia (part of modern Turkey) against attack by the Persians.

Delos one of the Cyclades, a group of islands in the Aegean Sea.

Delphi city in central Greece; site of an Apollo sanctuary and an oracle. The utterances of Pythia, the priestess of the oracle, had great influence on personal and political life.

democracy from the Greek *demos* (people) and *kratein* (to rule); government by the people, either directly or through elected representatives. This form of government arose at the end of the sixth century BCE in Athens.

diadochs military commanders who succeeded Alexander the Great.

Dionysia Greek annual festival in honor of Dionysus; characterized by processions, poetry competitions, and theatrical performances.

Dionysus Greek god of wine, ecstasy, reproduction, life force, chaos, and death.

dithyramb ancient Greek hymn of praise to the god Dionysus.

Dodona site, near Epirus in north-western Greece, of an oracle devoted to the god Zeus.

Dorians people from Macedonia and northern Greece who conquered parts of the Peloponnese and Crete between 1200 and 1000 BCE.

ecclesia the tribal meeting of Athens open to all citizens that, after Cleisthenes' reforms, made the final political decisions on internal and foreign affairs.

Elea ancient town in Italy founded by Greek refugees; famous for its school of philosophy; modern Velia.

Eleusis city on the Greek coast near Athens where mysteries were held between around 600 and 400 BCE.

Ephesus Ionian city in ancient Anatolia (part of modern Turkey).

Epicureanism philosophy founded by Epicurus (341–270 BCE). Its central tenets were the pursuit of happiness and the avoidance of pain.

Epidamnus colony on the Adriatic coast in part of what is now Albania; founded in the fifth century BCE by Greeks from Corcyra.

Epidaurus small but important city-state of ancient Greece; situated in the northeastern Peloponnese.

Eurymedon river in Asia Minor; site of a major battle in 466 BCE between the Persians and the Delian League.

Gaugamela, Battle of military confrontation in 331 BCE in which Alexander the Great defeated Darius III of Persia.

Gordian knot according to Greek legend, a complex knot that could only be untied by the man destined to become king of Asia. The young Alexander the Great cut it with one blow of his sword.

Granicus River, Battle of military confrontation between Alexander the Great and the Persian Empire near Troy in Asia Minor in 334 BCE.

Hades god of the underworld and brother of Zeus; also the name of the underworld itself.

Hanukkah Jewish midwinter festival that commemorates the restoration of Jewish rites in the temple at Jerusalem by Judas Maccabaeus.

hemlock poisonous herb; commonly thought to have been the cause of Socrates's death.

Heracles greatest and strongest of Greek mythological heroes; also known as Hercules.

Hermes Greek god of travelers, shepherds, trade, and cunning. The son of Zeus and the messenger of the gods, he guided souls to the underworld.

hoplites soldiers in the Greek heavy infantry, armed with swords, lances, and the large round shields known as hoplons.

Illyria ancient region of the Balkans; part of modern Albania.

Indo-European languages common family of European and Asiatic (Indian) languages.

Ionia coastal region of southwestern Anatolia (part of modern Turkey) that contained several Greek city-states.

Ishtar Semitic war goddess who merged with Inanna and became the goddess of love and fertility.

isthmus narrow strip of land, bordered on two sides by water, that joins two larger land masses.

Jason Greek mythological hero who sailed in the *Argo* in search of the Golden Fleece.

Logos divine force—also known as reason—that the Stoics believed directed the universe and humankind.

Lydia ancient province of Anatolia (part of modern Turkey). Its capital was Sardis.

Macedon alternatively, Macedonia; region of northeastern Greece that was for a short time during the fourth century BCE the most powerful state in the eastern Mediterranean region.

Maia in Greek mythology, the eldest of the Pleiades and the mother of Zeus's son, Hermes.

Mantinea ancient city in Arcadia; site of two battles. The first Battle of Mantinea, in 418 BCE, was the largest land battle of the Peloponnesian War. In the second Battle of Mantinea (362 BCE), Thebes defeated the allied forces of Athens and Sparta.

Marathon city on the east coast of Attica where the Persians suffered a devastating defeat in 490 BCE by a small Athenian army under Miltiades.

Medes Indo-European people who entered northeastern Iran around the 17th century BCE.

Mesopotamia area in western Asia surrounding the Euphrates and Tigris rivers. Floods and irrigation made the land fertile, and around 4500 BCE, the first agricultural settlements were founded there.

Minoan civilization Bronze Age civilization on Crete.

Muses in Greek—and later in Roman—mythology, nine sister goddesses (daughters of Zeus) who inspired human artistic creativity: Calliope (epic poetry), Clio (history), Erato (lyric poetry), Euterpe (music), Melpomene (tragedy), Polyhymnia (sacred poetry), Terpsichore (dancing), Thalia (comedy), Urania (astronomy).

Parnassus mountain of central Greece; in Greek mythology, the home of Apollo and the Muses.

Parthenon temple on the Athenian Acropolis dedicated to Pallas Athena; built between 447 and 438 BCE.

Peloponnese large, mountainous peninsula that is joined to the mainland of Greece by the Isthmus of Corinth.

Peloponnesian War (431–404 BCE) conflict of hegemony between Athens (generally allied with the Ionians) and Sparta (allied with the Dorians). The direct cause was a conflict about the island of Corcyra (modern Corfu). The army of Sparta annually destroyed Attica, while the Athenian fleet plundered the Peloponnesian coasts. Sparta finally triumphed over Athens with help from the Persians.

Pergamum ancient Greek city in Asia Minor; close to the modern city of Izmir, Turkey.

Persephone daughter of Demeter, the goddess of agriculture. Her recurring abduction by Hades and return from the underworld symbolize the growth and decay of life.

phalanx a battle formation in the Greek infantry, usually consisting of eight rows of hoplites fighting in extremely close ranks.

potsherd fragment of pottery, usually one that has been unearthed by archaeological excavation.

prytanes 10 groups of 50 men from the Council of 500; formed the daily administration of Athens for one-month periods.

rhetors orator-politicians in Athens. With their rhetorical gifts, they had a great deal of influence over Athenian politics.

Salamis island on the western coast of Attica where the Persian fleet was defeated in battle by the Greeks in 480 BCE.

satrap provincial governor in the Achaemenian Persian Empire.

satyr play Greek dramatic work with a heroic mythological theme, like a tragedy, but with a humorous tone and a chorus of satyrs (goatlike male companions of Pan and Dionysus who roamed the woods and mountains). Satyr plays formed the last part of a tetralogy and were thus always performed after three tragedies.

Seleucid Empire empire that, between 312 and 64 BCE, extended from Thrace on the edge of the Black Sea to the western border of India. It was formed by Seleucus I Nicator from the remnants of Alexander the Great's realm.

Skepticism philosophy based on the assumption that all assumptions should be doubted.

Sophists Greek teachers in the fifth century BCE who gave popularized (and eventually denounced) instruction in philosophy, political science, rhetoric, and literature.

Stoicism school of philosophy founded by Zeno of Citium in Athens in the third century BCE. At its core is the belief that people should do what is required of them by nature and accept their lot.

Thermopylae mountain pass between Thessaly and central Greece where Leonidas and hundreds of Spartans died covering the retreat of the Greek army from the Persians in 480 BCE.

trireme ancient galley ship with three banks of oars.

zeugitai social class of economically independent farmers in Athens; owners of *zeugos* (yokes of oxen). The *zeugitai* served as foot soldiers in the army and, after Solon's reforms, could hold minor political offices.

MAJOR HISTORICAL FIGURES

Aeschylus (525–456 BCE) Greek playwright; author of the *Oresteia* trilogy and *The Persians*.

Alcibiades (c. 450–404 BCE) Athenian politician and military commander whose policies contributed to his city's defeat by Sparta in the Peloponnesian War (431–404 BCE).

Alexander the Great (356–323 BCE) king of Macedonia from 336 BCE until his death. Alexander overthrew the Persian Empire and laid the foundations of a Hellenistic Empire.

Antigonus (382–301 BCE) Macedonian general who co-founded the Antigonid dynasty.

Archimedes (c. 287–212 BCE) Greek mathematician and inventor.

Aristophanes (c. 450–388 BCE) early Greek comic playwright.

Aristotle (384–322 BCE) Greek philosopher and scientist.

Croesus king of Lydia between 560 and 546 BCE; conquered Ionia and was in turn subjugated by the Persians; famous for his vast wealth.

Cyrus the Great sixth-century-BCE Persian ruler who founded an empire that stretched from the Aegean Sea eastward to the Indus River.

Darius I king of Persia between 521 and 486 BCE; started the First Persian War. His expedition against Athens ended in the Battle of Marathon.

Democritus fifth-century-BCE Greek philosopher.

Diogenes (c. 400–325 BCE) Greek philosopher; founded Cynicism.

Eratosthenes Greek mathematician and astronomer of the third and second centuries BCE who calculated the circumference of Earth.

Euclid (c. 300 BCE) ancient Greek mathematician; known as the father of geometry.

Euripides (c. 485–406 BCE) Greek dramatist; author of more than 90 plays, including *Medea*.

Herodotus (born c. 480 BCE) known as the father of Greek historiography.

Herophilus personal physician to Ptolemy I in the fourth century BCE; widely regarded as the father of the study of human anatomy.

Hesiod (c. 700 BCE) epic poet; author of *Thegonia*, on religion and mythology, and *Works and Days*, a manual for farmers.

Hippocrates (c. 460–377 BCE) ancient Greek physician; known as the father of medicine.

Homer (c. 800 BCE) legendary Greek poet to whom the epics the *Iliad* and the *Odyssey* are attributed.

Judas Maccabaeus leader of the Maccabaean revolt against the Seleucid Empire (166–165 BCE).

Leonidas (died 480 BCE) Spartan king who died in the Battle of Thermopylae.

Menander (c. 341–291 BCE) Athenian comic dramatist; author of more than 100 plays.

Miltiades general who led Athenian forces to victory over the Persians at the Battle of Marathon in 490 BCE.

Pericles (c. 495–429 BCE) democratic leader of Athens during its Golden Age.

Plato (c. 428–348 BCE) ancient Greek philosopher who, with Aristotle and Socrates, laid the foundations of subsequent Western thought.

Plutarch (c. 46–120 CE) Greek biographer and historian.

Pythagoras (c. 580–500 BCE) ancient Greek philosopher and mathematician whose religious, political, and philosophical doctrines strongly influenced Plato.

Socrates (469–399 BCE) Athenian philosopher. His ideas were passed down primarily through the writings of Plato.

Sophocles (c. 496–406 BCE) Greek playwright; author of tragedies.

Thucydides (c. 460–400 BCE) Greek historian of the Peloponnesian War.

Virgil (70–19 BCE) Roman poet; author of the *Aeneid*, an epic of the foundation of Rome by fugitives from the sacking of Troy.

Xenophon (431–350 BCE) Greek historian; author of the *Anabasis*, an account of how Greek mercenaries attempted to seize the Persian throne.

Xerxes I king of Persia between 486 and 465 BCE; destroyed Athens in 480 BCE during the Second Persian War.

Zeno (c. 335–263 BCE) Greek Cypriot who founded the Stoic school of philosophy.

INDEX

Page numbers in *italic* type refer to illustrations.

A

Achaean League 173
Achilles *37*, 38, *45*
Adonis 84
Aeschines 153
Aeschylus 88, 92–93, *92*, *93*, 95, 119, 154
Aetolia 166
Aetolian League 171
Agamemnon 26–27, 38
Agesilaus 152
Agesilaus II 151–152, *151*
agriculture 6, 8–9, 16, 19–20, 33, 50, 72, *72*, 73, *76*
Ajax *45*
Akrotiri 11–12
Alcibiades 143–144, *143*, *144*, 146
Alcmaeonidae 70, 72, 74
Alexander IV 166
Alexander the Great *135*, 153, 154–165, *155*, *159*, *160*, *161*, *164*, 166, 168
Alexandria 154, 161, 162, *162*, 168, *170*, 174, 176–180
Al Mina 47
alphabets 42, 46
Ambracia 112
Amon-Re 161, 163
Amyntas 156
Anacreon 75
Anatolia 26, *29*, 40, 42, 79, 96, 154, 159, 166, 169, *169*, 171
anatomy 181
Anaxagoras 118, 126, *128*, 132
Anaximander 122, 124
Anaximenes 122, 124–125, *125*
Antalcidas, Peace of 152
Antigonid dynasty 166, 169, 172
Antigonus 166, 168–169
Antigonus Gonatas *167*, 169, 171–172
Antioch 169
Antiochus I 171
Antiochus III 170
Antiochus IV 170

Antipater 158, 166, 171
Antisthenes 136
apoikiai 47–48
Appolonius 162
Aratus of Sicyon 173
Arcadia 44, 153, 176
Archaic colonization 45
Archaic period 40, 42–51, 64
Archidamus II 140
Archilochus 40, 51
Archimedes 178, *180*
architecture 50, 118, 119, 177
    Cyclopean masonry 28
    Doric order 68
    Minoan 19, *19*, 22
    Mycenaean *32*, *33*
    Sparta 58–59
archons 60–61, 63, 90, 114–115
areopagus 60, 114
Argos 43, *43*, 45, 143, 152
Aridaeus 166
Aristarchus 174, 179
Aristides 111
aristocracy 64–65, 74
Aristogeiton 75, *75*
Aristogoras of Miletus 97
Aristophanes 88, 95, 119, 148, *148*
Aristotle 122, *123*, 124, 131, 137, *137*, 154, 174, 182
armor and weapons 35, 45, 59, *59*, 74, 100, *138*, 157
army *see* warfare and armies
Artaphernes 97
Artaxerxes 160
Artemisium, Battle of *99*, 102–103
ascesis 127
asceticism 136
Asine *29*, 31
astrolabe 180
astronomy 124, 126, *126*, 174, 179–180
atheism 86–87, 122
Athens *29*, 43, *43*, 45, 47, 52, 58–63
    Academy 122, 135, 137
    Acropolis 58, *63*, 70, *79*, 110, 112, *116*, *117*, 119
    Alcmaeonidae 70, 72, 74
    archons 60–61, 63, 114–115
    areopagus 60, 114

army 74, 76
Athena *53*, 63, 82, 84, *114*, 121
    citizenship 60, 78, 120
    coinage 73, *74*
    Corinthian War 152
    Council of 500 74, 76, 77–78, 114
    Delian League 110, 111–112, 138, 140, 148
    democracy 64, 74–79, 114–118, 138, 149–150
    ecclesia (assembly) 61, 63, 76–77, 114, 115
    Erechtheion *79*, 119
    festivals 71, 88, 90
    government 60–61, 63
    Lamian War 171
    legal system 71, 114, 150
    Long Walls 140, 141
    Lyceum 122, 137
    metics 150
    Mycenaean culture 26, 31, 35
    naval supremacy 101, 110, 111, 138, 140, 146, 148
    ostracism 76
    Parthenon 110, *116*, 119, 121, *121*
    Peisistratus 70–71
    Peloponnesian War 110, 112, 114, 138–153
    pentakosiomedimnoi 63
    Pericles 110–121, *111*, 140–141, 143
    Peristratus 64
    Persian Wars 96, 99–107, 112
    phylae 76, 77
    plague 138, 140–142
    pottery 71
    Propylaea 119
    prytane 77–78
    rhetors 115
    slaves 78, 117
    social organization 60–61, 63
    Solon's reforms 61, 63, 64, 68, 74
    strategoi 115, 143, 147
    Temple of Athena Nike *117*, 119
    Theater of Dionysus 88, 90, *91*

thetes 60, 61, 74, 114
Thirty Years Peace 138
tyranny 64, 68, 70–72, 74–75, 148–150
wealth 101, 118
women 62, 78, 120
zeugitai 60, 61, 74, 114
athletics 77, 82
Atlantis 13
atomic theory 131, 182–183
Attica 44, 45, 52, 58, 60, 71, 103–104

B

Babylon 96, 163, 165, 169
Bactria 164, *169*, 171
Barsine 165
basileus 40, 43
Bessus 164
Boeotia 7, 50
Brasidas 143
Bronze Age 6–13, *8–9*, 16–25
bull-leaping 21, *21*, 23, *24*

C

Callias 112
Callimachus 100, 162
Cambyses II 79, 96
Cape Mycale, Battle of *99*, 106, 109, 110
Cape Sounion *85*, *99*
Carthage 51
Cassander 171
Catana 144
Celts 51
centaurs 81
Chaeronea, Battle of 153, 154
chariots 35, *59*
children 57, 62
Chios 42
Chrysippus 183
Cicero 105
Cimon 111–112
Cleanthes 183
Cleisthenes 64, 74, 76, 79
Cleomenes III 166, 173
Cleon 141, 143
coinage 73, 74, *82*, 98, *100*, *161*, *168*
colonies 45, 47–51, 119
comedy 88, 90, 95, 177, 182
comos 88, 90

Companions (*hetairoi*) 158, 159, 165
Corcyra 138, *139*, 140
Corinth 43, *43*, 47, 48, *67*, *68*, 107, *115*
  oligarchy 64, 68
  Peloponnesian War 112, 114, 138, 140
  Spartan Confederacy 112, 114
  Temple of Apollo *69*
  trade 65–66
  tyranny 64, 65–69
Corinthian League 155
Corinthian War 152
Corupedium, Battle of 166, 169, *169*
Cos 42, 44
craftsmen 6, 19, 33, 55, *60*, *68*, 71, 72–74, *73*
Crannon, Battle of 166, 171
Crete 11, 14–25, *17*, 26, 35, 40, 44
Croesus 98
Croton 122, 126–127
Cycladic culture 6, 7, 8–13, *11*, *13*, 16
Cynics 136
Cyprus 40, 44, 166, *169*
Cypselus 64, 66–67, 72
Cyrenaica 166
Cyrene 163
Cyrus the Great 96, 98

D

Damon 118
Dardanelles 154, 159
Darius I 75, 96, 97, 99–100, *102*, 163, *163*
Darius III 160–161, 163–164, 165
Dark Age 36, 40–42, *42–43*, 43
debt slavery 47, 52, 60–61, 64
Delian League 110, 111–112, 138, 140, 148
Delos 8, *9*, 11, 111, *115*
Delphi 80, 83, 85, *86*, *99*, 101
Demaratus 99
Demetrius of Phaleron 174
Demetrius Poliorcetes 166, 168–169
democracy 64, 65, 74–79, 114–118, 149–150
Democritus 87, 182
Democritus of Abdera 131
Demosthenes 141, *152*, 153, 156, 171

diadochs 166, 168–172
Diagoras of Melos 87, 122
diet 6, 8–9, 72, *76*
Diogenes 122, *123*, *134*, *135*, 136
Dionysia 71, 88, *89*, 90, 92
dithyramb 88, 90
divination 85
divorce 120
dodeca poleis 42, 52
Dodona 83
Dorians 35, 40, 42, 44, 52, 80
drama *48*, 82, 88–95, 119
  choregi 90
  comedy 88, 90, 95, 177, 182
  masks 88, *90*, 91
  satyr plays 90
  tetralogy 90
  theaters 88, 90, *91*
  tragedy 71, 88, 91–95, 182
dromos 31, 32, *32*

E

ecclesia 61, 63, 76–77, 114, 115
economy 72–74
education 57, 118, 131, 132, 181–182
Egypt 11, 12, 14, 36, 154, 161–163, 166, 168, *169*, 172, 174
Elea *49*, 125, 128
Eleusian mysteries 80, 85–86
Elis 143
emporion 47
Epaminondas 152–153
Ephesus 73
Epicurianism 181, 182–183
Epicurus 182–183, *183*
Epidamnus 138
Epidaurus 140
Erasistratus 181
Eratosthenes 150, 180
Eritria 97
ethics 132–133, 182
Etruria 50
Euboea *42*, *45*
Euclid 174, 177, *178*
Euripides 88, 94–95, *95*, 119, 126, 154
Eurymedon, Battle of the 111
Evvoia 44

F

festivals 71, 82, 88, *89*, 90, 92

G

Gaugamela, Battle of *158*, 163
Gaul 51
Gaza 161
geometry 124, 128, 177, 179
Gla 26, *29*, 35
gods and goddesses 80–81, 82, 84,
    122, 172
  Aphrodite 80, 84, 86–87
  Apollo 11–12, 80, *81*, 84, 182
  Ares 84, *84*
  Artemis 34, 84, *116*
  Athena 34, *53*, 63, 71, 73, *74*, 82,
    84, *114*, 121
  Demeter 84, 86
  Dionysus 34, 71, 80, 81, 84, 88,
    89, 90, 172, *173*
  Eos Aurora 80
  Hades 84, 85–86, *87*
  Helios 80, *82*, *127*
  Hephaestus 84
  Hera 80, 84
  Hermes 80, 84
  Hestia 82
  Minoan culture 20–21
  Mnemosyne 182
  Mycenaean culture 34, *34*, 35
  Olympian 80, 84
  Persephone 80, 84, 85–86, *87*
  Poseidon 34, 84
  priesthood 34
  Zeus 34, *71*, 80, 83, 84, 163, 182
  see also religion
Gordian Knot 160, *160*
Gordium *158*, 160
Gorgias 132
Gournia *17*, 21, *22*
government
  colonies 50
  democracy 64, 65, 74–79,
    114–118, 149–150
  oligarchy 64, 68, 118, 138, 145
  poleis 40, 42, 43, 45, 47, 52, 64
  Sparta 47, 52–57, 118, 138
  tyranny 47, 64–75, 96
Graces 182
Granicus River, Battle of 154, *158*,
    159–160
Grotta-Pelos 10
Gylippus 146

H

Harmodius 75, *75*

Helladic culture 6, 7, 16
Hellenism 172–173
helots 52, 54
Hephaestion 163, *164*
Heraclitus of Ephesus 125, 132
Herodotus 68, 69, 70–71, 74, 98,
    100, 101, 105, *105*, 106
heroes 80
Hero of Alexandria 178, *179*
Herophilus 181
Hesiod 40, 50, *51*, 83
Hindu Kush 164
Hipparchus 75
hippeis 60, 61, 63
Hippias 64, 71–72, 74, 75, 99
Hippocrates 122, 180–181
Hippodamus of Miletus 119
Hittites 36
Homer (*Iliad* and *Odyssey*) 26–27,
    36–39, 42–43, *45*, 71, 80, 83,
    154, 174, *176*
hoplites 59, *59*, 74, 76, 99–100,
    106, *106*, *138*, *146*, 152
housing 6–8, 13, 16, 17, 21–22, 28
Hydaspes, Battle of 154, 164

I

idealism 182
Ilium 39
Illyria 155
India 154, 164
Iolkos *29*, 31
Ionia 11, 42, 44, 96, 98, 138
Ionian philosophy 122–126
Ionian Rebellion 96–97, 99, 101
Ipsus, Battle of 168, *169*
Ischia 50
Issus, Battle of *158*, *159*, 160–161
Ithaca 26

J

Jerusalem 161, 166, 170
jewelry 23, 24, 30, 33, *45*
Judas Maccabaeus 166, 170, *172*

K

Kastri 11
Keftiu 14
Keros 7, 10
Knossos 14, 16–25, *16*, *17*, *18*, *19*,
    26, 35

krypteia 54
Kythnos 8, *9*

L

labyrinth 14, 20
Laconia 45, 52
Lamachus 144
Lamian War 171–172
languages 7, 26, 42–43, 44, 172
Laurium silver mines 101
Lefkandi *42*, *45*
legal system 47, 71, 114, 150
Leonidas 58, 103
Leotychides 106, 109
Lerna 6
Lesbos 40
Leto 84
Leucippus 131
Leuctra, Battle of 138, 152
Library of Alexandria 177, 180
Libya 166, *169*
Linear A script 23, 25
Linear B script 44, *46*, 80
literature 119
Locris 144
logic 132, 177
logographers 150
Logos 125, 183
Lycurgus 52, 56, *57*
Lydia 73, 96, 98, *100*, 106
Lysander 148–149, *149*
Lysias 150, *150*
Lysimachus 169

M

Macedon 96, 112, 153, 154–165,
    169, 171–172
  Alexander the Great 154–165
  Antigonid dynasty 166, 169, 172
Magna Grecia 48, 50
Maia 84
Mallia 16, *17*
Mantinea, Battle of 143, 153
maps 124
Marathon, Battle of 96, 99–100, *99*,
    103
marble 7, 9, 11
Mardonius 106, 107
marriage 57, 62, 120
mathematics 122, 124, 127–128,
    130, 174, 177–180
Medes 96

Media 164
medicine 122, 180–181
Megacles 70–71, 74
Megara 140
Menander 95, 177, *177*
Menelaus 26, 38
mercenaries 64, 73, 158–159
merchants 6, 19
Messenia 45, 52, *54*, 153
metempsychosis 127
metics 150
migration 40, 42, 44, 47–51
Miletus 73, 97
Miletus, School of 122, 124–125
Milos 8, 11, 13
Miltiades 100
Minoans 11, 12, 14–25, *16*, *17*
Minos 14, 18, 20
Minotaur 14, *15*, 20, *20*
Minyan culture 6, 7–8
mosaics *15*, *38*
Mount Olympus 80, 84
Mount Parnassus 83
Muses 84, 174, *181*, 182
Museum 174, 176, 177
music 118, 127, 128, *130*, 180, 182
Mycenae 26–28, *29*, *31*, 35, 37, 38
Mycenaeans 13, 14, 16, 25, 26–36, *27*, *29*, 39, 40, 58, 80
    tombs 29–32, *32*
Mykonos 8, *9*
mythology 80–81, 83, 84, 88, 92, 122, 124

N

Nabis 173
Naxos 8, 9, *9*, 111
Nestor 26, 31, 33
Nicias 143–144, 146
Nicias, Peace of 138, 143

O

Odysseus 26, *37*, 38, *38*, *176*
oligarchy 64, 68, 118, 138, 148
Olympias 154, 156, 163
Olympic Games 125
oracles 49, 80, 83, 84, 85, *86*, 101, 161
oration 110, 115, 150
orchestra 90
Orchomenus 7, *9*
ostracism 76, 112

P

Paestum *47*
Palestine 161, 163, 166, 170
Pallene, Battle of 71
Panathenaea 71
Parmenides 125, 128, 130, 131, 132–133
Paros 9, *9*
Partakes 171
Parthenon 110, *116*, 119, 121, *121*
Parthia 164, *169*, 171
Pasagardae 163
Pausanias 149–150
Pausanius 107
Peisistratus 70–71, 72
Peloponnesian League 138, 140
Peloponnesian War 44, 48, 110, 112, 114, 138–153
Perdiccas 156
Pergamum 171
Periander 64, *65*, 66, 68–69
Pericles 110–121, *111*, 126, 140–141, 143
perioikoi 52, 54–55
Peristratus 64
Persepolis *108*, 163, *163*
Persia 60, 151–152, 154, 159–166, *163*–164, 165, 171
    Seleucid dynasty 166, 169–171, 172
Persian Wars 58, 75, 79, 96–109, *99*, 110, 112
Phaistos 14, 16, *17*, 22
phalanx 157, *157*, 159
Pheidippides 100
Phidias 121
Philip II 153, *153*, 154, 156, *156*, 157
Philip III 166
Philistus 154
philosophy 118, 122–137, 174, 181–183
Phoenicia 42, 46, 102, 161
Phrygia 160, 168, *169*
Phrynichus 91–92
phylae 76, 77
Pindar 158
Piraeus 118, 119, 140, 141, *142*
Pithekoussai 47, 50
Plataea, Battle of 96, *99*, 106, 107, *107*, 109
Plato 58, 117, 118, 122, *123*, 131, 132–133, 134–135, *134*, 137, 182

Plutarch 154
poetry 40, 50, 51, 82, 83, 88, 176–177, 182
poleis 40, 42, 43, 45, 47, 52, 64
Polycrates 126
Polypechon 171
population 45, 49
Porus 164
Potidaea, siege of 140
pottery *37*, *45*, *60*
    Athenian 71, *78*, *119*
    Bronze Age 7, 13, *18*, 24, 33, 35
    Corinthian *68*
    Dark Ages *42*
    Kamares ware 17, 24
    Mycenaean *34*, *35*, *36*
    pithoi *18*
Priam 37, 38
priesthood 82, 83
Protagoras 119, 122
prytane 77–78
Psammetichus 64, 68
Ptolemaic dynasty 162, 166, 168, 172
Ptolemy I 166, 168, *168*, 174
Ptolemy II 168, 174
Ptolemy of Alexandria *175*, 179–180
Pylos 26, *29*, 31, 33, 34, 35, *46*
Pylos, Battle of 141
Pyrrhon of Elis 182
Pythagoras 122, 126–128, *129*, *130*
Pythia 83
pyxis *120*

R

religion 13, 80–87, 122
    atheism 86–87, 122
    divination 85
    Hellenistic empires 172–173, *173*
    Minoan 20–21, 24
    Mycenaean 28, 32, 34, *34*, 35, 80
    mystery cults 80, 85–86, *87*, 154
    oracles 49, 80, 83, 84, 85, *86*, 101, 161
    priesthood 82, 83
    Pythagoreans 127
    sacrifice 24, 32, 34, 35, 82, *83*, 84
    syncretism 80, 173
    temples 81–82, *85*
    see also gods and goddesses

rhetoric 115, 118, 131, 132, 181
Rhodes *36*, 42, 44, 166
Romans 39
Roxana 166

S

Salamis, Battle of 96, *99*, 104, *104*, 106, 109, *109*, 110
Samos *41*, 42, *101*, 126
Samos, Battle of 97
Sappho *44*
Sardis 96, 97, 160
satyrs 81
science 118, 122, 124, 128, 131, 174, 177–181, 182
seals 6, 16, 24–25, 30, 78, *109*
Sea Peoples 36
Seleucid dynasty 166, 169–171, 172
Seleucus 166, 168, 169, *171*
ships *25*, 35, 42, 101, 109, *109*, 110, 138, 140, *141*
Sicily 48, 143–146
Simonides 75
Siwa Oasis 161, 168
Skepticism 181, 182
slaves 33, 47, 51, 60–61, 62, 64, 78, 117, 177
Socrates 118, 122, 126, 131–135, *132*, *133*, 136, 143, 182
Sogdiana 164
Solon 52, 61, *61*, 63, 64, 74, 98
sophia 127
sophists 118, 131, 132, 181–182
Sophocles 88, 93–94, *94*, 119, 154
Sparta 26, 38, 43, *43*, 45, 52–58, *58*, 110, 166
    army and military training 55, *56*, 57, 58, 59
    Cleomenes III 173
    Corinthian War 152
    gerousia 56–57
    government 47, 52–57, 118
    helots 52, 54
    imperialism 151–152
    kings 56
    krypteia 54
    Lycurgan Constitution 52, 56
    oligarchy 138
    Peloponnesian League 138, 140
    Peloponnesian War 110, 112, 114, 138–153

perioikoi 52, 54–55
Persian Wars 96, 99, 102–103, 106–107
    social organization 47, 52–55
    Spartan Confederacy 112, 114
    Thirty Years Peace 138
Spartan Confederacy 112, 114
Stoicism 87, 174, 181, 183
Stone Age 6–8, 14–16
strategoi 93, 110, 115, 143, 147
sundial 124, 180
Susa 163, 165
Syracuse 48, *48*, 138, 143–144, *145*, 146
Syria 169
Syros 10, 11

T

Tarentum 144
textiles 33, 62, 72, *119*
Thales of Miletus 122, 124, *124*, *126*
Thasos 51
theater *see* drama
Thebes 26, *29*, 31, 43, *43*, 138, 152–153, 156, 158
    Corinthian War 152
    Peloponnesian War 112, 114
Themistocles 101, 104
Theocritus 162, 176–177
Thera *9*, *12*
    volcanic eruption 6, 11–13, 14, 25
Thermopylae, Battle of 58, 96, *99*, 102–103
Theseus *15*, 20, 52, 58, 91
Thespis 88
thetes 60, 61, 74, 114
Thirty Years Peace 138
tholos tombs 30–32, *32*
Thrace 71, 96, 154, 155
Thrasybulus 149
Thucydides 122, 141, 142, 147, *147*
Thurii 119
Tiryns 26, 28, *29*, 31, *33*, 35
trade 72, 73–74
    Archaic period 40, 42, 45, 47
    Bronze Age 6, 11, 16, 19, *25*
    colonies 47, 51
    Corinth 65–66
    emporion 47

Mycenaeans 26, 35
    Sparta 55
tragedy 71, 88, 91–95, 182
tragoidos 88
Treasury of Atreus 26, 32, *32*
trigonometry 180
triremes 109, *109*
Troy 26–27, 28, *29*, 36–39, *39*
tyranny 47, 64–75, 96, 148
Tyre 154, 161
Tyrtaeus 52

V

Virgil 176

W

warfare and armies 73, 74
    Athens 74, 76
    Bronze Age *10*
    Companions (*hetairoi*) 158, 159, 165
    hoplites 59, *59*, 74, 76, 99–100, 106, *106*, *138*, *146*, 152
    Macedon 157, *157*, 158–159
    Mycenaeans 26, 33, 35
    naval warfare 97, 101, 102–103, 104, 106, *109*, 138, 140, *141*, 146
    phalanx 157, *157*, 159
    Sparta 55, *56*, 57, 58, 59
    see also armor and weapons
women 57, 62, 72, 78, 91, *112*, *119*, 120
wrestling *56*
writing 23, 24–25, 40, 42–43, 46, *46*, 47, 85

X

Xanthippus 110
Xenophanes 125
Xenophon 73, 132
Xerxes I 96, 100–106, 160

Z

Zakro 16, *17*
Zeno of Cyprus 174, 183
Zeno of Elea 130, 132–133
zeugitai 60, 61, 74, 114